Reinventing
Diversity

Reinventing Diversity

Transforming Organizational Community to Strengthen People, Purpose, and Performance

HOWARD J. ROSS

SOCIETY FOR HUMAN
RESOURCE MANAGEMENT

Published in association with the
Society for Human Resource Management
Alexandria, Virginia

ROWMAN & LITTLEFIELD PUBLISHERS, INC.
Lanham • Boulder • New York • Toronto • Plymouth, UK

Published in association with the Society for Human Resource Management

Published by Rowman & Littlefield Publishers, Inc.
A wholly owned subsidary of The Rowman & Littlefield Publishing Group, Inc.
4501 Forbes Boulevard, Suite 200, Lanham, Maryland 20706
www.rowman.com

10 Thornbury Road, Plymouth PL6 7PP, United Kingdom

British Library Cataloguing in Publication Information Available

Library of Congress Cataloging-in-Publication Data

The hardback edition of this book was previously cataloged by the Library of Congress as follows:

Ross, Howard J.
   Reinventing diversity : transforming organizational community to strengthen people, purpose, and performance / Howard J. Ross.
      p. cm.
   Includes bibliographical references.
   1. Diversity in the workplace. 2. Cultural pluralism. I. Title.

   HF5549.5.M5R67 2011
   658.3008—dc22   2011011776

ISBN: 978-1-4422-1043-1 (cloth : alk. paper)
ISBN: 978-1-4422-1044-8 (pbk. : alk. paper)
ISBN: 978-1-4422-1045-5 (electronic)

Contents

One Song

Jalaluddin Rumi[1]

Every war and every conflict
between human beings has happened
because of some disagreement about names.

It is such an unnecessary foolishness,
because just beyond the arguing
there is a long table of companionship
set and waiting for us to sit down.

What is praised is one, so the praise is one too,
many jugs being poured into a huge basin.
All religions, all this singing, one song.

The differences are just illusion and vanity.
Sunlight looks a little different
on this wall than it does on that wall
and a lot different on this other one,
but it is still one light.

We have borrowed these clothes,
these time-and-space personalities,
from a light, and when we praise,
we are pouring them back in.

Foreword

Howard Ross is a gentle giant of a man with a passion for diversity that is unparalleled. He has written from his soul, and from his very essence. Weaving his twenty-five years of experience as a diversity professional with statistics, anecdotes, and perspective, he has produced a manuscript that challenges the reader to consider the ways we have been programmed to approach issues of diversity and difference. Within the challenge that he poses, he offers each of us the opportunity to explore the basis of our many biases and challenges us to be mindful in the face of the inevitable demographic changes that will shape our society.

This is a careful book. Howard uses conventional wisdom to build toward that which is unconventional, offering organizations a set of metrics through which to assess diversity matters. In some ways this work is disconcerting because it is so comfortably discomfiting. In other words, Howard begins with the familiar, then pushes us toward the challenging and unfamiliar. There is a wry sense of humor working here. Who else would lead a chapter opening (as in chapter 8) with reinforcing quotes from both Malcolm X and Oscar Wilde? In many ways, Howard Ross reminds us that we are more similar than we are dissimilar, connecting the thoughts of two extremely different men to make a point about perceptual reality.

I am honored that Howard asked me to write the foreword to *Reinventing Diversity: Transforming Organizational Community to Strengthen People, Purpose, and Performance*. We have a long association and friendship, through Leadership Greater Washington, where he was the lead trainer for my class, and through our mutual work in diversity issues, first working together to construct training for a Fortune 50 company, then through his work as diversity professor in residence at Bennett College for Women. In appointing Howard as diversity professor, it was my goal to make the point that diversity is not simply an issue for people of color and that it is essential that white folks "get it" and both talk the talk and walk the walk. Howard is one who not only gets it but also lives and breathes it. His openness of spirit, gentility, and humility make him a perfect person to push us past familiar diversity models to truly challenge ourselves and our organizations about ways we can effectively embrace those inevitable changes that will shape our collective futures.

In his seminal work, *The Souls of Black Folks* (1903), the African American philosopher, activist, and leader Dr. W. E. B. DuBois wrote, "The problem of the twentieth century is the problem of the color-line—the relation of the darker to the lighter races of men in Asia and Africa, in America and the islands of the sea." In these challenging economic times, with world relationships recalibrating based on economic power, the DuBois assertion is prophetic. We've taken twentieth-century problems into the twenty-first century, even as the kaleidoscope of our reality continues to shift, challenging interpretations of global dominance, cultural hegemony, and faux postracialism. Thinkers like Howard Ross remind us to resist the status quo, to embrace the creative dissatisfaction that comes when things change.

To be sure, there is much in this book that one might challenge, much that one might take issue with. That is a good thing. I applaud Howard Ross for raising the issues, for bringing his heart, soul, spirit, and passion to an issue he has devoted much of his life to. We have no choice but to embrace diversity, and Howard says we must confront our own biases in that embracing and in our effort to construct a more inclusive society. His words ain't nothing but the truth, embracing my Ebonics. This is mind-expanding and important work.

Julianne Malveaux
President, Bennett College for Women
March 2011

Acknowledgments

This book was cooking for a long time. There had been at least a dozen "serious" times over the past fifteen years or so when I was going to *really* get it done and God only knows how many other moments of inspiration, thought, or fantasy. While books can, and do, serve many purposes, for me, after more than twenty-five years in my profession, it serves as a milestone of where I have been and what my work has become. Since the first edition was published in August 2011, the response has been immensely gratifying, and I have had the opportunity to travel in and outside of the United States and meet thousands of new people who are interested in reinventing the way we see diversity work. And, as many people, I am nothing if not the product of the relationships I have been blessed to have and the people I have been blessed to learn from. And over a long life, there have been many.

I have had the opportunity to work with and learn from an amazing array of talented, passionate, and committed people over the years. Images of many of them fly through my thoughts as I write this: Hafsa Ahmed, Vital Akimana, Sandy Amato, Mary Arzt, Shayne Bauer-Ellsworth, Susan Bender, Lee Butler, Robin Carnes, Al Collins, Barry Certner, Sally Craig, Christine Cranston, Nicole Daley, Brenda Dancil-Jones, Janet Davis, Bob Devlin, Tarwea Duckett, Anne Ferrier, Michael Friedman, Chrisanne Garrett, Erik Granered, Robby Gregg, Michelle Hannon, John Honor, Clyde Horton, Buffy Illum, Emery Jones, Suzanne Lagay, Meredith Levert, Hannah Mack, Jim MacRae, Janie Marbley, Nicole Martin, Armers Moncure, Camille Mosley, Mugo Mutothori, Sonte Myers, Tara Nelson, Okezie Nwoka, Mark Pfeifer, Lizet Porter, Reema Rahman, Jim Rogers, Bryant Rollins, Joe Santana, Caitlin Saunders, Angella Savage, Howie Schaffer (to whom I owe a special debt because without him this book never would have gotten published), Jerry Schuerholz, Scott Shields, Peter

xi

Shiver, Bobby Joe Smith, Minjon Tholen, Lois Taylor-Holsey, Bill Woodson, and Jasmine Zhu all come to mind, with gratitude for each.

A number have made a huge difference: Dottie (Cook) Gandy, my original business partner, who had an enormous impact on the vision of our company and my own vision of how to lead it; Michael Reed, who was my colleague and partner for a dozen years; and Amri Johnson, who helped recreate professional possibilities at a time when I was satisfied to simply answer the phone.

There are so many clients and participants in workshops who have engaged in our programs—literally hundreds of thousands at this point—far too many to name but never too many to remember. I have witnessed amazing acts of human kindness and human courage before my eyes. I am very clear on what a privilege it has been to have had the opportunity to do the work I have done for the past twenty-five years. I am clear that I have rarely had to work for a living; I've simply had the pleasure of doing what I love to do and getting paid for it. Yet, none of that happens without somebody who is willing to sit on the other side and listen and engage. Thank you all for your listening.

There have also been countless friends and colleagues in my professional communities: hundreds of members of Leadership Greater Washington and hundreds of other diversity professionals, chief diversity officers, and other practitioners whom I have learned from and with over the years. These people have inspired me with their commitment and their willingness to fight the good fight every day, to keep moving forward again, and again, and again. Also inspiring to me is my Inner Journey community, particularly Gunnar Nilson, Penelope Bell, Kimberly Salameh, Michael Lucy, Kathleen Troust, Dee Rosenberg, Scott Watkins, Pascale Maslin, Tim Castallo, and especially, Neelama Eyres, the sister of my soul. A special thanks to Eric Hoffman, Jim MacRae, and Elliott Fielder for being there as brothers in heart and mind for more than thirty years, and Scott Paseltiner, who has been there almost every day for the past fifteen years.

And, of course, at the heart of it all have been my teachers. There have been far too many to mention, and they continue to show up almost every day, but some who were the most "core" include the following: Saul Alinsky, whom I spent less than one day with, but it was a day that rocked my world; Dick Hopkins, a college professor who taught in a way that I'd never seen before; Nancy Neall, whom I met as a twenty-one-year-old looking to work with young children and who taught me what education and compassion were *really* about; Dr. Arnold Meyersburg, a brilliant psychiatrist who advised me as a teacher and taught me insights into human behavior thirty-five years ago that stay with me today and whose commitment to community inspired me; Werner Erhard, from whom I learned about human transformation; Bob Allen, my mentor in the world of consulting, who gave me ten years of experience in two-and one-half short years; Fernando Flores, the brilliant Chilean linguistic philosopher whose work opened up a deeper understanding of the human mind than I had ever known; Michael Schiesser, my beloved friend who opened doors to human understanding and pathways to learning that I had previously dared not step into; and Osho, from whom I learned to turn toward life. Many more I have learned from through their writing but have never met are listed in the bibliography at the end of the text.

And so many heroes and she-roes. Mahatma Gandhi, Dr. Martin Luther King, Jr., Nelson Mandela, and Cesar Chavez, who I met for three hours when I was nineteen years old and whose aura of goodness was so profound that it stays with me today. Eugene McCarthy and Shirley Chisholm, whose presidential campaigns inspired me to action. Dr. Julianne Malveaux and Dr. Johnnetta B. Cole, who I am honored to call my friends. My students at Bennett College for Women in Greensboro, North Carolina, who opened their hearts to me and gave me a richer view of the world and hope for the future. My colleagues and friends at Operation Understanding DC, the Human Rights Campaign, PFLAG, and so many other organizations that fight for a just society every day, and so many other people like them who have had the courage to stand up for what is right. I can't list them all here, but many of them, and even more of their influence, drift through this book.

As I sit here now, I am in partnership with an amazing group, the People of Cook Ross, the best I have ever had the opportunity to work with. I want to especially acknowledge my partner Michael Leslie Amilcar, whose deep heart and passion for doing things well and doing things right inspires me and makes me look good daily; Laura Malinowski, who embodies loyalty, intelligence, dedication, and quality; and Rosalyn Taylor O'Neale, our newest addition but my sister from another mother. What an amazing gift it is to have a day at the office be a day with people I love.

People I love. That is what this has always been about for me and what it always will be about. It started, of course, with my parents: my father, Jack, who taught me that *all* people deserve respect and to be treated with respect, and my mother, Irene, who, underneath it all, taught me the most important values of all. Mostly, they both let me know that I was loved every day of my life. My stepfather, Bob Rosen, who I have loved for twenty years. And my sisters, Sharryn and Robbie, who both have inspired me with their continuing love, strength, brilliance, and passion for social justice.

To my amazing sons, Matt, Jason, Gabe, and Jake—there simply is no life without you. There have been so many times when it is you who have kept me going. You who made me smile. You who are at my side. You whom I turn to, even as you scatter far and wide to fulfill your own dreams. And to your wives, Monita, Kate, and Shauna—because they love you. And last but never least, to Christine Joachim, whose presence in our lives just makes life better.

I dedicate this book in memoriam to my family members in Trochenbrod, in western Ukraine, at least forty-three of whom were murdered on or about Yom Kippur 1942 because they were Jews, and my other family members and the members of so many other families of Jews, Roma, gays, and others throughout Europe who suffered the same fate; for Dr. King and those four little girls in a church in Birmingham, Alabama, and all the rest who lost their lives in the Middle Passage and the struggle for their humanity; to Harvey Milk, and all the gay, lesbian, bisexual, and transgendered people who have lost or taken their lives because our society is still not ready to see God's grace in all people; and to so many others whose names have been forgotten but whose pain and suffering was just as real and just as unnecessary in places like Rwanda, Cambodia, Uganda, Armenia, and around the world. May this book play a small part in creating a world in which others may not have to suffer your fate.

And I dedicate this book to the future, for my grandchildren, Hannah, Mayah, Sloane, Penelope, and Davis, in the hope that they one day live in a world in which the walls have tumbled to the ground.

Most deeply of all, to my beloved wife, partner, and dearest friend, Leslie. You are at the core of everything I am and ever want to be. I can't even begin to list all of the ways I am grateful to you. Thank you for helping me see what love and devotion truly is.

And finally, to the Great Beloved, in all of Your names, for shining grace on me every day. This work is Your work.

Introduction

A PERSONAL JOURNEY

> If we are to achieve a richer culture, rich in contrasting values, we must recognize the whole gamut of human potentialities, and so weave a less arbitrary social fabric, one in which each diverse gift will find a fitting place.

Margaret Mead[1]

Recently, I was at a conference and ran into a chief diversity officer I have known for quite some time. I congratulated her for her company's recent placement on one of the "Best Company for Diversity" lists. I asked her how things were going and she told me all about the kinds of activities that her company has been engaging in: training programs, executive presentations, global business initiatives, and a whole assortment of similar "best-practice" activities. Then I asked about her results, and her mood shifted. "We still have a long way to go," she said.

Later that day I looked at the newspaper and read a report about the impact of the economy on communities of color within the United States. Dramatic high-school dropout rates. Health disparities for virtually every major disease. An African American unemployment rate double that of the nation. A few days later, another report cited almost no movement in closing the gap between men's and women's salaries and, on the same day, just four months after Rutgers University freshman Tyler Clementi committed suicide after being filmed while making out with another man, members of U.S. Congress condemned the vote on overturning "don't ask, don't tell," the seventeen-year-old policy that allowed gay, lesbian, and bisexual soldiers to serve and die on foreign battlefields as long as they didn't share their sexual orientation, and swore to continue the fight against marriage equality. And in a country built on a foundation of religious freedom, protests still rage against mosques being built in various parts of the country.

Something is wrong with this picture.

This is a very personal book for me, about a very personal topic, and so before I go any further, it is important that you know who I am and why I am writing this book.

I have been doing diversity and inclusion work for most of my life and have made my living at it for more than twenty-five years. I believe that inclusiveness and cultural flexibility can be learned and developed and that it can lead to unprecedented growth and vastly improved productivity, morale, internal communication, leadership, and customer satisfaction. However, doing something for a long time, and doing it pretty successfully, can have a "shadow" side to it. It can make us attached to the ways we have done things in the past. It can make us resistant to new ways of moving forward.

I once heard a story about a man who got married and, coming back from his honeymoon with his wife, wanted to show her that he knew how to cook. He decided to make a roast beef dish that had been in his family for generations. As he prepared the meal, his wife watched him as he sliced a thin piece off of the front and the back of the roast beef. "Why did you do that?" the wife asked. "Because that's the way my mother has always done it," replied the husband. He went on to prepare the meal. A few nights later the wife had an opportunity to visit with her new mother-in-law. "I'm curious," she said, "why is it that when you make your roast beef dish you trimmed the front and the back of the meat before cooking it?" "I guess it's because that's what my mother always did," replied the mother-in-law.

Finally, a couple of weeks later, the wife was with the grandmother. "Can you please tell me," she asked, "why do you trim the ends of the meat before making your roast beef dish?" "Oh," she said, "that is because my pot was too small to fit the whole piece."

I believe that we have been basing our diversity and inclusion work on paradigms that were created long ago, and we have to realize that, like the roast beef, we can get familiar, habitual, and unconscious about our beliefs and actions. Ultimately, our success in dealing with these issues starts from our ability to be introspective, and that applies to both organizations and individuals. I know it has been true in my own personal experience. I have known hundreds of colleagues who are working on this issue and they are, consistently, among the most committed people I know. They have put their heart and soul into their work. And yet, if we are honest, we have to admit that there is more than a little strain of righteousness as to how many of us have gone about it. I know this has been true in my own perspective at times.

In fact, my personal journey is at the heart of my work and at the heart of understanding why a tall white guy from a middle-class, Jewish American home ends up building a career in diversity and writing a book on diversity, inclusion, and cultural competency.

When I first started doing diversity work more than twenty-five years ago, the early diversity training programs were still relatively new and rare. Many of them had been mandated by court orders for businesses to hire more women and people of color, or driven by concerns about discriminatory behavior. My interest in diversity had always been a strong driver in my life.

Growing up Jewish in the early 1950s in Washington, D.C., I felt a sense of duality in my identity. On one hand, I knew and was around many Jewish people and felt quite "normal" about being Jewish. On the other hand, I heard stories about how dozens, maybe hundreds, of my Eastern European relatives were killed in the Holocaust. My mother told me about how as a teenager, growing up in a German neighborhood in Baltimore in the 1920s and 1930s, she would have to wash away the swastikas on her father's grocery store windows every morning. As she shared her experiences and the beliefs that they led her to adopt, and as I learned about the history of people like me, part of me dismissed it as paranoia . . . perhaps as a self-protective mechanism. It wasn't until later in my life that I realized that I had developed a subtle sense of vulnerability about being Jewish. This was true even though I had never been exposed to any egregious forms of anti-Semitism. That vulnerability has taken me years to understand and be able to really see, yet underneath all that was an important message that came through loud and clear: bad things can happen to people who are different.

We had plenty of role models who taught us that you were supposed to give back, especially my maternal grandfather, Samuel Bulmash, who worked to purchase and outfit the *Exodus* ship in Baltimore Harbor and worked to get money and supplies to the resistance movement against the Nazis. There is a forest planted in his memory in Israel.

Yet the duality came from the fact that I was (and am) still a white-skinned man in a society that benefits white-skinned men. In subtle and not-so-subtle ways, I have benefited from that dynamic. Even as a young boy I remember being in five-and-dime stores with black friends and being able to do things they couldn't do. I remember things being said and kids being forced to wait outside while I was allowed to shop. I didn't begin to really explore the effect of white and male privilege on me until much later in my life, but these incidents did not go unnoticed. One impact was that it became far more comfortable for me to keep my Jewish identity hidden at times, when possible. That way I could fit in; I could, in effect, be just another white guy. Where race was concerned, my parents encouraged us to treat all people with respect and never to be insulting or disrespectful in our comments, yet even they clearly acted differently when they were around people of color.

Nevertheless, the dichotomy of the ways different people were treated in this society affected me. Living in Washington in the 1950s and 1960s, our experience was informed by societal events happening around us. Our local news covered national and international events, including reports of the civil rights movement. I got my first taste of social action as a teenager, attending civil rights meetings in churches in downtown Washington. It was a real awakening as to how ignorant I was about how Blacks were being treated in this country. Some of these meetings turned into Black-White encounter groups, with the black people expressing their anger at Whites and the white people feeling guilty. I had my own personal reactions, but at the core, the conversation drew me in like a bee to honey.

Later, I got a job at a department store downtown where most of the people who worked and shopped were black. Not only was I one of few white people there, I also was one of the only college students. It was a dramatic experience of getting to know people in a different, more intimate way. I could see how many advantages I had that the people I worked with did not. I found myself helping my fellow employees organize themselves in negotiations with management. On the day that Dr. Martin Luther King Jr. was assassinated, I got a call telling me not to come to work that day. The store had been burned to the ground.

Dr. King's murder was a pivotal moment in my life, as it was for so many others. I was deeply affected by the waste of it all. It wasn't that I wasn't paying attention before; it was that it became very real that day that something needed to be done. And, for some reason still unknown to me, at that moment it became very personal. And it became very clear to me that it was more than just "their" problem. It was, and is, "our" problem.

In college, I did volunteer work with children, primarily black children, and tutored them in their homes. That led me to take a job teaching at a day-care center with a preschool and before- and-after-school programs. We had a mixture of affluent white and low-income black students.

When I was asked to take over the job of running the school several years later, I failed miserably at first. I realized I knew very little about managing people. So I began studying management and organizational development. I learned what it took to create a particular kind of work environment, how some employee communication worked and some did not. And I learned about organizations and how they functioned. Over time, I started to change the "culture" of the school. Soon, the school was thriving. I tripled the staff within a year, created new programs, and expanded the number of students. As word got out, I began getting phone calls from other schools asking me to show them what I was doing. My life as a consultant had started.

In 1984, I was approached by a local hospital just outside of Washington, D.C., asking me whether I would run their new employee wellness program.

The program had been built on the work of organizational psychologist Robert Allen, who was to become one of my most significant mentors. When I first read his seminal book, *Beat the System! A Way to Create More Human Environments*,[2] it was like he was saying what I had always known to be true. The basic message of his work was that people don't change just because they're educated and motivated; they change because the cultures that they are part of begin to call them to new behaviors. Deep down I knew he was right, and this truth would change the way I began to work with people, and, ultimately, the way I do diversity, inclusion, and cultural competency work.

I began doing diversity work with telephone companies in New York and New England. In the late 1970s, a court order had forced them to hire large numbers of women and people of color, and the environments that were created were anything but collaborative. Diversity work was generally unknown to people in those days, and when it was known, it was generally seen as an opportunity for people to confront issues that very few wanted to handle. Needless to say, we were often greeted with cynicism, skepticism, and some fear.

I realize in looking back that part of the problem was the diversity model we were using in our workshops. As has often been the case, the design of the work was, generally, to support people in the dominant group (generally white men and women because the focus in those days was mostly on race and gender) in understanding the dynamics of others. It's easy to see, retrospectively, why white men, and often white women, sometimes reacted defensively to the notion of this kind of training. It often seemed to them to be based on the desire to have them feel guilty, and my experience has led me to see that guilt is a generally dysfunctional emotion. It can help us, at the moment, see the need for change, but when we hold on to it we inevitably either feel disempowered and bad about ourselves, or angry and resentful at those who make us feel that way. Neither emotion is very productive in moving toward constructive change.

Having grown up in social justice politics, I had come to believe that there were good people and bad people: "racists," "sexists," and so on. And I believed (and still believe) that all of these "-isms" were wrong and needed to be crushed. I worked very hard to be sure that I was one of the "good" people and that I didn't have any "-isms" in me, but with only mixed results. I still knew that, at some level, I am the product of my environment and upbringing and the sense of entitlement and privilege that I was born into. It wasn't until I started doing some personal work in the late 1980s and 1990s that I began to see that while there are clearly some people who are consciously biased, hateful, and hurtful, most people developed different ways of looking at the world that, at some level, made sense *to them*, because of the narrative of the world that they had grown up in. It wasn't a function of being a "good" or "bad" person; it was more a function of their cultural narrative, the story of their life: what they had been taught, what they were told, what they saw, and so on. It became clear to me that even obvious things can show up quite differently to others and, even more importantly, that I would probably be very similar to them if I had grown up in *their* story. As I once heard said, every villain is a hero in his or her own story.

I had a profound moment of awareness about this in the early 1990s. I had been hired by a large newspaper chain to lead a series of diversity trainings in newspapers across the country. Leading diversity trainings was nothing new for me. I had been doing so for almost ten years at the time. My dual tracks, coming from a social change background and from an organizational culture change background, had begun to integrate into a successful model. I had been mentored and trained and developed a consulting practice that was doing well. I had already led hundreds of trainings in all kinds of environments and my approach was a familiar one. I was pretty sure that what I thought was true, was, indeed, Truth. I was still basically using the same "oppression model" of training that I had used for a long time.

But this particular training would change the way I looked at my work forever.

The paper I was working at was in a small town in Louisiana. It was an old-style Southern town with old-style Southern attitudes. David Duke, a member of the Ku Klux Klan, had carried the parish during his run for governor, a campaign considered by most to be a throwback to the old "segregation today, segregation forever" Southern attitude.

The two-day training included a mix of people: reporters who had come from all over the country as well as some local ones, and others who worked for the paper who generally were from the town and its surrounding environs. The first day we got into the normal kinds of dialogues. People shared their experiences and argued points with one another. People of color, mostly African American at this particular training, talked about the pain of racism, how it had impacted them in their lives. Whites in the group were all over the place. Some understood, and some resisted. One man sat virtually silent the whole day, clearly listening, clearly engaged, but not speaking except in minimal comments in small groups. He was a pressman, dressed in a flannel shirt and jeans. White, probably in his mid-thirties, he could have fit the stereotypical picture of a local "Southern boy." His demeanor was pleasant, even friendly. He smiled a lot and seemed to interact easily, though quietly, with people at the breaks.

During the morning discussion on the second day of training, a couple of the African American participants were much more open than they had been about their life experiences, the challenges they had faced, and their fears for their children. It was deep and emotionally moving. Finally, out of nowhere, the man who had been silent said, "I have something to share."

His speaking surprised me, and I think others as well, and I have to say I remember feeling curious and a bit apprehensive about what would come out of his mouth. He leaned forward on his chair and started to speak, looking down mostly. I don't recall it word for word, but when he spoke he said something like this:

"I've been sitting here listening to what folks have to say and I feel a little confused and pulled in two directions. I can understand the kind of upset that people are talking about here. I haven't really heard black folks talk about it in quite this way ever before. I guess I haven't wanted to. But I know some of these folks and they seem nice. I also know that the kinds of things that they are talking about that have happened in these parts, particularly when I was a kid, were pretty scary. But I grew up right around here, on a farm not far outside of town. I've lived here my whole life. I know folks in this town, white and black. I grew up with them. There are good people here. It is hard for me to believe that those people did some of the things that you folks are talking about, but I know enough from what I've heard, and I believe you when you say they happened."

He paused for a few minutes and looked down at the ground. He stayed that way for what seemed like a long time, long enough so that the rest of us wondered whether he was finished. I remember that just as I was about to ask him whether he was finished, he looked up and he had tears in his eyes. I think everybody in the room was surprised.

"Here's my problem," he said. "My father and grandfather were the most important people in my life. They're both gone now, but they taught me everything I know. They took me hunting and fishing from the time I was this high." He motioned with his hand. "They were leaders in our community, helped people. My grandfather was the pastor of my church. They taught me to be a good father. . . ."

And then he dropped the bomb.

"But they were both members of the Klan. It wasn't talked about that much, but it wasn't hidden that much either. I don't know what they did, and I don't want to know, but as I sit here I feel the conflict inside of me. I know that what you have all been saying makes sense. Nobody should have to feel the way you're saying you feel. But I feel like when I say that, I reject the two people who were the most important people in my life, and I know, as well as I know anything, that they were good people."

The room was dead silent. I noticed that I had very little to say to the man. Normally I would have engaged him directly, but I was so touched by his authenticity and vulnerability that I found myself almost speechless. I asked him a few questions and then, after a short time, we decided to break for lunch. As the group dispersed I sat in my chair, processing what had happened. I noticed one of the most outspoken African American men in the group approaching the man, and they pulled up chairs and ate with each other, engrossed in conversation.

Even at that moment I realized that something profound had happened within me. In all the years I had dealt with the issue of race, worked on social change, and conducted trainings, my perspective had been clear: there are good people in the world who are open, accepting, nonbiased, and inclusive. Then there are bad people, who are biased, racist, sexist, anti-Semitic, homophobic, and so on. The lines, in my mind, were pretty clearly, and from my understanding today, naïvely drawn. Yet as I looked at the two men talking, and as I thought about what had transpired, I realized that this was a good and decent man, an honest man, even a courageous man. And I couldn't help but think that there is something else here to consider.

That "something else" is an important part of this book. If the diversity conversation is not simply about how good people are, what is it about?

That's where my experience in that small Louisiana town fit in. Soon I found myself shifting my approach from the oppression-based model, where organizations needed to fix the bad people, into what I call a transformation-based model, where the emphasis was on getting people to understand their own view of the world and to look outside of their own view to see and understand the experiences and viewpoints of others. I want to be clear: this doesn't mean that I am any less committed to, or willing to, intervene when it becomes clear that people are engaging in behavior that is hurtful, racist, sexist, heterosexist, and so on. These behaviors need to be confronted anytime they emerge. It is just that it became clear that by seeing another's view of the world, we could really create a dialogue. That transformational approach is at the heart of this book.

You see, the "bias equals badness" paradigm has been the foundation of most of the diversity conversation in our culture, and it is one of the reasons that most of our attempts to address diversity issues in schools, organizations, hospitals, and society have been frustrated or failed. Of course, there are good people and there are bad ones. But I have come to believe that the fundamental notion of determining who they are based on their views of diversity and inclusion is a flawed paradigm. In this book I intend to show you why. And what we can do about it.

The other problem I had with some of these early workshops was the fact that people would bring up sometimes very personal and troubling issues and then have to return to their same work environment, which had remained fundamentally unchanged. One of the things that became important to me was figuring out a way to integrate the diversity work I was now engaged in with the work I had learned from Bob Allen about creating new cultures in the workplace. I wondered whether it was possible to actually create cultures in which diversity could be immersed, rather than just train people about diversity. That search would lead me to studying systems theory and developing the Diversity Systems Map™, which I will discuss at length in chapter 12.

We have dealt with diversity in our society as long as it has been around. In fact, diversity is a fundamental dynamic of the human condition. We have tried so many ways to address it, and, while we have made progress, we continue to be frustrated in those attempts.

I have learned that we can make a difference in how we deal with these issues. I know that we can create organizations and a society where people are truly valued and included, and we can realize the possibilities of our society. There is the possibility that a diverse group of people can come together and create something better than they could by working alone.

I have to admit that I have at times felt self-conscious about being a white man and doing this work. Even being Jewish, I have rarely had to deal with any significant kind of bigotry. There have been many times when I have been told, or it was made clear in other ways, that I have not been chosen to do work for organizations for that reason, in that they preferred a woman or person of color, and others when my race and gender were undoubtedly an advantage.

Is it necessary to have experienced oppression firsthand in order to do diversity work? I don't know. But I do know that I have witnessed insensitivity from people of every diverse group. I know Jewish people who are terribly concerned about anti-Semitism but are overtly racist; I know African Americans who are terribly concerned about racism but are overtly homophobic or heterosexist; I know women who worry about sexism but are insensitive to the immigrant experience. Having said that, I can understand why people who have been the victim of societal oppression from a particular group of people might feel uncomfortable about having representatives of that group take the lead in promoting a discussion about the issues involved.

Unfortunately, we have often created a "hierarchy of pain," in which one person's experiences are considered more or less valid than another's because of their group identity when, in fact, we know that on an individual level that may not be the case. I remember leading a workshop many years ago in which we did an exercise in which participants were shown a film of various experiences that Whites and people of color were having, followed by a hidden camera. Participants were asked to react to what they saw and one white man in the group expressed surprise at how consistently the differential behavior occurred. He was shocked, he said, at how invisible it was to him. An African American woman in the group was furious with him, literally shouting at him, "That is the problem! You need to open your eyes!" and more. Later in the session the participants had an opportunity to share a bit about the origin of their views. The black woman said she had grown up in a very wealthy area, her parents were both highly regarded professionals, and she had encountered very little direct racism growing up. The man, on the other hand, described with tears how he had grown up in extreme poverty, so much so that he and his sister went to a school where the

Goodwill truck would come and the school's principal would announce their names to come out to the truck to get clothing. Who was the most oppressed? How can we know?

I have seen people weep at disclosing that they were left-handed and were forced to write with their right hand when they were younger; that they were unmercifully teased for being fat; for wearing braces; for having divorced parents; for having parents who didn't speak English, and so on. I am clear that people's experiences of oppression take many forms. The hierarchy of pain on an individual level serves very little than to continually separate us. Clearly, on a group level, certain people experience societal oppression that is far greater than others. On an individual level, we all have our own stories.

I've come to believe that it is critically important to have all people involved in the diversity process. If women and people of color overwhelmingly lead diversity and inclusion processes to the exclusion of white male involvement, the process replicates the marginalization that occurs in a normal societal system. It makes it difficult for the group not to be seen as "outsiders." In fact, it reinforces the "them versus us" paradigm. If we are to truly create inclusive, culturally competent environments for people to work and live in, then everybody needs to have a place at the table.

On a personal level, though, what it comes down to is this: *I love this work*. I love being able to make a living by making a difference in people's lives and by creating greater understanding. I love helping my clients be more successful. And I have five grandchildren. Two of them have one parent who is white and Jewish and another who is Indian and Hindu. Two others have one parent who is white and Jewish and the other who has a Filipino father who was raised Christian. The other grandchild has parents who are both white, but one Jewish and one Christian. I care a lot about the world they will live in, and I believe that the challenge of living in the world today requires *all of us* to step up and engage. And while this book is mostly directed toward developing a better understanding of how the dynamics of diversity and inclusion emerges from the United States, during the years I have worked in England, Canada, Switzerland, Puerto Rico, Singapore, Japan, Malaysia, Sweden, Austria, and Denmark. I have worked with multinational organizations and people from all over the world applying the same principles. These principles do work, and they work all over the world!

It takes more than good intentions. It takes a willingness to break open the paradigms we have been working within. It takes a willingness to look at ourselves. But it can be done. It is a possibility that, for many of us, has existed only in our fantasies, only in our dreams. A place in which organizations exist that value everyone. A place where people of all races, ethnicities, genders, sexual orientations, and more exist and work side by side.

Change is possible. Breakthroughs are possible. In this book, I will try to show you how to maximize the power of diversity, develop inclusion and cultural competency, and, ultimately, change the way you do business. The knowledge I share with you is what I have learned in more than a quarter century of doing this work with just about every kind of organization you can imagine, large and small, public and private, more than five hundred businesses, schools, grocery stores, charitable groups, not-for-profits, hospitals . . . in forty-seven states and seventeen other countries. I've even worked with a major league baseball team!

It is a new way of looking at things that leads to a new way of doing things and a new way of living. For me, it is a new way home. Home to an understanding that we all share a space on what R. Buckminster Fuller called "Spaceship Earth." And unless we begin to truly understand that (especially given the technologies of destruction that are now available to us), the results will be catastrophic.

The work begins here. It begins first with us, and then with our families and communities and workplaces. It starts by creating places to live and work in which people truly embrace both their similarities and differences in a constructive way.

This book is designed as a road map to get there.

CHAPTER 1

Why Does It Matter?

> Some may think that to affirm dialogue—the encounter of women and men in the world in order to transform the world—is naively and subjectively idealistic. There is nothing, however, more real or concrete than people in the world and with the world, than humans with other humans.
>
> Paulo Freire[1]

> The dogmas of the quiet past, are inadequate to the stormy present. The occasion is piled high with difficulty, and we must rise with the occasion. As our case is new, so we must think anew and act anew. We must disenthrall ourselves.
>
> Abraham Lincoln, December 1, 1862

Over the past generation we have spent hundreds of millions of dollars on diversity. We have put people through millions of hours of training. We have changed the name to "diversity *and* inclusion." We have created diversity and inclusion departments, diversity and inclusion councils, employee resource groups, diversity calendars, mugs, t-shirts. We've watched diversity videos, gone to diversity conferences. And yes, here I come with about the twenty thousandth diversity and inclusion book. We are practically diversity exhausted! Yet organizations continue to struggle to find effective ways to bring people from diverse backgrounds together with a sense of common purpose and commitment to create new possibilities for action.

This struggle is rooted in our collective inability to learn to live more effectively with diversity and create a society—a national identity—that is more inclusive and more culturally competent. But, more than ever before, it also is rooted in the fundamental reality that the world of business, whether it is the business of commerce, education, health care, or anything else, is now the world of diversity.

There may never have been a time when our need for new ideas has been greater. In all kinds of organizations, a new consciousness is emerging. People are beginning to truly understand that our separateness has an enormous cost in terms of productivity, teamwork, and effectiveness. In hospitals, we see a dramatic call for a greater ability to meet the needs of an increasingly diverse employee and patient base. In schools, we increasingly see the cost of our inability to effectively educate children from low-income and culturally and linguistically diverse backgrounds, and, at the college level, a greater diversity of students from around the world.

In many organizations, our attempts to build bridges of understanding have been limited to the creation and implementation of diversity and sensitivity training programs. Despite all of the time, effort, and money that have been spent, the reality is that diversity programs have, to a large degree, simply not yet fulfilled their promise. This is not for lack of effort and investment, and certainly not for a lack of good intentions. Powerful new evidence suggests that the traditional models for attacking issues, increasing awareness and tolerance, and instilling cultural literacy simply do not work as well as they should work. Yet most organizations continue to try to change by attempting incremental efforts that fail to challenge the fundamental operating notions that are producing a lack of desired results. The best definition I ever heard of insanity has been attributed to the author Rita Mae Brown, who defined it as "doing the same thing over and over and expecting different results."[2] In that sense, there is a certain insanity in the way we approach our current challenges. The bottom line is that what we are doing now, and even more importantly, *how we approach this work*, doesn't work well enough given the dramatic challenges we are confronting as a society and as a global community.

Human beings are creatures of habit and routine. We tend to rely on our past to guide us. Things that are new and different, especially *too new and different*, are generally jettisoned for more comfortable and familiar strategies. I have been hired by hundreds of organizations to help them address the issue of diversity. Together we have analyzed the situation and made recommendations, only to have people within these organizations resist practical and proven recommendations. The typical response is this: "That's not the way we do things around here." Exactly the point! Clearly, the continuous reliance on old, failed ways of operating can only continue to produce the kind of organizations that we have seen—organizations that stifle creativity and spirit and fail to rise to the challenges posed by exciting and unprecedented demographic shifts. On some level we know that we need different strategies and greater resolve. Yet we seem unable to achieve what we so desperately need. The rational, trained parts of ourselves continue to drive us toward the structures we were trained to participate in and keep us from risk or discomfort.

The purpose of this book is to feed the fire of dissatisfaction with the status quo and inspire new thinking that will lead to a reinvention of ideas and concepts about diversity and inclusion and a revolutionary impact on organizations and leaders.

Organizations across every part of the economic spectrum—hospitals, corporations, schools, religious institutions, banks, utility companies, law offices, architectural firms, government agencies, and nonprofits and charities—all share a common link. They are bound together in the acknowledgment that the way to a new future cannot be found by using the old models of limited leadership and participation. It can only be discovered by constructing a new way of *being with each other* in organizations, a way of being that is at the heart of this book. I refer to this missing ingredient as the creation of *organizational community*.

This book may be a challenge to many who have been trained in traditional organizations. It directly confronts the notion that organizations must be dominated by a few key people who must make all of the decisions and then find some way to be sure others follow their orders. It will test people within these organizations who ask questions such as "How can we afford to take the time to deal with issues like diversity when we're busier than we've ever been before?"

Some elements of this book are also certain to challenge many experienced diversity professionals. After working in the diversity field for more than twenty-five years, I am keenly aware that our intentions are great, our purposes are often noble, but our work hasn't always hit the mark. Unless we are willing to admit our failures and shortcomings, to do some self-reflection and reinvent ourselves, we will miss out on the opportunity we have to not only change the organizations we work with, but change the world.

This is my inquiry into the resounding question of how we can use inclusion and openness to catalyze change within our organizations so that they become more successful, more productive, and more effective. Some of the concepts examined may initially seem confusing. Many of them, when they are juxtaposed with each other, will be even more confusing. Good. The search for both questions and answers will continue long after the last page of this book is turned.

This book is intended to encourage people to think. It is not an academic study, although quite a lot of research and analysis went into it. It is the outgrowth of the years of personal experience I have had working in trying to change organizations, institutions, and communities, and a synthesis of the most powerful and persistent lessons I have learned along the way from a wide variety of teachers in many forms. It is a book of some philosophy and theory because, as one of the pioneers of organizational development, Kurt Lewin, once said,

"There is nothing more practical than a good theory."[3] Yet it also is a book designed to provoke action, because it is in action that we live our lives. We have to act where diversity is concerned because if we don't, the cost will be enormous.

I invite readers to digest this book skeptically, to challenge both in their minds and in application everything shared here. I am not attempting to confound people or deflect responsibility for my statements. Rather, I am attempting to articulate the specific way I intend for this book to be used—not as a source of data or facts, but rather as a catalyst for insight, thinking, reflection, creativity, and action. Many of you who are reading this book have more knowledge than I do, more experience in organizations, and far more academic study to your credit. I don't claim superior knowledge. My intention is perhaps best described by a story I once heard about Igor Stravinsky.

After Stravinsky composed his revolutionary music for the ballet *The Rite of Spring*, he purportedly gathered an orchestra to play it for the first time. The musicians looked at the music dumbfounded, having never seen any music before that was written in the way Stravinsky had arranged the piece. Finally one of them told the maestro, "I don't think I can play this music." Stravinsky is reported to have replied, "I'm not interested in you playing this music. I'm interested in the sound that is made when musicians of your quality try to play it."

I do not know whether that's a true story, but it reflects my intention in writing this book. I don't want people to *believe* it. I want it to inspire people to begin to make sense of their lives, particularly with one another. We are at a pivotal point in human history. The threat to our global peace and prosperity is simply too dire to imagine if we cannot find new ways to work with organizations to help build productive, collaborative work environments in which *all* people communicate effectively, recognize their value, develop themselves as leaders, and contribute powerfully to their organizations and communities.

I am attempting to open up the diversity conversation in a broader way to a broader array of people. I want to be clear that I do not claim any exclusive hold on the concept of creating inclusive organizations, of creating successful diversity efforts, or of bringing community alive, in organizations or anywhere else. There are people all over the world who are engaged in this same search, and some of their work has contributed to my work as it has developed. Nor do I claim to have completely figured out how to do it myself, for in our company we have struggled with many of these same issues over the years. We do not have traditional models of these kinds of cultures to fall back on. We are inventing, exploring, creating, and validating as we go along.

This book will follow a path of learning for the reader that I hope will allow people at all levels of organizations to take responsibility for creating a new way of existing in organizations. And it is not only for those people who have executive-level titles. I believe that we have evolved to the point where the notion that only those with titles can create change in organizations is an outdated one. This book is a clarion call to people to take hold of their lives and their organizations and begin to create inclusive organizational communities by involving all levels of people, and if necessary, one at a time.

The challenge, of course, is that doing things in new ways is not easy for us. Let me give you an example of what I mean.

Many years ago, when I was in elementary school, I learned to type. I remember being curious as to why it was that typewriters were built with that strange keyboard. You know what I mean. Wouldn't it make more sense to have a typewriter keyboard that was alphabetical or designed in some coherent order rather than the QWERTY keyboard that has become a ubiquitous part of our lives on typewriters, computer keyboards, iPhones, BlackBerry devices, and virtually any other keyboarded technology? It might, but that assumes that "what makes sense" is the driving force behind the typewriter keyboard, or, for that matter, many decisions that we make on a regular basis. In fact, it is often not a function of "what makes sense," but rather "what *made* sense."

The QWERTY keyboard was the creation of Christopher Latham Sholes, the main inventor of the first widely used commercial typewriter, the Remington Standard. Early typewriter mechanisms were quite awkward, and the keys tended to jam quite frequently, so much so that the process of typing was slow and laborious. Working with his assistant, James Densmore, Sholes created the QWERTY keyboard by separating the letters that tended to be typed together (the technical term for this is a digraph). In addition, Sholes wanted the word *typewriter* to be able to be typed using only the top row in order to make it easy for salesmen to demonstrate the machine. The resulting keyboard had the unintended effect of being awkward and confusing to typists. Only 32 percent of the typing time was spent on what is referred to as the "home" row, and they were thus slowed down. However, the slower typing speed actually reduced key sticking and contributed to people being able to type faster, which was a brilliant, if accidental, stroke of counterintuitive technology. After the Remington Standard was patented in 1878, it became the industry standard and has remained so for the past 130 years, not only on typewriters, but also on almost anything else with a keyboard.

The interesting thing is that the need for the QWERTY keyboard was eliminated relatively quickly when the use of springs in the keys corrected the jamming issues to a great degree. However, by that time the Remington had in fact become the standard and was widely in use. For years, other models were promoted, with perhaps the most popular being a model developed by Augustus Dvorak on a Carnegie Foundation grant in the 1930s. The Dvorak keyboard was designed with a scientific attention to placement of the keys. The key vowels were set on the left side of the home row, the key consonants on the right. While the Sholes keyboard allows fewer than one thousand words to be typed from the home row, the Dvorak model allows ten thousand. It was easier to learn, more logical . . . superior by virtually any standard. Yet after it was patented in 1936, it was largely unused, except by a cultish following that continued for years. Why did the new innovation go unused? Because the QWERTY keyboard is "the way we do things around here"!

So what does a curious story about a typewriter keyboard have to do with diversity? It actually has more to do with the title of this book, *Reinventing Diversity*. As Mr. Sholes's typewriter has taught us, it is difficult to change things once they have become the norm. Our pattern is to continue to do them the same way we have always done them unless there is a glaring, obvious reason not to. Reinvention is often challenging.

The state of diversity[4] in our country and in our organizations is at a point of crisis. And I use the word *crisis* quite specifically in the sense that we are at an incipient point of history in which we have the opportunity to either move constructively into a new future in which we constructively deal with the inevitable and irrevocable movement to a more diverse society and an ever-changing world, or one in which we decline into a deeper and deeper sense of tribalism, one that threatens to tear our society apart.

The opportunity is all around us. As most people can see all around them, the demographics of the world are changing with staggering rapidity. In 1967, when the two hundred millionth American was born, approximately 78 percent of United States residents were classified as "white." By 2006, when the three hundred millionth American was born, that number had dropped to just over 60 percent. Most demographic predictions are that by the year 2050, that number will have dropped well below 50 percent.[5] Ninety percent of the population growth in the United States over the next forty to fifty years is expected to come from people of color. And during that same period it is expected that the white population will increase only 7 percent, and that includes Whites born in other countries.

In addition to higher birth rates among people of color, immigration is a major factor in this demographic revolution. The past twenty years have brought us an extraordinary influx of immigrants. As of this writing, approximately 12 percent of the residential population of the United States is made up of people who were born outside the borders of the country, the largest percentage since the nineteenth century. More than 50 percent of them have come to this country since 1990! And these numbers don't even include millions of people who are currently residing in the United States without documentation.

I have had the opportunity to talk with and work with demographers over the years, and I find it to be a fascinating field. Demographers track population changes in extraordinary detail and find noteworthy patterns in changes of one-tenth of one percentage point per year. We are talking about one-half of a percentage point per year, over a forty-year period . . . which is *five times that pace!*

Not only that, but patterns of immigration are different, too. When we look at earlier periods of robust immigration we see vast differences in the makeup of the immigrant pool. At the turn of the past century, for example, when all of my grandparents came to this country, more than 60 percent of the immigrant population was European. Today that number has dropped below 30 percent, as more immigrants are coming from South and Central America, Africa, Asia, the Middle East, the Caribbean, and other places. People not only look a lot more different but also have cultural models that are more distinct than ever before.

In addition, people are not "melting" into American culture in the way they once did. Travel around the country. You will see surprising pockets of different cultures in places that one might not suspect. Omaha, Nebraska, has one of the largest intact Sudanese populations in the country. Penobscot, Maine, and Columbus, Ohio, have large Somali populations. Hmong populations flourish in Minnesota and Wisconsin. Even in Utah, for a long time considered one of the whitest states in the country, one in ten residents is now Hispanic.[6]

I know that the xenophobes among us rail against immigration. They bemoan the loss of our "national identity." Perhaps a few minutes with a history book will remind them that the national identity of the United States is the story of immigrants coming together and of different people growing together in different ways. Yes, in an earlier time a greater percentage of them were white. The differences weren't as great. That's why we have to learn how to make it work in this new reality today.

When I started my career in diversity consulting in the early 1980s, we struggled sometimes to make the "business case." Those of us who were studying the information knew that the trends were there, but we simply didn't have the research to back up our assertions. Today the business case could not be clearer. Unless somebody is deeply committed to not seeing the impact of diversity (and, let's face it, we know that some still are), it is virtually impossible to ignore the impact of these numbers on market share, on staffing, on employee retention . . . on having a successful business. That's why virtually all Fortune 500 companies engage in some kind of diversity effort today.

The opportunity also lies in the vast network of diversity professionals who work in companies all around the world today. Years ago when I began in this field, you could count diversity professionals in the hundreds. Now organizations have made enormous commitments of personnel, resources, time, and training programs. It is more the norm than the exception for an organization of any substantial size to have some diversity focus. And beyond that there are industry-wide networks, conferences, and websites. Diversity has become part of the daily vernacular of American and global business.

Patterns of diversity are changing similarly all over the world. The world is becoming less Westernized, more urbanized, and more connected. Patterns of immigration flood the planet. The global nature of business, in fact the increasing level of our global perspective in general, is dramatically increasing the need for us to become culturally intelligent, flexible, and competent. Consider these facts:[7]

- If you're one in a million in China . . . there are 1,300 people just like you. If you're one in a million in India, there are 1,100 people just like you.
- The 25 percent of the population in China with the highest IQ is greater than the total population of North America. In India, it's the top 28 percent. They have more honors students than we have students.
- In 2006, there were 1.3 million college graduates in the United States, 3.1 million in India, and 3.3 million in China.
- All of the college graduates in India speak English.
- In ten years China will become the number one English-speaking country in the world, if it is not already.
- If you took every single job in the United States today and shipped it to China . . . China would still have a labor surplus.
- In the next eight minutes, sixty babies will be born in the United States, 244 babies will be born in China, and 351 babies will be born in India.
- More than half of twenty-one-year-olds in the United States have already put material on the Internet.
- Seventy percent of U.S. four-year-olds have used the Internet.
- Through radio, it took thirty-eight years to get information out to fifty million people; through television, that number was cut to thirteen years; through the Internet, it can be a matter of days.
- There are now more than one billion Internet devices in the world.
- More than one in eight married couples last year met online . . . many met and married people from different countries.
- The number of daily text messages now exceeds the population of the planet.
- Facebook now has *five hundred million* members worldwide, with 240,000 joining each day.
- Three thousand books are published daily.
- Two billion children live in developing countries, and one in three will never complete the fifth grade. Nicholas Negroponte's One Laptop per Child[8] project is already distributing millions of computers to children *who have never held a book in their hands.* And now they will hold the world.

Toto, I have a feeling we're not in Kansas anymore.

That's why we have to create organizations that work for the people in them and diversity efforts that make that happen. I'm not saying they never work, or that they don't work somewhat. There are some outstanding examples of companies that have been successful in many of their diversity efforts. I'm also not saying that people don't want them to work. As I said before, there are a lot of good people, smart people, conscientious people who have tried very hard to make them work. There are good leaders who would like to see their organizations reflect the racial and demographic makeup of their communities; they would like to see them become more inclusive, and they would like to have *all* of the people in them be more successful and productive. And in the best of all possible worlds, they wish they could wave their magic wands and say, "Great! Our diversity improves the level of quality and performance that we are now operating at as a corporation."

Yet most diversity programs have not produced the kinds of breakthroughs that organizations and the people in them have sought. So we often find ourselves frustrated and asking the question, "Does anything really make a significant, sustainable difference?"

Perhaps even more importantly, on a societal level we know that despite our best efforts we still see dramatic examples of our failing to make a difference. We never seem far away from the next conflagration over some diversity-related issue.

In organizations, despite the success of a few, the numbers still tell a bleak story. Promotions and retention rates are lower among women and people of color. And at the very top, the results remain strikingly unchanged: there are still only thirteen women and four African Americans among the Fortune 500 chief executive officers. Yet in the face of these facts, some people still believe that white men are now the victims of discrimination. Yes, we now have plenty of vaunted lists and coveted awards, but often organizations receive them as much for how well they market their efforts as for the actual effectiveness of the efforts.

No wonder some people are hesitant to invest, financially and emotionally, in trying to make these efforts work. No wonder so many have developed a cynical attitude, thinking of diversity as "soft stuff" or, in the "technical" words of a business executive I once knew, "touchy-feely bullshit." No wonder so many people are suffering from "diversity fatigue." They believe in the fundamental idea; they've heard it presented countless times; they would like to see it happen, but they're tired of dealing with it and resigned and hopeless as to the possibility that anything can *really* change.

It is time for a revolution in the way we approach diversity.

We are at a historical watershed about diversity in our society and in our organizations. Many people have worked hard to get more and more people into organizations; to create diverse schools and diverse communities. It is folly for anybody to suggest that diversity is not a regular part of our lives and that it won't continue to be even more so in the future. It is, whether one likes it or not, an inevitability of nature. But the question becomes, what does it leave us? How will having the diversity we are increasingly living with impact our societal and organizational structures?

We have recently seen the results of several studies that give us some perspective on this question. In 2006, Robert Putnam, a political scientist at Harvard University, discussed the findings of a study that he had conducted regarding the impact of diversity on "social capital," a term that he had popularized with his widely read and well-thought-of book, *Bowling Alone*, in 2000.[9] Social capital, as Putnam defines it, is the value of the "social networks and the associated norms of reciprocity and trustworthiness" that impact the lives of people.[10] It is important to preface his findings by stating that Putnam is a self-described advocate of diversity, so his study is not one that set about to debunk the value of diversity. Despite that, his findings were troubling.

Putnam and his team interviewed more than thirty thousand people who live in increasingly diverse communities around the country. In his own words, what he found was this:

> In the long run immigration and diversity are likely to have important cultural, economic, fiscal, and developmental benefits. In the short run, however, immigration and ethnic diversity tend to reduce social solidarity and social capital. New evidence . . . suggests that in ethnically diverse neighborhoods residents of all races tend to "hunker down." Trust (even of one's own race) is lower, altruism and community cooperation rarer, friends fewer.[11]

His findings indicate that the fact of integrating various racial, cultural, and ethnic groups in our societal structure does not, in and of itself, create a greater sense of social inclusion or, in his terms, social capital. In fact, it may be doing the opposite. This finding contradicts some of the most foundational beliefs about diversity, beliefs that have been at the basis of some of our most aggressive social and organizational efforts. As far back as the early 1950s, social scientists, particularly Gordon Allport in his landmark work *The Nature of Prejudice*, have promoted what has often been referred to as the "contact theory" of race relations, the belief that when people were put together within a social environment, the increased contact would begin to create more trust and greater social comfort.[12] Perhaps that is true. Certainly many of us who have children in schools with a diverse population notice that their social circle is far more diverse than ours was when we were younger. Perhaps, eventually, more trust and greater social comfort will emerge. But how long can we wait to find out?

Putnam's findings suggest "the more ethnically diverse the people we live around, the less we trust them."[13] Even more disturbingly, he found that not only do we trust others less, but we also experience degradation in the trust we feel toward people who are members of our own groups. In other words, "diversity seems to trigger *not* in-group/out-group division, but anomie or social isolation"[14] in general. He described it as a "turtling" effect, much like the way a turtle pulls into its shell in the face of uncertainty or fear. In the case of communities, it is characterized not only by less interaction and less trust, but also by reduced participation in social institutions that contribute to the development of social capital (e.g., civic associations, PTAs, and so forth). It's not so much that diversity damages race relations or increases racial hostility per se,

> rather, inhabitants of diverse communities tend to withdraw from collective life, to distrust their neighbors, regardless of the color of their skin, to withdraw even from close friends, to expect worse from their community and its leaders, to volunteer less, give less to charity and work on community projects less often, to vote less, to agitate for social reform *more*, but have less faith that they can actually make a difference, and to huddle unhappily in front of the television. . . . Diversity, at least in the short run, seems to bring out the turtle in all of us.[15]

Some opponents of diversity seized on Putnam's findings with great gusto. The *Wall Street Journal*, in a piece by Daniel Henninger titled "The Death of Diversity," declared that the study was "the last nail in the coffin of diversity," and that it confirmed that diversity is a "solution without a problem."[16]

However, these reactions actually run counter to what Putnam is suggesting. Putnam's findings do not suggest that diversity cannot be a force for greater community and cooperation, but rather that by the way we have gone about it, by throwing people together in diverse groups and largely expecting them to "work it out," we are not achieving our aims. In fact, Putnam actually strikes a more optimistic chord when he looks at what is possible:

> In the long run, however, successful immigrant societies have overcome such fragmentation by creating new, cross-cutting forms of social solidarity and more encompassing identities. Illustrations of becoming comfortable with diversity can be drawn from the U.S. military, religious institutions, and early waves of American immigration . . . dampening the negative effects of diversity by constructing new, more encompassing identities. Thus the central challenge for modern, diversifying societies is to create a new, broader sense of "we."[17]

This more optimistic view was substantiated by another recent study released in 2007 by Scott E. Page, professor of complex systems, political science, and economics at the University of Michigan. Page has a background in theoretical mathematics from the California Institute of Technology and has studied whether mathematical theories of diversity in problem solving also apply to human systems. He found that, in fact, they do. He found that diverse groups, when formulated effectively, and when people have taken the time to learn to understand one another, communicate and work together effectively and produce better results with higher productivity and more creative problem solving.[18]

Similarly, James Surowiecki, in *The Wisdom of Crowds*,[19] suggests that diverse groups of people make better decisions than individuals or homogeneous groups in solving three major kinds of problems: *cognition problems*, those that have or will have definitive solutions; *coordination problems*, those requiring members of a group to figure out how to coordinate their behavior with one another; and *cooperation problems*, those involving the challenge of getting people to work together.[20] Surowiecki suggests that the essential factors in this benefit in decision-making come from three major characteristics: points of view that are diverse; independence from the opinions of others; and a lack of enforced centralization, which allows people to draw on local knowledge.

In reality, virtually all of us know that there is truth in Page's and Surowiecki's assertions. Anybody who has a hobby and has had the opportunity to practice it with some new people on occasion has experienced the phenomenon. We learn from one another, and out of that learning we expand our abilities. I am a musician and play some percussion instruments. I remember sitting in India with a man playing the tablas, the small lap drums that Westerners often associate with sitar players. He taught me a different style than I would normally use to play my congas. When I returned to my congas, that style had been integrated. The whole now included some elements of both . . . and was better. Perhaps you noticed the same when you were cooking with a friend or when you were designing an engineering project.

These studies are showing us the crossroads that we face. If we ignore the increasing diversity in our society and expect that it will "work itself out," we are likely to end up with the turtling phenomenon described by Putnam. On the other hand, if we find ways to understand each other better, work together more effectively, and deepen our connection, we will reap the benefits that Page and Surowiecki describe.

That is why this is such an important moment in our history. Where will we choose to be on the "Putnam to Page pipeline"?

So while I have begun this book with the assertion that most diversity programs don't work, I want to be clear that I'm not saying that diversity programs can't work. What I am saying, though, is that there is a reason they usually don't work. It lies in a historic set of paradigms that has dominated our ways of thinking and our action in addressing the issue of diversity and in an unchallenged background to the way we think and feel about the subject. In some cases, it is a set of paradigms that may have served us well in getting to the historical moment that we are in, but that must be revisited if we are to move forward, if we are to create a future not only of true diversity, inclusion, and cultural competency, but also of a healthy society with successful organizations.

Today, it is politically correct to say that your company, your school, your hospital, or any other kind of organization is committed to diversity (and, to some degree, dangerous to not say it). Yet only rarely have these organizations created cultures in which people have experienced a real breakthrough in their ability to create environments in which large numbers of people can work inclusively and with a high level of cultural flexibility.

Most organizations, even those that are conducting large-scale diversity efforts, are driven more by what they feel they need to do than they are by a commitment to create an inclusive environment for their workers and a high level of cultural competency. They have lost touch with their commitment to diversity, or perhaps they have never really understood or articulated their commitment to it. Instead, they have gotten caught up in the details surrounding it, arguing over affirmative action, debating policies and practices, and avoiding embarrassing and costly lawsuits and discrimination charges. But generally, they have not really understood the actual impact that diversity has on the way their organization functions. The reality is that when it comes to diversity, a lot of us don't know what we don't know. It's like having a very large blind spot, one that is costing companies millions of dollars.

Yet, as I said earlier, we can no longer afford for diversity not to work given the changing demographics of our everyday world. In 1964, approximately 65 percent of the American workforce was made up of white men. Today, the number of white male employees is less than 50 percent. And, according to U.S. Department of Labor findings, only 15 to 20 percent of new hires entering the workforce in 2010 were native-born white men.[21] At the same time, the economic base within communities of color[22] continues to grow. The combined spending power of African Americans, Asians, Hispanics, and Native American Indians has more than doubled in the past twenty years, about twice as fast as the increase in spending by Whites.[23] In addition, it is now estimated that more than forty million Americans have disabilities, and, according to a Harris study, as many as fourteen to sixteen million Americans self-identify as gay, lesbian, or bisexual.

The changing workforce and expanding marketplace has created enormous opportunities for those companies that can offer their products and services in new ways, and companies looking for the best talent better be thinking of creating environments in which *all people* see some possibility of a future for themselves. It might seem elementary today, more than fifty years after the landmark *Brown v. Board of Education* decision, but the reality is that most American businesses still exclude people from full participation, some doing so without even realizing it. And that is only the tip of an iceberg that includes poor hiring decisions, poor promotional decisions, and then leading to revenue lost to turnover along with marketing, sales, and service delivery issues. In an increasingly diverse organization, leaders who do not manage that diversity will no longer be seen as simply poor managers of diversity; they will be seen as poor managers.

In some ways, our diversity "programs" are like diets. Any expert on weight loss and fitness will tell you that diets don't work in the long run. Sure, you can see short-term benefits or temporary results. We finish a training program and feel good about it. People seem to learn and understand. Yet how many times has it been like a car wash? A couple of weeks later it is like a faint memory, a dusty course book on the shelf, and we find some new language to describe the same old behavior. The car has begun to get dirty yet again. We have learned that the only way to ensure long-term weight loss is to change the way you eat and exercise. In short, you have to change your lifestyle. And generally, understanding what it takes to change requires a willingness to engage in some introspection to get a better understanding about why you eat. And to maintain the results, you have to constantly renew the process. Making diversity work within an organization requires the same kind of thinking. We have to change the "lifestyles" of our organizations if we are going to create real, substantive change.

To make real, lasting change requires organizations to completely rethink the way they view diversity. They have to be willing to make systemwide culture change. Essentially, they have to change the way they do business. And because change is constant, they have to constantly renew the process. Creating diversity "programs" won't do it; trying new or different activities won't do it; trying new names for it won't do it: creating a permanent diversity commitment can, and will, do it.

The exploration of the topic of diversity is one that increases almost daily on the national scene. At the same time as the diversity of our community expands dramatically, the clear sense of fear and isolation that so many feel drives more and more people to turn to questioning our notion of a common connectedness. So, in that sense, the question of diversity is inherently correlated with the question of what community means to us. I will discuss this drive in chapter 4, what diversity and community mean to us, why we find a resolution to it so persistently elusive, and, finally, where we begin to create the possibility of a reemergence of community in our work lives and daily lives.

I start in chapter 2 by looking at why diversity programs aren't working. Then, in chapter 3, I explore the way we think and how our background gives us a particular sense of the world we see. I talk about how things are within societies and organizations that have us facing some of the issues we currently grapple with, and I try to help the reader understand what it is about our development as a culture that has permitted our organizational and business environment to develop the way it has developed. In chapter 5 I uncover the background of the way we look at diversity itself and some of the myths that we have created about community, and I look at the human and organizational needs we are confronting. I also try to explain why we, as human beings and most particularly as Americans, have created the kinds of organizations we have created.

In chapters 6, 7, and 8 I explore the nature of how human beings see the world and the power that language has in that worldview. I attempt to integrate a rather eclectic body of studies, philosophies, and teachings to identify and understand key elements in the development of our organizations and identify what paradigms we've created that limit our opportunities to be successful in our diversity efforts. And in chapters 9 and 10 I offer some ways to develop a better understanding of ourselves and a sense of mastery around issues of diversity.

In the remaining chapters, I discuss the concept of creating *organizational community* in a more complete way, developing an understanding of how the concept plays itself out in the organizational experience and including a case study. I attempt to create a new possibility for the future of our organizations and a new set of paradigms to guide us in moving diversity forward into the twenty-first century.

I am committed to having this book be more than just a new philosophy. I want it to create action so that once we've identified what we are trying to create, we will begin to distinguish how we can create it. I will identify a particular model for creating organizational cultures that value diversity and inclusion and are culturally competent, along with some key concepts that we have found to be critical in stewarding an organization through the development process. You, the reader, will have an opportunity to engage in your own exploration of your organization to see what kinds of things you can begin to do to create a sense of *organizational community*.

I know how many books there are on the shelves about organizational change and management development, and even about community. It is understandable if, as you are reading this book, you experience déjà vu at times or, in a more direct sense perhaps, feel as if you've "heard this before." I make no claim that every thought or idea expressed in this book is original. I have attempted to be rigorous in acknowledging the thinkers that have contributed to my own learning. Yet some thoughts have been with me for so long and have come from so many places that I no longer know where I learned them. I also ask that you not feel the need to abandon old thoughts and ideas that you have in order to consider the ones that are expressed in this book. By the time you read it I can almost promise you that my own perspective will have altered, changed, or evolved.

You also should know that I don't want you to read this book as if I think I am the pope or a guru on the subject of diversity. I know that this is a journey of discovery that I continue to be on as a businessman and a consultant. I am still experimenting and discovering new ways to create *organizational commu-nity* in my own company, in my client organizations, and in the community in which I live. I do ask that you listen to what I write here with the understand-ing that I have operated three separate businesses, worked in large and small organizations, and consulted with organizations all over the country for more than twenty-five years. During that time I have probably worked directly with two hundred thousand people. The assertions that are made in the book come from that experience. That doesn't make them true, just heavily (and sometimes painfully) researched.

I have tried to make this book as useful as possible. I have written it to be interacted with your own experiences. My hope is that you will stop at times and talk to the people you work and live with to explore these concepts and see whether they ring true in your life. Play with this book. Use it as a tool.

The notion of *organizational community* is a leap of faith for many. It re-quires a belief that reinventing our ways of being with one another will produce a breakthrough that makes it worth the pain and discomfort that the change can cause. I recognize that even though organizations have already started producing results, this does not guarantee the absence of that fear.

I believe that we have come to a place in time where we have no choice but to reach across the gulf of fear to touch one another. We have to dare to chal-lenge the norms that tell us to play it safe, because there is no safety anyway. Helen Keller perhaps said it best when she said, "Security is mostly a supersti-tion. It does not exist in nature, nor do the children of man as a whole experience it. Avoiding danger is no safer in the long run than outright exposure. Life is either a daring adventure, or nothing."[24]

When I suggest to people in workshops that they reach out to people around them, it is shocking how often people respond, "I can't do *that*!" But it is rarely because they don't want to or even long to do so. People are concerned about how others will respond. Will they be offended? Will they file lawsuits? How can we afford the time?

Yet those are exactly the things that are happening now. We have to begin to see that we are standing at the window of a burning building, waiting to see whether or not it's safe to jump into the firefighter's safety net. It looks scary as hell, *but we're going to die if we don't jump.* This book is an invitation to jump.

The desired fruits of our labor are more inclusive: culturally competent organizations and a more inclusive, culturally competent society. I believe that such a society is a closer expression of the truest nature of the human soul. It embodies the reality that even though we live in an illusion of separateness, we are actually interdependent, interconnected by our nature. We are like the large aspen forest in Colorado—seemingly separate trees, but actually one large organism connected by a common root system. We are an intact community; we just haven't seen it yet.

The tree analogy brings me back to where I started. Does *reinventing diversity* mean that we are casting out all that we have done in the past? Does it mean that our efforts go unvalued and unacknowledged? No. It is springtime as I sit and write this, and the trees are just beginning to bud with new leaves. Last year's leaves were jettisoned during the fall, *but not because they served no purpose.* They were jettisoned so that new growth could occur . . . the new leaves of spring.

We are at a similar time in our diversity journey. We have to create a new way of approaching this issue that honors the work of the past but creates an opportunity for new growth moving forward.

It is time to *reinvent diversity.*

CHAPTER 2

Why Most Diversity Programs Haven't Succeeded

Because many professionals are always successful at what they do, they rarely experience failure, and because they have rarely failed, they have never learned how to learn from failure. So whenever their strategies go wrong, they become defensive, screen out criticism, and put the "blame" on anyone and everyone but themselves. In short, their ability to learn shuts down precisely at the moment they need it the most.

Chris Argyris[1]

It can be really off-putting when you lose your way somehow.

A. A. Milne, from *Winnie-the-Pooh*[2]

Faced with the choice between changing one's mind and proving that there is no need to do so, almost everyone gets busy on the proof.

John Kenneth Galbraith

I know that in suggesting that most diversity programs haven't worked, I may upset some colleagues who have labored hard and seen some results. So in making that suggestion, it seems reasonable to begin by defining what determines a successful diversity program. To my mind, a diversity program that "works" is a very high and important standard to meet. Definitely, there are organizations that are meeting that standard, but when looked at in the context of the thousands of businesses, schools, hospitals, and government agencies, they are a woefully small percentage of all diversity programs. One challenge in defining diversity program success has been that diversity professionals have often focused more on activities than results. For instance, why do we recommend training so often with regard to improving diversity within organizations? Because training is good. How do we know it's good? Because we say so.

In fact, a study published in 2007 by researchers Alexander Kalev of Harvard University, Frank Dobbin of the University of Minnesota, and Erin Kelly of the University of California, Berkeley, found that diversity training, particularly when offered independent of other measures, could not be proven to contribute to an increase in diversity.[3] I have some concerns about the research methodology and subsequent assertions due to the fact that the researchers studied relatively few programs and tended to treat diversity training as a monolithic entity, when diversity training is actually conducted in many different ways by many different practitioners. One would be dismissive, for example, of the assertion that "restaurants are bad" and might naturally respond, "Which restaurants are you referring to?" Nonetheless, any honest assessment, even by those of us in the diversity business, has to be that there is some legitimacy to their findings.

Simply throwing training programs at the diversity problem and forcing people to attend doesn't generally seem to have resulted in much long-term sustainable impact upon organizational behavior regarding diversity. Some organizations have conducted mandatory training, introduced it in a constructive way, and realized success. Success, unfortunately, is too often defined as fewer diversity complaints raised with human resources and making a half-hearted commitment to increasing diversity in future hires. Unfortunately, more often than not, training has created a backlash, resulting in an increase in cynicism and resistance to a more diverse workforce. Diversity becomes trivialized as "the program du jour" cooked up by the human resources staff in an effort to try and improve the organization's public face.

With all of this said, we really haven't yet created any consensus measures of diversity program success, and so we return to our own individual determinations of success. We are left to decide what works and what doesn't by employing relatively subjective standards. But what happens if different people have different needs for their diversity initiatives? How do we know when a diversity program is *really* working, and how can we then say that most are not?

I am not declaring myself the arbiter of standards for diversity program success. The true and ultimate measure of success for any program is whether it meets the needs of the people implementing it and who stand to benefit from it. For example, if the sole purpose of conducting diversity and inclusion activities is to fulfill an expectation or a requirement that it be done, then the simple act of conducting the training is, by that definition, a success. While most of us would agree that this alone is not sufficient to create a well-functioning inclusive organization, if that is all the particular organization is seeking, then it has, in its own sense, "succeeded."

I do want to offer a description of the standards that I have set for success, standards against which I believe most diversity programs fall short. I believe that diversity efforts can be reasonably measured against a number of standards, some of which are quantifiable. It is important to note that quantifiable results are not inherently more valuable than nonquantifiable or anecdotal results. I remember spending some time with Edwards Deming (the renowned organizational quality guru) toward the end of his life. Deming, of course, was well known for his use of quality measurement. By introducing quality measurement practices, he transformed the Japanese business environment after World War II. Later, he introduced hundreds of American businesses to the total quality management (TQM) movement and its use of metrics. Yet after a career of instituting measurable quality programs, he said he had come to believe that less than 10 percent of the things leaders do that really matter could be quantified.

Many of us implicitly know this, too. For instance, most of us value interpersonal "teamwork" (by which I mean the quality of interactions between team members). We inherently believe that teamwork is better than divisiveness, even though it is difficult to absolutely prove that teamwork has a direct impact on typical organizational success. In fact, we have a good deal of evidence to suggest that interpersonal "teamwork" is not always necessary to organizational success. The Oakland A's and New York Yankees baseball teams of the 1970s and 1980s were famous for bickering, fighting, . . . and winning. Yet we rarely need to establish the ROI (return on investment) of working on creating a better team.

Before I move deeply into discussing success standards, it is important to clarify language. By language, I'm not just referring to creating a new name or sets of names, and I'm definitely not talking about becoming politically correct. I'm talking about creating a whole new way of understanding diversity and how we relate to diversity.

The term *diversity* has generally represented an acceptance of difference, a lack of discrimination due to difference, and a presence of different kinds of people in organizations. Historically, it has been related to as more of a means to erase or fix problems than as a way to create a new future vision. That is why it often seems that when an organization announces it will have a diversity program, people begin whispering as to whether the organization has been sued.

It reminds me of what it was like back in the early 1980s when I was working in a large hospital. One of my responsibilities involved developing an employee and community wellness program. My colleagues and I were frustrated in our efforts because the very concept of a hospital doing wellness work was anathema to the cultural paradigm that largely existed in the normal American health-care system of the time. Hospitals in those days were there to do one thing—heal sick people. Of course, we now understand the limitations of that approach. Most of the best hospitals now have wellness programs for their communities as well as their employees.

The diversity conversation has evolved in a similar way. It began in earnest in the early 1980s with an increased awareness of the level of challenges (or "illness") that some people were facing: bias, discrimination, lack of access, oppression, physical and emotional violence, and so on. As a society, we responded to that awareness by first passing laws and then instituting compliance measures to make it illegal to continue these practices. Eventually, we attempted to create a state of social diversity, where people were not denied their rights, were more appropriately represented in organizations, and were not actively discriminated against. In other words, in the health-care metaphor, we now work to create organizations in which people are no longer "sick." Despite our efforts, we have not achieved true levels of "wellness" in too many of our organizations.

In order to really reach our potential, we will need to not only get people in the door but really develop a sense of *inclusion*. What is inclusion? I believe it means creating opportunities for people to be part of the fundamental fabric of the way the organization functions—decision-making, responsibility, leadership—and then creating organizations that are *culturally competent, culturally intelligent*, and *culturally flexible*. We have to develop a certain level of competence in understanding the needs of various people we are working with and serving, and beyond that, we have to develop the flexibility to be able to know where to apply our various competencies to achieve their most effective impact.

Cultural flexibility is more than just a component of a diversity program. It's a systematic approach to incorporating an awareness of diversity and skills related to diversity into everything an organization does. It may sound straightforward, but teaching companies to create inclusion and cultural competency is tricky. It's not like teaching team building or leadership skills. People often come into a program with the notion that "diversity is a lot of politically correct BS that people are going to shove down my throat, and the only reason they're doing this is so they can hire more Blacks and more women and fewer people like me." If people don't see the bigger vision of how the work will serve the organization they are part of, they can be given the best simulations, interactions, information, reasons, and so on, and those things will not change their vision. In fact, they will actively find ways to discount it or disregard it because it doesn't fit within their self-protective psychological mechanism.

One of the challenges we face today is that the level of misinformation people have acquired about diversity is quite staggering. The myth perpetuates among many people that, as a result of diversity efforts of the past thirty years, and particularly affirmative action programs, white men are now "an endangered species" in organizations and are denied access to jobs and opportunities. "After all," people say, "if Barack Obama can get elected president, then we obviously don't have a diversity problem anymore." This has led to a cry from some for a rollback in diversity efforts.

Of course, affirmative action is a particular target of people who resist the need for diversity and inclusion. And the subject is one in which there are tremendous misconceptions. Most people think of affirmative action as a relatively new historical phenomenon and one that is used only to increase the hiring (or in the case of schools, admission) of women and people of color. In reality, affirmative action has been with us informally for years and has been used in many ways in many organizations. For example, many school systems actively recruit male teachers because of the belief that students benefit from a gender mix in faculty. Businesses actively hire people who speak different languages in order to be able to serve a multilingual customer base. Many of us went to colleges and universities that have had affirmative admission programs for years, but not the types of programs that bring in students of color. I'm referring to the programs that bring in students who are 6'11" tall and can dunk a basketball really well, or others whose parents or grandparents went to the school, or especially those who have a building on campus named for their relatives. We refer to these programs as "sports recruiting" or "legacy admissions," but both are affirmative action programs. However, you may notice that when the superstar student athlete, or the student who comes accompanied by a big donation, enters the school with slightly lower grade point averages, there is very little outcry about "lowering the standards" of our schools. In fact, the goal of affirmative action is very simple: it is the desire to create a population within our organizations that, for whatever reason, seems to better serve the purpose of the organization. The desired results can include a wish to provide a broader, more multicultural educational experience to prepare students for the multicultural world that they will be living in, or have representation within an organization that helps the organization meet the needs of an increasingly multicultural customer base.

And yet, despite the actual "normalcy" of making decisions in this manner, some people still see it as aberrant. This idea points to a fascinating human phenomenon, which has been called "inattentional blindness."[4] Human beings, given a particular focus or interest, can miss seeing things that are right in front of their faces. We'll examine this and other aspects of how the mind processes these dynamics in subsequent chapters, but in the case of affirmative action, the self-interest of some people simply makes it easy to see things differently from the reality in front of their faces.

A noteworthy example of this was the reaction to the appointment of Supreme Court Justice Sonia Sotomayor in 2009. After Sotomayor was nominated by President Obama to be the first woman of color to be nominated for the highest court in the land, many people complained about it being an "affirmative action appointment," even though Sotomayor clearly was as qualified as any previous appointee. Consider the perspective. Up to that point in history, there had been 111 Supreme Court justices. A total of 106 of them had been white men. All were appointed by white male presidents. All were confirmed by overwhelmingly white male U.S. senators. Yet, somehow, that doesn't seem like affirmative action? Do people believe that presidents for years went out searching for the best possible justices and just by coincidence they were overwhelmingly white men? We have affirmatively created our organizations for years, and we may still need to affirmatively do some work before we have organizations that truly reflect our society.

But the deeper question is whether or not our society has truly achieved equality. Let's consider that question. As of 2008, if America had full racial equality in jobs, African Americans would have held nearly two million more professional and managerial jobs. Unemployment among them would have been 6.4 percent instead of 11.8 percent. They would have held sixty-five chief executive officer positions in Fortune 500 companies instead of only six. African Americans would have earned nearly $200 billion in wages. If America had full gender equality in jobs, women would have held 246 chief executive officer positions of Fortune 500 companies instead of a mere eight. Their salaries would be the equivalent of their male counterparts instead of 73 percent of those salaries. Amazingly, African Americans would own three million more homes. They would earn two million more high school diplomas and an additional two million college degrees. African Americans would make up 13.2 percent of the teaching population instead of 6.8 percent. They'd boast $760 billion more in home equity value. Their stock portfolios would contain $200 billion more. This group would have an extra $120 billion in their retirement funds and $80 billion more in the bank. All of these figures would total more than $1 trillion more in wealth. And, of course, the notion that gay men and lesbians would be allowed to die for their country but not allowed to do so while honestly acknowledging their sexual orientation would be thought of as absurd.

We still have a long way to go.

Interestingly, though, it isn't only people who are opposed to diversity, or can't or won't understand diversity, who are problems for organizations. My experience has been that it is often easier to work with people and organizations that are failing miserably on the diversity issue than it is to work with those who are strongly self-identified as progressive or liberal on the issue. The "burning platform" that they're standing on is clear. Most of them know something has to change. The fact is that the more challenging organizations are often those that are successful to a certain point, possessing the "if it ain't broke, why fix it?" attitude. As a result of their perceived success, they believe they don't need change, and they never see the huge opportunity losses that they suffer. In the words of the French playwright Molière, "the enemy of the great is the good."

These fundamental paradigms of how we approach diversity and inclusion work must be defined and addressed before we can ever hope to be as successful as we need to be in today's highly diverse world. To move beyond the realm of diversity for a moment, let's look at computer training. In the early days of personal computer use, there was a dynamic not often touched upon. It was referred to as "cyberphobia," the notion that people were scared to use computers for fear of not doing things well or losing information. People spent an enormous amount of time developing nifty systems, but other people ended up not using them *because they were afraid to go near the computer.*

> "A leading, inclusive culture cannot be manufactured by technical processes that check the boxes on every diversity issue. That's just 'old system' thinking and has a long track record of underachievement. What we all need now is a vivid, intelligent global insight process that values skilled people, embraces change and tracks progression potential. We have to develop the consciousness that an aggressively competitive ambitious world does not need our old habits or protective biases and will not stomach hierarchy instead of capability."
>
> Lord Michael Hastings CBE
> Global Head of Citizenship + Diversity
> KPMG International

In the diversity arena, we must address people's mindsets, scope of awareness, and the way they see the world before we can realize diversity "success." That's why just providing information to people doesn't result in fundamental change or lasting transformation. All of the information in the world about diversity, inclusion, or cultural competency is insufficient to get people really engaged in change. It's like dieting. How many of us know everything there is to know about losing weight and still are out of shape?

This is somewhat vexing for many of us in the world of diversity and inclusion, particularly those of us who are successful "doers." We want to move quickly to take action, institute programs, and put systems in place. The challenge is that "doing things" is only successful after there has been a shift in our way of being about whatever it is we are trying to transform. Tips and techniques are valuable, but only when we are clear about what we are doing with them and why.

So for our purposes here, I will use the following definitions:

Diversity will generally be used not only to describe the broad field of issues related to difference, but also to more specifically identify the various aspects of those differences as well as issues relating to how many people of different kinds are participating in a particular organization or society. Diversity also generally speaks to the more corrective functions of the issue, such as protection against discrimination. and other issues.

Inclusion is a function of how fully involved people are in the structures of their organizations and societies. It is not enough, for example, to have a substantial number of people of color in an organization if they are still under-represented in leadership and if the dominant group does not embrace their issues, concerns, and needs. Inclusion is a function of connection. It is the ability of people to feel fully integrated into the cultural dynamics, leadership, and decision-making structures of the organization.

Cultural competency is the organizational ability to have and utilize the policies, appropriately trained and skilled employees, and specialized resources to systematically anticipate, recognize, and respond to the varying expectations (language, cultural, and religious) of customers, clients, patients, and co-workers of diverse backgrounds. Cultural competency requires a certain amount of *cultural intelligence* in that people need to have the knowledge of both distinctions of culture and of the specific traits of different cultures. It requires a certain amount of *cultural humility* in that we need to be able to recognize that our cultural models may simply be different from, rather than better than, those of other people. And people also require a degree of *cultural flexibility* to facilitate interaction with others on their own terms.

Ultimately, if we wish to achieve a greater sense of inclusion and cultural competency, what does such inclusion and competency look like? What should an organization do to have that happen? And how will we know it when we see it?

Later in the book I address the importance of clear metrics. For now, here are just some of the things I look for with regard to standards to measure diversity program success:

- What is the organization's demographic composition?
  The reaction to this standard is interesting because it often tends to create somewhat of a backlash. People may ask whether "quotas" are being set. I find this reaction to be a fascinating one because how can you know you are successful in drawing from a broader range of talent if measurement is not done by checking and seeing how many people are actually hired? The real issue should be, is this *all* that you are doing? To that end, what are some of the specific areas we look for in determining organizational demographics? To start:
  - Is the organization drawing the best talent from a mixed pool of people that represents the marketplace it serves?
  - Is the organization retaining the talent it draws, or are there patterns indicating that more of some groups are leaving than others?
  - Is there a diverse mix of people in the leadership team?
- What kind of organizational practices are in place to support diversity, inclusion, and cultural competency? For example:

- Are there consistent standards and behaviors regarding mentoring and career development?
- Are there consistent communication structures in place that keep all people informed as to what is going on within the organization?
- Are people given clear performance standards and feedback that allow them to know how to be successful and know whether or not they are successful?
- How does it feel to work in the organization?
  - Is there a high level of employee satisfaction across diverse groups?
  - Do people interact comfortably with people of diverse backgrounds and feel free to discuss diversity issues when they emerge?
  - Are there constructive ways to deal with conflict?
  - Are people culturally competent and culturally flexible? Do they understand that people from different backgrounds may have different cultures, ways of communicating, and so on, and are they able to adapt accordingly in dealing with different people?
  - Is the organization inclusive? Are people from diverse groups able to involve themselves at all levels?
- How does the organization relate to the marketplace and the community?
  - Does the organization capture its share of the multicultural market?
  - Is client/customer/patient satisfaction high across diverse groups?
  - Does the organization do a good job of representing itself to various communities in its marketing and public relations?
  - Are diverse vendors used to provide services to the organization?

As I said, this is a partial list of the things to look for in truly diverse organizations. In chapter 11, I talk more specifically about a complete systems approach. Even these questions may seem like a high standard to set, but the reality is, as I've indicated previously, diversity programs have been conducted for many years. They have been conducted at a cost of millions of dollars and thousands of hours of time. Is it unreasonable to expect that we should have begun to see more than a few organizations demonstrating true diversity excellence?

I don't think it is unreasonable at all to expect more. I think a fair assessment is that we have achieved, at best, limited success. In fact, there are some organizations that have done an outstanding job of shifting their organizational culture to be more inclusive and culturally competent. Still, I'm often struck by how little is being achieved, even by some of the organizations that regularly make the popular lists of "Best Companies for Diversity."

If the results don't seem to match the level of investment, intention, and commitment, we then need to ask why they are not doing so. I suggest there are three major paradigms that have shaped how we have approached our work that have contributed to the limitations of our success. The first is that we have based our work on a U.S.-based model that has been drawn primarily from our work in civil rights and the women's movement and remains, despite all of the variations of "diversity wheels" that we see, based on the way we have approached those movements. The challenge with this approach is not that we still do not have to address the societal inequities that we face. It is that in a global environment we are dealing with two distinct lenses of the challenge toward a more diverse, inclusive, and culturally competent society and organizations that reflect that same diversity, inclusion, and cultural competence. On one hand we have the issues of social justice, inequity, dynamics of power, and status upon which there has been impact. On the other, we have another domain of culture, perspective, and normative behavior. Rather than seeing the depth of both of these, our approach has traditionally bifurcated them and, in doing so, done a disservice to how we have addressed both.

The second paradigm, and perhaps the most predominant of all, has been that we have addressed the issues too heavily from a corrective approach. Now, I want to be clear that I believe, as I have indicated earlier, that there are still many aspects about the way we have dealt with diversity and inclusion that need to be fixed. Yet our overwhelming emphasis has created a "good person-bad person" paradigm. There are those people (especially those of us in the field of diversity and inclusion) who "get it." And then there are the others who do all of those things we see, hear about, and read about . . . you know, the *bad* people. This has created a "find them and fix them" mentality for a lot of our work. This is problematic for a number of reasons. It assumes willful intent on the part of people who engage in exclusive behaviors. It assumes that exclusive behaviors are the dominion of only some groups. It creates a mindset of "fixing" rather than "creating," and it makes diversity advocates seem self-righteous, as if we believe that we are better than other people. All of these contribute to, rather than alleviate, resistance to people's full engagement and to "diversity fatigue."

The third paradigm is that we have tended to take an event-based approach to developing more diverse, inclusive, and culturally competent organizations. I'm sure you know what I mean. We conduct some diversity trainings, we have a Black History Month celebration, we sponsor international food day in the cafeteria, and we think that is what a diversity program looks like. What we have largely failed to do is effectively apply systems thinking and comprehensive culture-based change approaches to an issue that is clearly rooted in a systems and culture-based dynamic. As a result, our efforts, even when done well, don't lead to sustainable change.

We will explore these dynamics in more depth in later chapters.

If we are to truly create a breakthrough in our ability to work collectively, we will have to shift these paradigms and create a real sense of organizational community. Let's look at what that really means.

CHAPTER 3

The Background Is Background

> A man wanted to know about mind, not in nature, but in his private, large computer. He asked it, "Did you compute that you will ever think like a human being?" The machine then set to work to analyze its own computational habits. Finally, the machine printed its answer on a piece of paper. . . . "That reminds me of a story." Surely the computer was right. This is indeed how people think.
>
> Gregory Bateson[1]

> You can out-distance that which is running after you, but not what is running inside you.
>
> Rwandan proverb[2]

Let's begin by looking at the background of how we approach diversity, and, in order to really understand that, what's behind the way we understand what a *background* really provides for us.

In the introduction I quoted the remarkable Helen Keller. An author, and later an activist for people with disabilities, women's suffrage, and other causes, she was the first deaf/blind person to ever graduate from college in the United States, graduating magna cum laude from Radcliffe College in 1904. Many readers are probably familiar with the story of Keller's life, famously recounted in *The Miracle Worker*, a play written in 1957 by William Gibson that since that time has been shown all over the world on stage, screen, and television.[3]

The story centers on the relationship between Helen and her teacher, Anne Sullivan. Helen had lost her vision and hearing due to illness at the age of nineteen months, and for the next five years had lived in what has been described as "an almost feral state," without any way of communicating with the outside world and, according to her own later accounts, with almost no sense of the very concept of language.

Though she had begun to learn a few basic words before her illness, Helen was completely unable to see or hear and, as a result, unable to speak. When she was six years old, her family, through the assistance of Alexander Graham Bell, hired Sullivan to work with Helen. Sullivan secluded herself with Helen and spent weeks trying to get the child to respond to a "game" of making finger symbols into her hand while exposing her to different objects. Occasionally the child would repeat the symbols, but with no sense that she understood that they were "words." And then something happened. In her autobiography, Helen described it in this way:

> My teacher . . . had been with me nearly a month. . . . One day she handed me a cup and spelled the word. Then she poured the liquid into the cup and formed the letters w-a-t-e-r. She says I looked puzzled, and persisted in confusing the two words, spelling cup for water and water for cup. Finally I became angry because Miss Sullivan kept repeating the words over and over again. In despair she led me out to the ivy-covered pump house and made me hold the cup under the spout while she pumped. With her other hands she spelled w-a-t-e-r emphatically. I stood still, my whole body's attention fixed on the motions of her fingers as the cool stream flowed over my hand. All at once there was a strange stir within me—a misty consciousness, a sense of something remembered. It was as if I had come back to life after being dead! I understood that what my teacher was doing with her fingers meant that cold something that was rushing over my hand, and that it was possible for me to communicate with other people by these signs. It was a wonderful day never to be forgotten. . . . Now I see that it was my mental awakening. I think it was an experience somewhat in the nature of a revelation. I showed immediately in many ways that a great change had taken place in me. I wanted to learn the name of every object I touched, and before night I had mastered thirty words.[4]

What had happened? A new world, a new reality had opened up for Helen. After that moment, nothing ever looked the same to her again. As she went on to say:

> It was as if light came where there had been no light before, the intangible world became a shining certainty. The horizons of my mind widened to bright destinies where the race would still be swift, the battle strong.[5]

Helen had learned the word *wa-wa* for water before her illness, and so, perhaps, a vague memory was reignited, but for one reason or another, at that moment she realized that *things have names*. She repeated the sign back to her teacher.[6] She then was quickly able to move to learning new words, and then sentences, which opened her native intelligence to a world of awareness, comprehension, and language. Her fundamental character changed dramatically, as did her life.

What is critically important to understand in Helen's story is that it wasn't the fact of knowing what water *was* that changed Helen Keller's life, and it wasn't the fact of knowing the name of water. What radically changed her life was realizing that *things have names*. Before she had that background of understanding, adding more *content* or more symbols relating to more different things did not teach her to understand or to speak. It was shifting the *context* by creating the *world* of language where previously there had not been one that gave her that whole new world to explore. That is the power of our background of understanding. It creates a visible or known world from what was previously concealed, or it can transform the way we look at our existing world.

The background of understanding gives us the *context* through which we experience the *content* of our world. Because the essence of this book is to create a new *context* for viewing the conversation about diversity in our society, I want to talk a bit more about how context shapes our way of looking at and experiencing the world.

We have examples every day of the way our background of understanding impacts the world that we see. For example, two people approach a roller coaster. One says, "Roller coasters are exciting!" The second says, "Roller coasters are scary!" Which is right? In actuality, of course, roller coasters are neither exciting nor scary—they are just roller coasters. They are inanimate objects, which exist in time and space, made up of wood or metal and other materials. So where does the excitement or the fear live?

In this case, it is pretty obvious. The excitement or fear is a function of the experience that each of the people has had with roller coasters. The first person has a background of understanding about roller coasters that was created by a particular history. It might have been personal experiences that were the reflections of the experiences of others. It might be a fantasy that has been created based on certain expectations. Regardless of where it came from, it created a background of excitement that had the roller coaster itself appear exciting. The same can be said, in the opposite, for the other person. That person's experience came from a background of fear.

This background provides a frame of reference, a lens through which the roller coaster is seen. What really happens when the people see the roller coaster? What we see as an individual thought ("Roller coasters are scary!") is actually the result of a series of realizations that have occurred in sequence so quickly that they become collapsed in our conscious mind as one thought or feeling. If we were to really break down, step by step, in slow motion, what is happening in the mind of the second person, for example, it might be something like this:

1. I see an inanimate object.
2. This inanimate object seems similar to other inanimate objects I have seen in the past.
3. Those inanimate objects were called roller coasters, so I assume that this, too, *is* a roller coaster.
4. When I experienced the other inanimate objects in the past, I had a series of physical sensations in my body: rapid pulse, heart palpitations, heavy breathing, dramatic increase in adrenaline, and more.
5. I refer to that collective group of physical sensations as fear. (By the way, these sensations are virtually identical to the ones that the first person called excitement!)
6. Based on that past experience, I anticipate that I would have the same series of physical sensations if I were to experience this inanimate object.

And all of those steps, all of that logic, get instantly translated in one thought, one feeling: "roller coasters *are* scary!" The *content* is an inanimate object made of wood or steel; the *context* is fear.

Ultimately, it doesn't matter much what we think about roller coasters, but the same way of seeing the world governs how we think about almost everything and almost everybody.

Consider the potential impact of this dynamic when it is applied to people. Imagine, for example, that I am interviewing two potential people to hire. The first interviewee comes into my office in the morning. As soon as I meet him, I like him. We have all had that experience. "There is just something about that person that I like," I say. It happens in milliseconds. If we think about it logically, it can't really be about that person. I have only known him for a second. Even if I think I'm a good judge of character, how reasonable is it to think that I'm *that* good? What actually is happening, of course, is that something about that person probably reminds me of something or somebody I like: the shape of their eyebrows, their kind of smile, the sound of their voice. Or it might be the mood I'm in, or any number of other things. Some might be conscious, but most are likely to be unconscious. For me, all I know is that I like the person.

So I ask that person the first question of the interview, and like a lot of people, he is a little nervous. He hems and haws a bit. And without even thinking about it I say, "Relax . . . it's only an interview," and ask the question again, giving him a second chance to make a good first impression. So now he nails the answer, and the interview goes great from there on. I'm smiling a lot, making a lot of eye contact, laughing at his jokes. You get the point.

Later that afternoon the second candidate comes in. Perhaps something about her strikes me the opposite way: "There's just something about her I don't like." Or maybe it's been a bad day. I just found out that a report that I thought was due in a week is due in three days. My wife called and told me that our son is having a problem in school. I've had a low-grade headache all day. Who knows what it is, but when I sit with her and ask her the same question and she responds the same way, this time I just sit. Or even worse, I make one of those quick glances at my wristwatch that she's not supposed to see. Now she's sweating bullets, and the interview goes in a completely different direction.

The next day one of my colleagues asks me, "What did you think about the two of them?" Predictably, I respond, "He was great . . . smart, open." As for the other, I'm more lukewarm: "She was okay." And I have no idea that my background completely affected both interviews. In fact, if you gave me a lie detector test and asked whether I interviewed them any differently, I would probably pass when I answered, "No."

Is there anyone among us who doesn't do this every day to the people we work with or meet? When you walk down the street, what makes you say "Good morning" to one person but look the other way when another comes along? It is a natural human reaction, because it is fundamental to how we see the world. And it has a huge impact on how we see, evaluate, and work with people. And, in this case, it may have determined who gets a job.

This dynamic is actually not at all unusual. There are dozens of circumstances in which the same unconscious dynamic occurs. One thing, one idea, or one person appears to us in a particular way. That "appearance" is a function of the background of understanding that each of us has that creates a filter through which we interpret what we see. The philosopher John Searle describes this "background" as "the set of non-intentional or pre-intentional capacities (abilities, dispositions, tendencies, and causal structures) that enable intentional states of function."[7] Searle goes on to say that this *background* "enables linguistic interpretation to take place . . . enables perceptual interpretation to take place [and] . . . structures consciousness."[8] The "background" that Searle discusses here is what has us see the roller coaster in the way that we do. We perceive it as exciting or scary (perceptual interpretation), we think of words (*exciting* and *scary*) to identify what we are experiencing (linguistic interpretation), and those interpretations create a mindset that we have about roller coasters (structures of consciousness).

The linguistic interpretation is especially important because it communicates so much to the world. Consider the difference between somebody saying, "The United States *invaded* Iraq in 2003," and "The United States *liberated* Iraq in 2003." There is a world of difference in one word that could give us an entire view of a person's politics.

We often even go about searching for reassurance that our particular perspective is the right one ("You think roller coasters are scary too, don't you?"). And we create actions that correlate with our perspective: we ride roller coasters more, or not at all; we go to the park with friends who also ride roller coasters, and so on. In other words, we reaffirm what we already believe. Anthropologist Carlos Castaneda described this reaffirming phenomenon in this way:

> We talk to ourselves incessantly about our world. In fact we maintain our world with our internal talk. And whenever we finish talking to ourselves about ourselves and our world, the world is always as it should be. We renew it, we rekindle it with life, and we uphold it with our internal talk. Not only that, but we also choose our paths as we talk to ourselves. Thus we repeat the same choices over and over until the day we die, because we keep on repeating the same internal talk over and over until the day we die.[9]

We filter what we see through the very beliefs we have, so the world we see is shaped by those beliefs. The beliefs create a background in the sense that I referred to earlier. This background is so omnipresent that we may not even notice it is there before us. We might say it is concealed by its obviousness. It is so clear to us, so *true*, that we not only don't question it, we don't even see it anymore. As is the proverbial fish to water, we are to our own beliefs. It is not something that we see ourselves seeing through; it becomes, in effect, *the one that does the seeing*. We can see only through that lens, and it is difficult for the lens to see itself.

Imagine that the moment you were born, the doctor popped a set of blue contact lenses into your eyes and they were never removed. The entire world would have a blue tint for you. However, in your experience, it would not be a world with a blue tint; it *would be a blue world*. In your mind, the world *is* blue, and you probably could not be talked out of that point of view until somebody managed to show you that you had blue lenses in your eyes. *Only at that moment would you would finally be able to see that you are looking at a world that is colored blue by your perspective.*

It develops through a series of stages. All human beings have basic ideologies through which we see the world. By an *ideology*, I am referring to "a body of doctrine, myth, belief, etc., that guides an individual, social movement, institution, class, or large group."[10] It is the only way we can traverse our daily existence; otherwise, we would be paralyzed by all of the decisions we have to make. In fact, the very purpose of our identity structure is developed around what keeps us safe, what helps us navigate the world and survive. We have ideologies about what a good person is (honest, caring, dependable) and what a good family is (loving, supportive, communicative). In fact, when our different ideologies don't match, they can be a source of stress or even conflict. For example, what if one person has an ideology that says, "A good family eats dinner together at least once a week," and the person marries someone whose ideology is "A good family eats dinner together every night"? We can see that they are set up for six days of hell every week! We also have ideologies about good workplaces, and even huge human systems (democracy, socialism, freedom, etc.). Ideologies give us our basic framework for evaluating the world.

These ideologies give us *schema* that help us see the world clearly. Schema are "concepts or conceptual frameworks by which an object of knowledge or an idea may be apprehended."[11] Schema are the lenses through which we see our world. In fact, they determine what we see and what we don't. Let me give you an example. Read the following paragraph and see whether you can determine what it is referring to:

> The procedure is actually quite simple. First you arrange things into different groups; of course one pile may be sufficient, depending upon how much there is to do. If you have to go somewhere else due to lack of facilities, that is the next step. Otherwise you are pretty well set. It is important not to overdo things; that is, it is better to do too few things at once, rather than too many. In the short run, this might not seem important, but complications can easily arise. A mistake can be expensive as well. After the procedure is completed, one arranges the materials into different groups again. Then they can be put into their appropriate places. Naturally they'll be used once more and the whole process will have to be repeated; however, that is a part of life.[12]

Did you know what it was referring to? It's about doing the laundry. Perhaps you got it, and if so, you were one of less than 10 percent of people who do. If you didn't, go back and read it again and see how much sense it makes now. This is the way schema work. They give us a particular perspective that can have a world appear that was not there before. They help determine what we see and don't see and how we interpret what we see.

While this is an interesting philosophical conversation, there is growing scientific evidence to indicate that it is phenomenologically identifiable as well. Bear with me here because I know that to some this may seem somewhat esoteric, but I think it's important that we see this beyond just being a matter of philosophical or psychological opining. There is something fundamental in the way we see the world, the discovery of which can dramatically shift our perspectives.

Fernando Flores and Terry Winograd, researchers and scholars in natural language systems and human-computer interaction, refer to this as our "background conversation," or the set of beliefs and assumptions that make up the way we interpret the world. They describe it this way:

> Background is a pervasive and fundamental phenomenon. Background . . . allows us to listen to both what is spoken and what is unspoken. Meaning is created by an active listening, in which the linguistic form (spoken word) triggers interpretation, rather than conveying information. The background is not a set of propositions, but is our basic orientation . . . to the world.
>
> The world is (actually) encountered as something always already lived in, worked in, and acted upon. World as the *background of obviousness* is manifest in our everyday dealings as the familiarity that pervades our situation, and every possible utterance presupposes this. . . . What is unspoken is as much a part of the meaning as what is spoken.[13]

Said considerably more simply, we do not describe the world we see, even though at the moment it appears to us that we are doing so. We actually *see the world that the things we already know and believe allow us to describe.* The "background" that Winograd and Flores describe is the framework through which we interpret everything that we see. As that ubiquitous old aphorism goes, "We see the world not as it is, but as we are."[14]

A fascinating example of this occurs in the 1981 film *The Gods Must Be Crazy.* In the film, a pilot flying a small plane over the Kalahari Desert throws a Coke bottle out of his cockpit. The bottle lands on the desert floor and is recovered by a member of the Sho, a tribe of Bushmen. Because they have never seen anything like it before, it quickly becomes a disruption to their societal structure and one of them, a Bushman named Xixo, determines that "the gods must be crazy" for bringing this to them and goes searching for a way to return the bottle to the gods. During his trek he encounters "civilization" for the first time. One moment captures how his background of understanding creates the world that he sees.

Stopping to rest, Xixo is awakened by a Land Rover zooming past him at high speed. He awakens with a start but doesn't see a Land Rover at all. In fact, he doesn't even see a car. As the narrator says, "A very noisy animal rushed past where Xixo was sleeping. It left very peculiar tracks, as if two enormous snakes had slithered past."[15]

We might say that was just the fact that Xixo didn't know what he was seeing. Of course, at some level that is true. But at a functional level, he did know what he was seeing . . . a very noisy animal that left tracks like two enormous snakes. Inside his background of understanding, only animals move independently; therefore, the Land Rover *is* an animal.

So our background of understanding has us see certain things in certain ways, but it also governs whether or not we see some things at all. Let me give you an example of what I mean. A number of years ago I met a guy at a ranch out in Colorado. Having grown up in urban and suburban environments, I was not a natural horseman. Sam, on the other hand, is every bit of that kind of man. His father used to lead hunting trips in Wyoming, and when Sam was little he was taught many distinctions in tracking game that I did not even know existed.

We became good friends, and he taught me how to ride. I spent time during five summers visiting with him and riding horses at high elevations in the Colorado Rockies. One day we were out riding at more than ten thousand feet of elevation, and we came through an area that had a dirt path. Generally there had been evidence of riders throughout the trail, but when we reached this higher elevation, they diminished. However, on this particular part of the path I noticed some horseshoe prints in the dirt, which I mentioned to Sam. Sam turned his horse around and looked down at the prints and said, "Oh, it looks like Chuck and Ted [two of his ranch hands] were here a few hours ago with three other people . . . and it rained."

I thought he was joking and laughed at Sam's comment, but then he got off his horse and showed me that he actually could determine all of that information by looking at the prints. He knew that one print was Chuck's because it had a broken corner; he pointed out how the others were distinct in various ways that I hadn't even noticed, giving him the clear sense of how many people had been there. He showed me how he "dated" the prints and how he knew that it had rained. There was a whole story on that path for Sam that I couldn't see, not because I wasn't looking at it, *but because the background given by my inexperience was insufficient to really understand what I was looking at.*

This background creates a lens of our own that sees things or doesn't see things, depending on the schema that it creates for us to interpret. That is why my friend Sam saw more in the horseshoe prints. He saw something that I didn't see. I once watched an Olympic diving event with a diver and was amazed at what he saw that never occurred to me. A shoeshine boy sees shoes in a completely different way from the rest of us. It is in this sense that Winograd and Flores say that "the world is encountered as something already lived in." All of our experiences and history shape what we are able to see.

"I've come to understand that 'background' shapes our lens and thus how we look at the world. This is equally true for individuals and communities.

"The experience of growing up in the post-Reconstruction South shaped the experiences of many in the Baltimore community; and the stories of human experimentation and discriminatory health services on African Americans have colored how many today still view research and health care. Whether apocryphal or not, the collective experiences of a group have become imprinted on a community and the image of the research institution has come to be viewed as the image of abuse; and science has come to be viewed as genocide. Clearly, in every myth there is reality; and the interface of the African American community with American medicine has all too often been tainted with real abuse at times of stunning proportions.

"So after years of community work I have come to understand that the only way to garner respect is to be absolutely honest. I have taken actions such as closing a 'free clinic' because the standard of care was sub-par; and I told community representatives if I could not send my family there I could not send theirs to that center either. It took two years to develop an alternative system where all in the East Baltimore area can get 'Hopkins quality' health care whether they are insured or not, documented or undocumented. Following through, transparency, delivering on a promise, doing what you say you will do are the critical characteristics for a community that has a collective conscience that tells them daily that what emanates from big institutions is all a charade."

Robert William Blum, MD, MPH, PhD
William H. Gates Sr. Professor and Chair
Department of Population, Family and Reproductive Health
Director, Johns Hopkins Urban Health Institute
Johns Hopkins Bloomberg School of Public Health

This phenomenon is critical to understanding the way both individuals and groups process the world. We all have a collection of beliefs, truths if you will, that come from our experience *or the experience of others as reflected to us*. That those beliefs have the capacity to shape what we see is something that should be patently obvious to most of us. Winograd and Flores, building on the work of a whole slew of philosophers, linguists, and biologists, take the assertion to another level. Their contention is that we actually see the world conditional upon what they refer to as our *background of obviousness*—that is, the background assumptions that we make that are so automatic that we are never even aware we are making them. They simply "are" the way the world is for us.

Biologists Humberto Maturana and Francisco Varela, as well as many quantum scientists, have extended the notion that our "perception of reality" may be shaped by our way of seeing or interpreting. They suggest that *reality itself* exists as a function of our perspective, our way of seeing. In fact, they suggest, even though we might find others, in some case many others, who agree with us, our sense of what is real, true, and so on, is created from our own personal framework.

> All cognitive experience involves the knower in a personal way, rooted in his (or her) biological structure. There, his (or her) experience of certainty is an individual phenomenon blind to the cognitive acts of others, in a solitude which . . . is transcended only in a world created with those others.[16]

When we have a sense of a shared identity with a group or a cultural pattern of looking that has been a part of our lives since their inception—in other words, "the world created with others" that Maturana and Varela speak of—the impact of this perception is particularly powerful. If we are members of a group that has a common agreement as to what is real, *we begin to see it as real.* At some point we stop distinguishing between what we see and what others see. *Reality appears to us as the way people around us see things*, and unless there is some dramatic reason to change, that becomes our world.

How is it, for example, that throughout history entire societies have repeatedly demonstrated signs of mass homicidal madness? Nazi Germany, Rwanda, and the treatment of the Native American Indian population or African American slavery in the United States constitute just a few examples. Education, culture, history, or any other rational information seems to have little ability to intervene in such cases. Normal people somehow justify, in their own minds and hearts, that their behavior, whether it be participatory or simply looking the other way, isn't as abominable and immoral as it obviously is when looked at outside of that context.

We believe, we *want* to believe, and perhaps even more accurately, *we have been taught to believe* that our thoughts and actions are our own, particularly in the context of our American societal model. Our sense of individuality, for better and for worse, is one of the core, defining characteristics of the American cultural model, and while we long for connection, we are, ironically, in many ways societally encouraged to avoid it. As sociologist Philip Slater wrote in his brilliant study of American culture, *The Pursuit of Loneliness*:

The avoiding tendency lies at the very root of American character. This nation was settled and continually repopulated by people who were not personally successful in confronting the special conditions in their mother country, but fled in the hope of a better life. By a kind of natural selection, America was disproportionately populated with a certain kind of person.

In the past we've always stressed the positive side of this selection, implying that America thereby found herself blessed with an unusual number of energetic, mobile, ambitious, daring, and optimistic persons. Now there's no reason to deny that there were differences between those who chose to come and those who chose to stay, nor that these differences must have reproduced themselves in social institutions. But very little attention has been paid to the negative side of the selection. If we gained the energetic and daring, we also gained the lion's share of the rootless, the unscrupulous, those who valued money over relationships, and those who put self-aggrandizement ahead of love and loyalty. And most of all, we gained an undue proportion of persons who, when faced with a difficult situation, tended to chuck the whole thing and flee to a new environment. Escaping, evading, and avoiding are responses which lie at the base of much that is peculiarly America, including the suburb, the automobile, the self-service store, and so on.[17]

The core elements of what we are as a culture consist of that rootlessness. Our mobility, our lack of connection to the older members of our families, our readiness to flee our neighborhoods when they begin to "change," all of these elements are the flip side of our "pioneer spirit." And so, built into our cultural psyche is the willingness to find ways to avoid dealing with that which is uncomfortable to us.

One of my favorites of Charles Schultz's *Peanuts* strips showed Snoopy walking past some calamity, directly to his dog food bowl, with a caption that reads, "There is no problem so large that you can't avoid dealing with it." Unfortunately, this is all too often the truth. Slater referred to this as the "Toilet Assumption—the notion that unwanted matter, unwanted difficulties, unwanted complexities and obstacles will disappear if they're removed from our immediate field of vision."[18]

So we have both a set of background understandings about "the way things are" that govern how we see the world, and a particular sense of individuality and separateness in that background. We wrestle with this dichotomy, a desire on one hand to be a part of something and the desire, on the other hand, to fulfill the expectation of individualism that American heritage has structured for us. The irony is that the two contradictory needs become interwoven and dependent upon each other; a duality that keeps both alive. We stress individuality; we emphasize it, glorify it, and yet we also suffer at the loss of connection that it brings us and, often at an unconscious level, strive to belong, to be part of the larger whole. We are, at the core, social creatures who respond and react to the world based on a worldview that is formed not only by our individual experience but also by the experience of those with whom we interact throughout our lives. The result is that we often develop blindness to our own need to conform to the background that we are a part of culturally. This is not a new phenomenon. It was at the heart of Erich Fromm's epic post–World War II study, *Escape from Freedom*, in which he wrote:

> On the one hand it (freedom) is a process of growing strength and integration, mastery of nature, growing power of human reason, and growing solidarity with other human beings. But on the other hand this growing individuation means growing isolation, insecurity, and thereby growing doubt concerning one's own role in the universe, the meaning of one's life, and with all that a growing feeling of one's own powerlessness and insignificance as an individual.[19]

And so this "pull" toward individual freedom and a sense of choice is a very conscious one, but it is in constant conflict with the unconscious desire to connect. We have been trained to believe that we should "think for ourselves," even as we are thinking and believing just as so many around us are and as we were raised to think and believe. This creates an internal contradiction and self-deception, according to Fromm: "Because we have freed ourselves of the older overt forms of authority, we do not see that we have become the prey of a new kind of authority. We have become automatons who live under the illusion of being self-willing individuals."[20]

Most of us have experienced this ourselves in the peer influence of children "needing" to have a particular brand of shoes or acting a particular way. Why? Because the collective culture that I am a part of (my peer group) sees them as important, *and so they become important.* Those outside the peer groups see them as simply "a fad" or "an opinion," but inside of that group they seem necessary for survival.

Fromm's work inspired several studies that have shown this pattern to be true. Two in particular are worth noting here. In 1951, Solomon Asch created a series of experiments in which he exposed students to a set of three lines and asked them to determine whether the line at the left (see figure 3.1) was longer or shorter than the ones on the right.

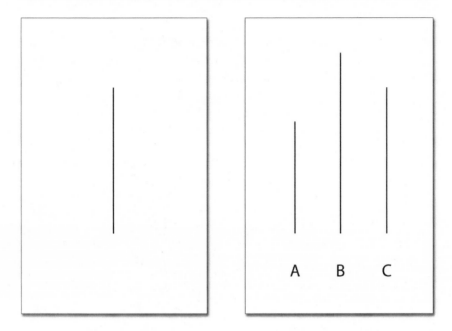

Asch Lines, 1951

Figure 3.1

What the students didn't know was that the other students in the group had been instructed how to respond before the experiment. The other students all responded unanimously, but clearly, with the wrong answer. The students being tested observed the obvious, that the line on the left was larger than A, smaller than B, and the same as C (there is no cognitive illusion in this exercise). Yet in the face of the (manipulated) findings of the large group, they agreed with the group and gave the wrong answer *more than one-third of the time.*[21]

This phenomenon of "going along with the tide" is one about which we all know. Most of us learned about it when we were young children and were told the Hans Christian Andersen fairy tale about the emperor's new clothes. The story is a classic. An emperor, rather charmed with himself, is convinced by some shady tailors that they can make him a suit that is so beautiful and magical that only the most intelligent, virtuous, and so on can see it. The emperor, in his vanity, goes along with the ruse rather than admit that he cannot see the clothing and is convinced to "wear the suit" (actually, of course, his birthday suit!) in a public parade. The entire population seems to buy into the scam, everyone afraid that they will be the one deemed somehow incapable of seeing the magical fabric, until a small child, innocent to the ways of the world, yells out, "He has no clothes. The emperor has no clothes," and the gig is up.

It is easy for us to understand this dynamic from afar. It makes sense and, after all, we have seen lots of *other* people fall into the trap. Yet it is a dynamic that occurs so regularly within organizations that it must be considered commonplace. A staff meeting in which all parties say what they think the boss wants them to say. A project development session in which somebody figures he just must not understand the situation as well as the others, all of whom seem to agree. A decision that is made because it is assumed that is what the boss would want. All of these are examples of the power of people's perception of group to influence both our own perceptions and our willingness to express our opinions.

We also know that the influence of authority has a dramatic impact on what people are willing to participate in. Stanley Milgram took the study of group conformity and adherence to authority to another level with his experiments in the 1960s.[22] Milgram was interested in testing Fromm's assertion that our desire for group conformity also would lead to a tendency to go along with authority, even when we knew what we were doing was wrong. He posed the question, "Could it be that Eichmann and his million accomplices in the Holocaust were just following orders? Could we call them all accomplices?"

Milgram's research was designed to determine how far the average person would go in inflicting pain on an innocent person when told to do so by an authority figure. He set up a mock testing station. The test subject, a volunteer, sat in front of a board with thirty levels of electric shock, the last eight labeled as "harmful" and "life threatening." There were three more levels that were higher than the scale.

Milgram asked the subjects to participate in delivering a test to another person on the other side of a shield. The testing volunteer could not see, but could hear, the other person. With a technician (also a researcher) by his or her side, the participant was told to press a button that would give a shock to the other person if that person answered a question incorrectly. The volunteers did not know that the people on the other side of the shield were part of the experiment and were actually responding to the shocks in scripted ways.

The volunteers were told to increase the level of the shock after each wrong answer, and the actors increasingly gave loud verbal reactions to the shocks, at some point even moaning in pain. The testers often asked the technicians whether they should continue, often showed visible discomfort with continuing, and yet overwhelmingly continued to do as they were told.

Before the test was conducted, most experts who were polled predicted that less than 1 percent of the test subjects would go past the tenth level in administering the shocks. In actuality, 65 percent administered shocks that were "off the scale," even while demonstrating strong distress and protesting what they were asked to do. Not a single test subject stopped before administering what they thought were three hundred volts of electricity! Milgram later said, "Stark authority was pitted against the subjects' [participants'] strongest moral imperatives against hurting others, and, with the subjects' [participants'] ears ringing with the screams of the victims. Authority won more often than not. The extreme willingness of adults to go to almost any lengths on the command of an authority constitutes the chief finding of the study."[23] The experiments were repeated many times, all over the world, over the course of a year. The findings were remarkably consistent, with 61 to 66 percent of the test subjects administering what they thought were fatal doses in virtually every study, regardless of when or where the study was conducted. Researchers also found that women were as likely to administer the shocks as men, although they tended to demonstrate more distress.

Now many of us might say, "That's not true of me . . . I think for myself; I make decisions on my own." Do you? Watch yourself for a day and see how many things you do automatically. When do you eat? What do you eat? How many meals? What kinds of clothes do you wear? Do you wear shoes? Do you shake hands? How firmly?

I could go on and list hundreds more examples, but I hope I have made the point. We do hundreds of things every day that we don't even think about doing. These actions are the result of a certain background of understanding that we live our lives from and show up in actions from the mundane to the deeply significant. Interestingly enough, even the point of view that we make our own decisions can be a reflection of a cultural view or worldview, one that is more prevalent in the United States, as Slater points out, where we pride ourselves on our individuality, than, for example, in many Asian cultures, in which people are raised in a more collectivist perspective. We'll discuss more about this later.

These patterns of group identification and response to the structural authority around us shape what we see. They affect our view of the world and our interpretation of the world. I want to be clear that I'm not suggesting physical phenomena aren't present around us. We just may not see them, or we may see them in an entirely different way than others, depending upon how our perceptive lens filters them. Even our physical world, and especially our understanding of it, is "deciphered" by our background of understanding. Consider this passage from *The Evolution of Physics*, by Albert Einstein and Leopold Infeld:

> Physical concepts are free creations of the human mind, and are not, however it may seem, uniquely determined by the external world. In our endeavor to understand reality we are somewhat like a man trying to understand the mechanism of a closed watch. He sees the face and the moving hands, even hears it's ticking, but he has no way of

opening the case. If he is ingenious he may form some picture of a mechanism, which could be responsible for all the things he observes, but he may never be quite sure his picture is the only one that could explain his observations. He will never be able to compare his picture with the real mechanism and he cannot even imagine the possibility or the meaning of such a comparison.[24]

Almost all of us have had physical experiences that affirm our sense that things are going on around us that we don't see. Our awareness of them is shaped by something that brings them into visibility, or something that alerts us to their presence. When I was a child, for example, I was fascinated by the dust that floated in the light coming through the Venetian blinds in my bedroom. I watched the dust particles float endlessly. I experienced what was for me a very clear reality: "Beams of light have dust in them." That was the way I literally saw the world until my mother explained that the dust was in the air all the time and that *the sunlight made it visible*. This seems so simplistic, yet it shapes the way we see things all the time. Waiting for a plane in the Detroit airport recently, I was making a phone call in a main corridor of the airport. As I spoke I watched the people walking by. I noticed a mother with a young baby in her arms, a middle-aged businessman carrying a briefcase, a tall teenager, and others. At some point I noticed that on the other side of the aisle a shoe shiner at his stand also was observing the same group of people, but I could tell what he was looking at, and by how he was looking I could see that his experience was distinctly different from mine. As he watched the people walk by, it was clear that he was seeing a pair of sneakers, a pair of black high heels, one pair of cordovan wingtips, and so on. His perspective shaped his view of the world, and in this case, his financial survival. Who needed a shoeshine did not appear on my radar screen, but it was virtually all he saw.

Our lenses, then, get developed throughout our lives. Our biological and social histories begin to develop the lens for us, and our world then begins to be shaped, mostly outside of our conscious knowledge. It doesn't then look to us like *our* perception, or *our* truth; in fact, it is not even a perception at all; it is simply *the* truth. The way things are. The story of our lives is seen in a way that is self-defined, self-justifying, and clearly "true" to us. And we then live our lives inside of that story, without realizing that it is not objectively true, but rather a construction of our own social reality.

One can see a great representation of this in the Jim Carrey movie *The Truman Show*.[25] Carrey plays Truman, a man who has been raised inside a constructed world for the entertainment of the viewing audience. From the time of his birth he has lived inside his "world" and has no sense that it is anything else than a natural phenomenon. Relationships, experiences, fears, all confirm that his world is just the way it is, and his life continues happily until one day he sees, for the first time, that something is amiss, and then he awakens to the reality of what has been going on.

I'm not suggesting that Truman's life is directly analogous to ours, but perhaps it is not as far off as we think. The notion of living inside of a constructed reality is very much the pattern of our lives. We develop an entire set of values, beliefs, interpretations, perceptions, preferences, and so on that are constantly filtering our experience and helping us sort out the vast array of information we are exposed to.

So what does any of this have to do with diversity? Just about everything. Our background of understanding gives us not only the way we see our lives, but the interpretation and reaction to how we see the lives of others. It also gives us the very background through which we see the field of diversity itself. And, most importantly, it creates a set of paradigms that dominate our thinking . . . and our results.

Before we look at those, though, let's consider what background of understanding gives us an interest in diversity anyway. After all, why bother? Most of the world's population lives in some kind of tribalism. What is in it for us to create a broader, more diverse and inclusive sense of community?

CHAPTER 4

The Conundrum
of Community

> A community is the mental and spiritual condition of
> knowing that the place is shared, and that the people who
> share the place define and limit the possibilities of each
> other's lives. It is the knowledge that people have of each
> other, their concern for each other, their trust in each
> other, the freedom with which they come and go among
> themselves.
>
> Wendell Berry[1]

Have you noticed any of the following trends in your organization?

- Declining profits, increased costs, decreasing market share, and a need to challenge the fundamental ways you have been conducting business.
- Loss of productivity and resources due to a lack of understanding between people of diverse groups leading, in its extreme, to Equal Employment Opportunity (EEO) complaints, sexual harassment lawsuits, or other diversity-related concerns, and more often to a generalized sense of lower-than-desired output.
- A lack of employee loyalty and sense of ownership, leading to less-than-optimal attitude, poor morale, declining work performance, absenteeism, tardiness, insufficient collaboration, and teamwork.
- A concern about managers who lack fundamental skills and who are frustrated by the difficulty they are having in motivating, evaluating, communicating, directing, and holding diverse employees accountable.

If you don't face any of these challenges, you are one of the lucky few. In most cases, attempts to address these issues have amounted to Band-Aid approaches, addressing one concern but not leading to any integrated understanding of the overall impact on the organization, and that often seem fundamentally reactive in nature. Management training that is skills-oriented but doesn't seem to really change the fundamental relationship between managers and the people they supervise. Diversity work that often seems to inherently reinforce in people a "them versus us" reaction, a sense of "walking on eggshells," or "diversity fatigue," and, in most cases, is dealt with as a corrective approach rather than a business initiative that is building toward a new possibility for the organization. Attempts to improve customer service that often have minimal impact.

My conversations with scores of people within organizations, as well as observations of the social environment, yielded a consistent pattern. Corporate chief executive officers expressing concerns about the territorial nature of their managers and workers, especially during times of economic challenge. People looking out for themselves, stuck in a paradigm of separateness, having lost touch with their interdependence and the impact their behavior was having on their overall organizational productivity and their ability to achieve their objectives. As a society and within our organizations, we have lost touch with a fundamental human element: the need to feel connected, the desire for a sense of community.

The concept of *organizational community* is one that arose out of attempts to address this fundamental need for organizations to look at themselves from a larger perspective, one that addresses the interdependence of all people and all areas of the organization: a community approach. As I began speaking about this concept to organizational leaders, I found a remarkable degree of interest and affirmation. The concept of community speaks to a basic human desire to break through the sense of isolation we are feeling and bring things together but is confronted by a profound resignation, a sense that we can never really get there, and a fear of investing in trying yet again.

What is *organizational community* anyway? The words individually have meaning for us. The *American Heritage Dictionary of the English Language* defines *organization* this way:

> **or-gan-i-za-tion**, *n.* **1.** The act of organizing or the process of being organized. **2.** The state or manner of being organized: *a high degree of organization.* **3.** Something that has been organized or made into an ordered whole. **4.** Something comprising elements with varied functions that contribute to the whole and to collective functions; an organism. **5.** A number of persons or groups having specific responsibilities and united for some purpose or work.[2]

While we are most used to using it in its noun form, organization is actually somewhat performative in nature. It calls forth a sense of activity, a sense of consciousness. To a certain degree, in many of the organizations I have observed and experienced, that performative nature has been lost. Rather than existing as a living entity, as *an organism*, organization has become a thing, and through its objectification we have developed frustration about our ability to influence it. Some of this frustration characterizes itself as anger and is acted out in active or passive ways (e.g., theft, tardiness, resistance to authority, poor performance, poor service, lawsuits), but most of it is characterized as resignation and hopelessness. People quit while still on the job, retreating into themselves (and perhaps those they perceive like themselves), and all too often they see themselves as separate from the organization, protecting themselves from it.

We develop effective methods of justifying or rationalizing our behavior, including making historical references to times when others or we have tried to change things and failed. Lowering our interest or ambitions (e.g., "I wouldn't want to be a partner around here anyway!"). Cynicism. All to avoid confronting the powerlessness and hopelessness that we feel.

Yet, as we see in the rare success stories, or in our occasionally successful departments or moments, vital organizations retain the power to unify our attention, our focus, and our actions. While people usually operate separately in large corporations and develop territoriality and "them versus us" mentalities, we have moments in which we experience the fact that we are *united for some purpose or work* and are identified by that relationship. As an employee at one of my client companies once shared with me,

> Our company was involved for many years in a lawsuit alleging racial and sexual discrimination. During the entire time the suit was going on I didn't give it much thought at all. I really didn't even have a strong opinion one way or the other about it. We even used to joke that if administration worried more about the suit they would stay off our case. But then on the night that the story was in the paper I went over to a friend's house and the whole evening all I heard were jokes about the company. That night I realized that, whether I like it or not, a big part of who I am is an employee of [company name].

Too often, negative experiences like this are the ones that bring us together and remind us of our connectedness. On a societal level, we see it when we are threatened nationally. During the first Gulf War, for example, or after the attacks of September 11, the approval rating for both Bush presidents went through the roof. Outside influences can reinforce our "inside" connection.

In businesses, the objectification of the organization has enormous costs—both literally and figuratively. Management and labor look out for their own best interests instead of collaborating to determine what is best for the company. Leaders of organizations fight to get their budget allotments at the expense of others without any overall sense of the net impact on the company. The production and sales departments argue with each other and try to win rather than collaborate to determine the best approach to developing and marketing a new product. "It's not my job" becomes an all-too-frequent refrain. And people of different groups maintain a polite distance, avoiding talking about the things that are right under the surface. Is it any wonder that most people have relatively low job satisfaction and loyalty to their employer?

Similarly, *community* is a word with established meaning for us:

> **com-mu-ni-ty**, *n.* **1. a.** A group of people living in the same locality and under the same government. **b.** The district and locality in which they live. **2.** A social group or class having common interests. **3.** Similarity or identity: *a community of interests.* **4.** Society as a whole; the public. **5.** *Ecology.* **a.** A group of plants and animals living in a specific region under relatively similar conditions. **b.** The region in which they live. **6.** Common possession or participation.[3]

We think we know what the word means. For many of us it harks back to a past time that we mythologize, remember, or may have heard about at one point or another, a time when people's actions were supposedly driven not only by their immediate needs but by the needs of the whole. Of course, in most cases the "good times" we look back to were good only because we are so myopic. Everybody got along because so many who weren't "like us" were excluded, in some cases violently. We weren't in a community as much as we were in tribes or clans.

We have very little sense of the ecology of community. Our primary experience of our relationship with our environment is reactive. We deal with or respond to our environment rather than feel a part of it. What we call community is often more a sense of tribalism. In actuality, it is more a demonstration of the breakdown in our sense of overall community. That's why protest movements, whether they are the civil rights movement or the Tea Party, hold such emotional appeal. More times than not they serve to define us as different, to ensure our safety from the community as a whole, and to give us a sense of power in relating with the movements.

In fact, in my experience, this is an extremely misunderstood aspect of the diversity and inclusion conversation. People exist in dominant and nondominant groups. These groups aren't necessarily defined by their numbers, but more often by their power and influence. To illustrate, in the days of apartheid, black South Africans were the majority in number but nondominant in power and influence. The same could be said to be true about women in many hospitals or educational institutions. People in nondominant groups tend to be more keenly aware of their group identity for the very reasons I described earlier. Their identification as "the other" naturally encourages a looking for and connection

"I have been thinking about the paradox of community, particularly if it is defined as a unified body of individuals. As much as the soul yearns to be part of a greater whole, so too does it want to be separate and apart. In organizations this can cause a real disconnect between the part of me that 'looks out for #1' and the part that wants to be part of a team. I am reminded of the lines from the play 'The Me Nobody Knows' that speaks to the longing for community—'I have felt lonely, forgotten and even left out. Set apart from the rest of the world. But I never wanted out. If anything, I wanted in.' And yet there's the fierceness associated with being one's own person, most eloquently by the late Frank Sinatra: 'I've got to be me.'"

Tiane Mitchell Gordon
Chief Diversity Officer
AOL

to "other others" to form a subcommunity and related representative institutions around. In addition, an awareness of one's "otherness" may be essential to survival. It helps one know when one is safe or when danger is present. You'd better believe that during the Holocaust my ancestors had to always remember that they were Jews.

So Black History Month, for example, becomes important to African Americans because every other month is mostly about white history. Women's support groups become important to women because most other groups are generally dominated by men, at least in power if not in number. And the Tea Party movement arises because people perceive themselves to be outside of what they perceive to be the "liberal establishment." Obviously, the content of each of these groups is quite different, but the psychological context in which they are created, *in their own minds*, is actually quite similar. This phenomenon then creates a distinct background through which members of these groups see the world, giving them a different perceptual lens and, therefore, a different worldview and interpretation of people, events, and circumstances.

A woman who was part of a group of women that formed a support group within one of the law firms I've worked with had this to say:

> When we started this it was not in any way designed to be subversive. On the contrary, we made very specific rules for ourselves that this would not be a "bitch" session. We did it because we wanted to remember that we weren't out there alone dealing with some of the frustrations we encountered. The interesting thing was

that once some of the company's leaders found out about what we were doing and started to ask questions, we all suddenly felt very powerful. A little nervous, but very powerful. It was like all of sudden we were a force to be reckoned with. At least we weren't being ignored!

Our frustrated desires to be included result in a search for ways to protect, defend, and be validated as people. But in doing so, they separate us even more. As with *organization*, by objectifying *community* we have lost our ability to see its power as a way of being. We want power to be a way of looking at the world that includes not only our interests and concerns but the interests and concerns of the community of which we are a part.

So what, then, is the power of synthesizing these two familiar words? *Organizational community* is not proposed as a kind of organization to create. Nor is it proposed as a kind of community to create. It is proposed as a way of being, a way for people to work together that creates the possibility of dramatically enhanced success and satisfaction.

The good news is that this kind of transformation is possible for organizations. There are businesses and nonprofit groups, health-care providers and newspapers, and even small cities that are engaging in the process of creating *organizational community*.

Understanding the way we individually and collectively think and feel about diversity provides the background of understanding of our struggles with it and thus is critical to understanding how we act about it. Before getting more deeply into the organizational conversation about diversity, it is worth exploring the very underpinnings of the concept and, especially, our relationship with and desire for community because that is at the core of the conversation about diversity. Why do we care how people get along? Where does our desire to live in some semblance of peace and acceptance with one another come from? How can we create a sense of community within the organizations that we live and work in?

There is no question that it is deep within our individual and shared value systems. In his *Wall Street Journal* piece, Daniel Henninger begins by stating, "Most people already knew that the basic idea beneath diversity emerged about 2,000 years ago under two rubrics: Love thy neighbor as thyself, and Do unto others as they would do unto you."[4] However, in actuality, the desire for connection, for community, began well before biblical times. The earliest philosophical and religious tracts that have been found, dating back thousands of years before Henninger's reference, all talk, in one way or another, about the importance of community.

That need to not be alone is at the heart of our quest for community, and it is an excellent place for us to begin an inquiry. Where does our perception of community come from? Cultures are built on a collection of normative behaviors. In recent years a neologism called the "meme" has developed for these behaviors. Richard Dawkins originally constructed the term in his book *The Selfish Gene*[5] based on the Greek word *mimeme*, meaning "something imitated." He chose the word specifically because of its similarity to the sound of *gene* because as genes are a unit of biological evolution, memes are a unit of cultural evolution. Memes *are* the various behavioral, emotional, and cultural traits that define us as groups. Dawkins defined the meme as "a unit of cultural transmission, or a unit of imitation," and he and others, such as Susan Blackmore,[6] Keith Henson, and Daniel Dennett,[7] speculate that memes are like viruses that exist and survive in a culture because of a natural selection phenomenon. Some of the more common examples of memes might include scientific theories ("The world is flat"), traditions, fashions, superstitions, fads, trends, urban legends, fundamental philosophical beliefs ("Freedom is good!"), biases, languages, and so on.

Northern European cultures, for example, tend to be very time conscious, as opposed to Central American cultures. Why? If we look back ten thousand years to Northern Europe, we see an environment in which the greatest threat to people's survival was the cold. Nine months out of the year people would die if they weren't prepared for the cold. Time becomes very important. In such a short growing season, if the crops get in the ground late or are picked late, there might be no food. The threat of death has a profound impact on people's behavior, and so consciousness about time becomes "the norm." That meme survives, even after technology diminishes the threat. At some point, it becomes a matter of "That's the way we do things around here."

We're all familiar with memes that come and go: Hula Hoops, Cabbage Patch dolls, or other popular toys of the moment; popular musicians, television shows, movies, or books; games (World of Warcraft, or, at an earlier time, Trivial Pursuit); and technology (the use of e-mail, so ubiquitous now, but rarely known or used a generation ago, or Facebook and the social networking revolution). Many memes, though, have survived for generations. We will discuss that more later, when we talk about globalism and cultural competency.

The challenge is that the memes, or cultural traits, that are most beneficial to us may not be the ones that spread rapidly, much in the way traits of destructive diseases may proliferate. The reality is that the ones that become the most prolific are the ones that spread the most easily, even though they may not only have no value but be inherently destructive or false. This is particularly true in the information age because it is so easy to rapidly spread information, valid or not. This makes us culturally susceptible to the conscious infusion of memes used to send a message. For example, as America entered the Iraq war, studies showed that close to 70 percent of the American population believed that

Saddam Hussein was involved in the September 11 attack, even though it had been established that there was no evidence to support that notion.[8] Similarly, as of this writing some 20 percent of Americans believe that Barack Obama is a Muslim, despite all of the information to the contrary.[9]

The function of memes is critical to our understanding of diversity because so many of our attitudes and behaviors regarding diversity are built on memes: beliefs about ourselves, beliefs about "other" people, our sense of what is normal, likes and dislikes, exposure to various cultural behaviors, our language or life behaviors, and value systems, not to mention our values about dominance and nondominance among groups. The list is almost endless. We'll talk more in later chapters about various memes, but it is clear that virtually every culture has some set of memes around what community is, because it is clear that despite what some may want to believe, it is virtually impossible for most people to live without interacting with others.

In our American cultural experience, we brought together a vast array of different people within a relatively short historical period of time and so have created memes that are both about coming together as a unified community and living separately at the same time. We can recognize that, as a result, an interesting dichotomy exists between our need to identify with people like ourselves and our desire to see ourselves as part of a larger universe. Struggles around issues of diversity exist throughout the planet, and in that sense there is nothing unique about Americans. However, our particular challenges with diversity are distinctive in that, perhaps more than any large country in the world, we have developed a national ethos around our ability to be "the home of the brave and the land of the free." We celebrate and teach about our diversity at the same time as we suffer from the struggle of it.

Of course, how we define community may differ dramatically, and often without our even seeing the contradictions. We can recognize that, particularly in American culture, an interesting dichotomy exists between our need to identify with people like ourselves in a smaller, identity-based "community" and our desire to see and experience ourselves as part of a larger, universal definition of community.

The desire to link with others with a familiar background is understandable. This clannishness provides a basis for support and strength for human beings. We can see this in our observations of indigenous people around the world. People seem to form groups that are extensions of family and that are exclusive rather than inclusive. In the case of Native American Indians, for example, the strong affiliation for the clan provided safety, support, shared resources, and spiritual sustenance. In fact, it is only usually in the most dramatic breakdowns of indigenous societies that this sense of clan identity seems to fall apart.[10]

This same desire for connection can be seen in observing patterns of immigration to the United States by many different ethnic groups. Despite our long adherence to the notion of the "melting pot," most people who have immigrated to the United States have found strength and solace in connecting with people like themselves. We can see examples of this phenomenon in the development of the Irish community in Boston, the Italian communities in Philadelphia and Baltimore, the Polish community in Chicago, the Chicano community in Los Angeles, the Jewish community in New York, and the Chinese and Japanese communities in San Francisco. This also is true for the earlier-mentioned Sudanese population in Omaha, the Hmong population in Minneapolis and St. Paul, and hundreds of others. These groups, brought together by their like affiliation, served (and in many cases continue to serve) several important functions. Some are obvious. Common needs are fulfilled, including religious and communal practices, financial support, places to get foods that are special to the culture, a place where the language is spoken, appropriate medical services, or a place to get one's hair done in a particular way or buy a particular kind of clothing, and so on.

All of these are critical to assisting in the day-to-day functioning of life, allowing people to have ease in daily routines rather than constantly confronting the strangeness, the "differentness" of the dominant culture around them. Of course, those in the predominant cultural group have similar things available as well, but because they are so predominant they often aren't seen as "cultural" at all, but simply as the way things are. I'll discuss this more, later in the book.

However, there are other dynamics that are not so obvious. On a psychological level the existence of community provides an emotional touchstone for people. The security of a place where my culture can live fulfills a particularly primal part of my personality. *I can deal with the difference of the world outside if I have a place where I can remember that I am not alone and isolated.* This emotional and psychological underpinning is essential if I am to engage in a broader community context, particularly if it is one where I feel different *all of the time* (for example, when I go to work every day). This begins to explain why it is that groups of people of color or nondominant groups joined by ethnic, religious, or sexual orientation seem to express more of a need to demonstrate their group identity than what might be found among predominant groups. If I feel included in the whole, the larger community, and if I feel like "what I am" is not an impediment to my acceptability in that larger community, then I can begin to take my attention off of my clan identification and see myself more as part of the whole. My struggles may still exist, but they are not related, in my conscious mind, to that particular identity. If I struggle, for instance, because of poverty, poverty is the issue, not my race/ethnicity. I begin to see myself as relating to a larger clan. Yet if my "minority" or nondominant identification leaves me vulnerable or powerless or leaves others like me feeling that way, the desire to identify with those others is a strong attraction, either consciously or unconsciously.

This phenomenon of identification is, of course, always changing, as the memes of our culture are changing, depending on history and depending on where we are at a particular moment in time. The evolution of culture occurs just like the evolution of biology, only faster.

We sometimes forget that some of those in the dominant group were not always so included. Irish and Italian immigrants were famously discriminated against and in conflict with each other in some places until generations after they became "mainstream." However, during those past times they also were "the other."

And so the "them" and the "us" are often and always changing, depending on where we are at a given time, how included we feel, how many of us there are, and how much of a struggle we face in surviving. I may feel fully included in the mainstream as a tall, white-skinned man but feel somewhat marginalized because I am Jewish. Most of us have some element of both inclusion and exclusion in our identity consciousness.

I once had dinner with I. King Jordan, at the time the president of Gallaudet University, the school for the hearing impaired in Washington, D.C. Jordan described a perfect example of this shifting dynamic of identity. He stated that African American female students on the Gallaudet campus focus on different aspects of their identity, depending on the challenges they face. Off campus they might focus primarily on their deafness, because it is the single aspect of their identity that creates the greatest challenge in the larger world. On campus, they might focus more on their African American identity in the face of a predominantly white student body. On the other hand, within the black community on campus they might focus more on their gender. Which has the most impact? It depends on the moment.

Figure 4.1

We might see this shifting identity phenomenon in this way (depicted in figures 4.1, 4.2, and 4.3). As individuals we are distinct from one another. There is an individual "me" and an individual "you" who might react with attraction or repulsion but are reacting from our individual personalities.

However, our individual selves almost always consciously or unconsciously identify with a subgroup or identity (White, Black, Asian, Hispanic, male, female, Christian, Jewish, Hindu, Muslim, gay, straight, etc.). As I mentioned earlier, this is more likely to be true if the subgroup identity is a nondominant cultural one. While we are identifying with that group, we become a "we" who are interacting (again, either positively or negatively) with the "they." We haven't lost our "me," as it is a part of the "we," and, similarly, we recognize that they are individuals, to some extent, but we also see them as part of the "they."

There can be multiple layers of this identity dynamic. Let's consider the feeling that many Americans had after the September 11, 2001, attacks on the World Trade Center and the Pentagon. I see myself as an individual, living in a house with other individuals (me/you), and I also see myself as part of a group, living in a society with other groups—for example, as a Jew living with mostly Christians (we/they)—but during the time after the attacks, I most strongly see myself as an American living in a world with others who want to hurt Americans (we might call this the "us/them" distinction).

So our identities become layered over the course of our lives. How many do we have? Almost an infinite number. How many do we focus on? It depends on the moment and the stimulus. And each of them may give us a distinct perspective based on the fact that at that moment in time we are seeing the world through the lens which that identity creates for us to look through.

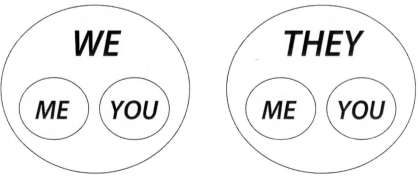

Figure 4.2

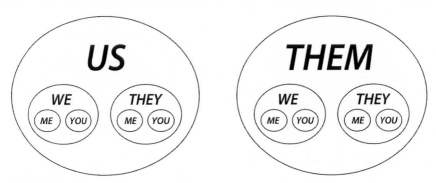

Figure 4.3

These identities are much more complex than simply race, ethnicity, religion, and so on. They also extend to aspects of ourselves that we adopt over time. "Diversity consultant," for example, is an identity that can give me both a particular view of the world and an entire set of reactions and responses to things that I encounter. Even in reading this book, somebody might react and/or respond to that identity (or to how that identity is framed).

Here is where the particular dichotomy emerges. These clan affiliations serve a distinct, and we might even say necessary, purpose. They provide security, support, and nurturing. Yet their very existence becomes problematic inside of the context of our classic American isolationism. If we are inclined to fear or feel less comfortable with people who are different from us, as I would suggest most people do at some level, and to feel like we have to make it on our own, then we are confronted with an inherent conflict. We like to be with people whom we feel comfortable with, yet that desire becomes increasingly articulated as "people like us" versus those "others" who are not like us. The extension of our personal sense of danger or discomfort about others is extended on this group level to a personal fear or discomfort of people who are from other groups. The "us/them" paradigm simply translates to a larger and even more dangerous scale. It is more dangerous because our inability to relate to other individuals remains at least semipersonal. It is directed at an individual or individuals at a time. When we expand this perception to a group level we can begin to see large numbers of people as a threat and to collaborate with large numbers of people like ourselves who see "those people" as a threat as well. This phenomenon explains why some groups of people become the targets of seemingly mass movements of those who feel uncomfortable with them at a given time, as happened in the United States over the past several years with Hispanic/Latino immigrants or with Muslims and Arabs after the September 11 attacks.

When this dynamic is at play, even seemingly innocent activities can seem threatening. Consider, for example, when a group of Latino and Latina artists came together in April 2006 to sing a Spanish version of the U.S. national anthem. The effort arose at a time when anti-immigrant sentiment in the country was growing, and the artists were trying to send the message that they, too, loved America. But that, of course, was not how the message was received. In fact, there was a great deal of reaction. The *Washington Post*, for example, ran a headline on April 28, 2006, that read, "An Anthem's Discordant Notes: Spanish Version of 'Star-Spangled Banner' Draws Strong Reactions." Of course, the reaction was not simply to the anthem being sung in another language, as it has been for years. (I remember years ago, in Hebrew school, singing it in Hebrew at an assembly.) It was in the context of the rampant anti-immigrant feeling that was sweeping the country, particularly focused on Spanish-speaking immigrants, and the fear of the country "being overrun" by that immigrant group, as symbolized by the looming threat of bilingualism. Imagine, for example, if, at the time, President Bush had gone to a Midwestern town and had a local school group sing the national anthem, and that school had been a Greek Orthodox school. Can you imagine the *Washington Post* running a headline that read, "An Anthem's Discordant Notes: Greek Version of 'Star-Spangled Banner' Draws Strong Reactions"? Not likely. No fear, no threat, no big deal.

This conflict continues to exist in the way even the most well meaning of us attempt to address the dynamic. People still talk about "teaching tolerance," or about "prejudice reduction," or "fighting racism," for example, when in reality those words have some built-in ambiguity in the sense that they are built on the acceptance of the sense of danger caused by those issues. The orientation of most of these definitions exists on the assumption of difference, and in some cases on the assumption of danger. At best, they allow for an absence of conflict but very little opportunity for true appreciation and inclusion of those differences.

There might be a different conceptual framework to examine. What if the existence of others, different from ourselves, was viewed as part of the whole, a larger whole than what we presently refer to as "community"?

To explore this notion, it may be beneficial to understand more clearly where our cultural sense of community comes from because the notion of separateness is not coincidental to the development of our American culture. In fact, it is one of the very fundamental bases for it.

From where did our country come? The indigenous people who lived on our continent just five hundred years ago (and relative to the cultures of most of the rest of the planet, that is indeed a short period of time) were not the ones whose basic life orientation created our primary culture. In fact, the development of our culture came close, both consciously and accidentally, to obliterating those people. On the contrary, our culture was formed by the infusion of large numbers of people who were not wedded to our land or who developed and grew it naturally. They came here having left behind their culture, their families, and their land. They were people who left by choice or were driven out for economic, political, and social reasons, or who were captured and forced to come to fulfill the economic and social desires of others.

As I noted earlier, this mix of people created a particular hybrid culture; a culture that was not rooted in a clear community, but that was rather joined only by the lack of those kinds of roots. And with that very sense of rootlessness came a natural tendency to avoid the establishment of community.

Yet people form groups. In some cases these groups are obvious in that they form along racial and gender lines, among levels of class, status, profession, and so on. The issue is not that they form, because people *will find ways to act out their clannish nature.* The question then becomes whether they will be inherently separatist and, therefore, protective in nature, or whether they will be seen as included in the whole and seen as a strength by the larger society *because they provide individuals with the ability to come to the larger community with a stronger sense of support and a stronger sense of self.*

These subgroups then become an extension of our individualism. They allow us a place where we can be, at the same time, connected and apart. And it is our very identification with that subgroup that begins to shape the world we see. In terms of the distinctions I discussed in the previous chapter, they are the background of understanding that frames our ways of dealing with one another. They provide the *background of obviousness* that Winograd and Flores examined.

This fundamental concept is difficult for us to grasp, primarily because one of our prime experiences is that of being taught that there is an objective world "out there," a world of facts and objects, and people who see the world otherwise might even be considered delusional. Yet just like Xixo, the Kalahari Bushman, we are incapable of interpreting the world we see unless it refers to something we already know. Robert Greenleaf described this phenomenon:

> Alfred North Whitehead once said, "No language can be anything but elliptical, requiring a leap of imagination to understand its meaning in its relevance to immediate experience." Nothing is meaningful until it is related to the hearer's own experience. One may hear the words, one may even remember them and repeat them, as a computer does in the retrieval process. But *meaning*, a growth in experience as a result of receiving the communication, requires that the hearer supply the imaginative link from the hearer's fund of experience to the abstract language symbols the speaker has used.[11]

The subcommunities we relate to provide this background for us, the basis of interpretation we use for understanding and defining the world. Who we are, as functioning human beings, is a result of the communities that we relate to, grow up in, and are therefore influenced by. Albert Einstein reflected on it in the following way:

> The individual, if left alone from birth, would remain primitive and beastlike in his thoughts and feelings to a degree that we can hardly conceive. The individual is what he is and has the significance that he has not so much in virtue of his individuality, but rather as a member of a great human community, which directs his material and spiritual existence from the cradle to the grave.[12]

Our experience of the world is shaped by fundamental messages we receive our entire lives, and those messages help define the lens through which we see reality. Our "cultural narrative," the collection of stories, values, experiences, lessons, and observations that make up our lives, color the way we look at the world every bit as much as the pair of blue contact lenses put on the baby. We are, for the most part, unaware of the messages we have received. Many of the "truths" that we experience in our lives are nothing but memes; a system of shared values that have been adequately and repeatedly communicated to us over the course of our lifetime, and, having incorporated those messages into the way we see the world, we begin to gather evidence to support those points of view.

Because we see our subgroups as so separate and maintain that separateness, our cultural narratives, our interpretations, our *vision of the world*, if you will, are equally separate. And so we see instances like the O. J. Simpson trial in which Whites and African Americans get the same information *but interpret it in totally different ways*. I discuss this phenomenon of *perceptual identity* later in the book.

The interesting thing about all of these components is that they all live in our dialogue with one another. None of them can truly exist unless people are willing to engage with one another in their discovery. None of them is an entity that one can hold in one's hand. They are reflected in our language, and that very language, rather than being descriptive, actually structures the world that we see. It shapes how we look at things. George Orwell described this in discussing his classic futurist novel, *1984*:

> The purpose of Newspeak was not only to provide a medium of self-expression for the world-view and mental habits proper to the devotees of Ingsoc (English Socialism), but to make all other modes of thought impossible. It was intended that when Newspeak had been adopted once and for all and Oldspeak forgotten, a heretical thought—that is, a thought diverging from the principles of Ingsoc—should be literally unthinkable, at least so far as thought is dependent upon words. Its vocabulary was so constructed as to give exact and often very subtle expression to every meaning that a Party

member could properly wish to express, while excluding all other meanings and also the possibility of arriving at them by indirect methods. This was done partly by the invention of new words, chiefly by eliminating undesirable words and by stripping such words as remained of unorthodox meanings, and so far as possible of all secondary meanings whatever.[13]

So as long as we have "antiracism training," for example, we must inherently have racism. In this sense we are stuck in a repeating loop. We are prisoners of our language. It is a language that is based in the individual and clan orientation paradigm and creates for us, even in our thoughts, a sense of ourselves as separate from our larger community, even as we are linking up with our subcommunities.

It is not so much that we disregard or denigrate our connection to our community; *we don't really even have the language to think it.* And, lacking that language, we attempt to create ourselves hopelessly in relation to others, constantly searching for the way we can make that relationship work while at the same time unable to define, describe, or experience it except through the very language that has no place for it. We even build defense mechanisms against new language when it is created, as is demonstrated in the cynicism that many express in reaction to people who are too "kumbaya" or "Polyanna-ish." The cynicism allows the language of the status quo to continue to exist. It is a fascinating dichotomy.

This dynamic is one of the most difficult we face in attempting to get people to engage in fundamental change regarding diversity issues. The very language that we have created is both a function of and a creator of the dynamic of which we are a part. It reflects the values and norms of society at the same time as it reinforces and shapes these values and norms. Language doesn't just define a world, it creates one. With regard to diversity, we have tried the two extremes: we have built structures on our differences (during segregation, among other times), and that didn't work. We have tried to ignore our differences (you remember all of those 1960s songs), and that didn't work either, because both were built in reaction to not feeling comfortable with the fact that we are different. The essence of awareness that we must come to is that *we are connected by the reality that we are different.*

Accepting the impact that this has had on our thinking is counter to the myth of individualism: the belief that people create their own experience of the world. Fromm wrote, "The most important factor for the development of the individual is the structure and the values of the society in which he was born."[14] Yet as a society we attribute an inordinate amount of our success to our own behavior and relatively little to the place where we began. I have a friend named

Clark who is a limousine driver. Clark is African American and grew up in one of the toughest parts of Washington, D.C. One day Clark and I got into a discussion about growing up. "When I was a boy," he told me, "my mother used to tell me that if I kept my nose clean and did well, I could be a truck driver like my dad when I grew up." My experience was very different from Clark's. In my home growing up I was told that "after you go to college," I would choose which profession to study. According to our general societal standards, I am the more "successful" of the two of us. I have gone to college and some graduate courses. I have built a business, using the skills I learned in college and graduate school. Yet when I look at my experience, the reality is that I had no choice but to go to college. In fact, I took one semester off when I was a junior and it almost killed my parents (and they me). For me, going to college was like putting one foot after another. It is what I was trained to do from birth. For Clark to go to college would have been a momentous achievement. He would have been the first person in his family, and perhaps even in his neighborhood, to go. He would have had to break out in a way I have never dreamed about having to confront. As a society we don't value what we accomplish in the context of where we came from, we evaluate it in the context of what we have produced.

This way of perceiving the "reality" of the world is more than just an existential conversation. Maturana and Varela began to look at living systems in this same way—and that was to question whether systems functioned in the context of a "real" environment or whether it was the processes of those systems that "realized" the surrounding environment. "We propose a way of seeing cognition not as a representation of the world 'out there,' but rather as an outgoing bringing forth of a world through the process of living itself."[15]

In other words, Maturana and Varela go past the notion that our "perception of reality" may be shaped by our way of seeing or interpreting. They are suggesting that *reality itself* exists as a function of our perspective, our way of seeing. If we are members of a group who have a common agreement as to what is real, *we begin to see it as real*. At some point we stop distinguishing between what we see and what others see. *Reality actually is, for us, the way people around us see things*. Comedienne/philosopher Lily Tomlin put it another way. "Reality," she says, "is a collective hunch."[16]

Think about it. What makes Cabbage Patch dolls silly toys one day and something for people to fight over the next? What makes people kill other people for their tennis shoes? Value is a determination of cultural language, repeated over and over by my group. At some level, this affects even our core institutions. What is the stock market other than a collection of conversations that people have on a daily basis about the value of a piece of paper? If you have any sense that there is much more rationality to it than that, you should spend thirty minutes on the floor of the Chicago Board of Trade.

Our world occurs within the limitations or the expanses of our experience, but we are, for the most part, unaware of the degree to which our vision is affected by our history.

Much of this reaction is shaped by our emotional experience. As I discuss later, our feelings, consciously and unconsciously, begin to shape our perceptions of the world more than any cognitive or behavioral knowledge we possess. This is no mystery to most of us if we just stop and look. Few of us cannot remember a time when a friend or loved one (it's always easier to see it over there than over here) "loses it." At these moments it is crystal clear to us that their perception, their very experience of the world, has been shaped by their feelings. This may be expressed in fantasies about the horrible things that might befall them or in delusions of grandeur. In any case, their reality and ours are vastly different at the moment. How often do we ask how much our reality is shaped by our feelings?

We even see times when masses of people form agreements over less-than-rational beliefs. Consider, for example, the movement against marriage equality. People who maintain that marriage should be allowed only between a man and a woman generally give four major reasons. The first is that marriage is for procreation. Yet when my mother remarried at the age of seventy-three I don't recall anybody contending that the marriage should not have been allowed, but I promise you there was no possibility of procreation occurring!

The second, and most widely held, is that homosexuality is a sin. The most often-cited reference is from Leviticus 18:22, "You shall not lie with a male as with a woman; it is an abomination." However, why do we adhere to that particular passage so stridently when we ignore so many dozens of others? For example, do we stone our neighbors when they mow their lawns on Sunday, as is explicitly required in Numbers 15:30–31 ("So if someone sinned in that manner against God's commandments, that person would be completely cut off from his people—killed for their sin")? Not to mention the question of whose religious law becomes civil law in a country in which Thomas Jefferson famously said, "I contemplate with sovereign reverence that act of the whole American people which declared that their legislature should 'make no law respecting an establishment of religion, prohibiting the free exercise thereof,' thus building a wall of separation between church and State."[17]

The third often-stated reason is that it is not good for children, though the latest research from the American Pediatric Association indicates that the children of lesbian parents are the healthiest in terms of school behavior and performance.[18]

The final reason is often a simple one: we have been doing this for so long that we should be hesitant to change it. But that reasoning, of course, was also applied to ending slavery, giving women the right to vote, and every other major social change.

So how is it that in the face of this seeming irrationality so many good people go along with this restriction on the rights of their fellow citizens? Because it is not a rational argument at all. It is what I call "the yuck factor." Marriage between gay and lesbian couples makes me feel "yucky"; therefore, the arguments make sense to me. Our reality is shaped by our feelings.

This "blindness" is especially difficult for people from a Western cultural tradition to grasp. Our cultural perspective is fundamentally geared toward a worldview that is based on the notion of an external reality, separate from us. Because we are geared toward action and reaction rather than reflection, our personal way of looking at things is to be generally blind to ourselves, *and we are blind to that blindness.*

This orientation in Western culture grew out of the metaphysical revolution of Galileo and Descartes in the sixteenth and seventeenth centuries. The Galilean and Cartesian orientations established a sense of mind-body dualism, the existence of two distinct domains of reality. The first is the objective world of physical reality that we see, feel, touch, hear, and smell, and the second is the subjective world of our thoughts and feelings. This way of looking at the world, which has basically defined our orientation for the past four hundred years, is based on several assumptions:

> 1. We are inhabitants of a "real world" made up of objects bearing properties. Our actions take place in that world.
> 2. There are "objective facts" about that world that do not depend on the interpretation (or even the presence) of any person.
> 3. Perception is a process by which facts about the world are (sometimes inaccurately) registered in our thoughts and feelings.
> 4. Thoughts and intentions about action can somehow cause physical (hence real-world) motion of our bodies.[19]

Most of the philosophy that has been written during these four hundred years has reflected an attempt to understand the relationship between the objective and subjective worlds. Our relationships with communities that we have been a part of have reflected this struggle.

As a result of this conflict we find ourselves in a state of ongoing dissonance in relationship to our identities and experiences, and that very dissonance keeps us separate from one another. On one hand, we can see that our knowledge, our perceptions, our feelings, our entire inner perspective, our biological-social-emotional histories actually shape our world. The more we live out of those perspectives, the more we gather evidence to confirm their reality. On the other hand, we are told that our relationship with our community and social groups must exist apart from those personal perspectives. *The very things that are affecting us the most cannot be spoken about and, in fact, should not be spoken about because it is considered "elitist" or "naval gazing."* Is it any wonder that our feelings about being in a community are so confusing?

On an interpersonal level this dynamic also occurs. Often a person's response to a particular situation is being directed by some unspoken agenda about which the person may not even be aware. Consider what happens, for example, if a group of people is generally mistrustful and angry at "the system," be it a government, societal, or organizational structure, and files a complaint. The response of the system to that complaint, however well intended and however much it seems to satisfy the demands of the complainants, will probably end up being considered insufficient. People in power are left feeling like "people are never satisfied" and give up trying to please them, when in fact the reality is that people may be either unaware of, unable to express, or unwilling to express their true fundamental concerns. What they really want is a sense of connection, a feeling of trust and support, but they may not be able to articulate that need or even know what it is they should ask. Attempts to mitigate the symptomatic issues are, therefore, unsatisfying, no matter how much effort is made to appease. No amount of what you don't want can ever satisfy you.

This dynamic plays a part in our societal debate about reparations to African Americans for slavery, especially when juxtaposed against the truth and reconciliation commissions that were created by Archbishop Desmond Tutu and others after apartheid fell in South Africa. The conversations about reparations have both a tangible, financial side to them and another side. The other perspective reflects the fact that, as a society, the United States has never fully embraced the horrors of and repercussions of slavery and then taken responsibility for it. In South Africa, on the other hand, the creation of a structure in which people could do just that was instrumental in dramatically reducing the difficulty of the transition.

At some level, we just want all of the stress around diversity to go away, yet we don't realize how much we are the ones keeping it in place. This is why the "cultural narrative" that is given to us by the history of our ancestors is so pervasive in the way we look at things. We are fascinated by the notion that we can learn to function in some collective format. We see the value of it. We really believe that "two heads are better than one," that "when you help one person up to the top of the hill you get there yourself," and dozens of other similar aphorisms. Yet there is something about the notion of teamwork, collaboration, consensus, and all those similar concepts that seems as though it may be fundamentally contrary to our cultural learning.

Think about it. We grew up into a story that was given to us by our ancestors. Those ancestors came from any number of places, but few of them came from anywhere else in this country. As I said earlier, many left their home country because they fled political or religious oppression. My own grandparents were in this category. My grandfather made it here to this country by himself at the age of twelve after the yeshiva he was studying in was burned to the ground. My grandmother's grandfather was the distiller to the czar, and her father and his family were allowed to flee the pogroms only because her grandfather agreed to stay and continue to supply the czar with booze.

Others, like many of the Irish, left because they simply could not survive, could not feed their families or themselves in the face of famine or other natural or economic conditions. Some were crusaders for a new political order. Others were explorers looking for the streets paved with gold. Still others were simply criminals of one kind or another who found a way to get out and start all over again. Many were ripped from their families, put on ships in chains, and taken to a land where they were forced to forget everything they left behind or suffer the sometimes fatal consequences.

Whichever they were, they all possessed the qualities we hold dear in our culture: adventure, risk taking, independence, self-reliance. We grew up on their tales. It was the great American frontier mentality. Frederick Jackson Turner, one of our most famous historians, created an entire school of history around it.[20]

But it doesn't end there. Who are the heroes we were told about? George Washington and the early patriots? All individuals. The wars were fought and won by Patton, and Eisenhower, and those who came before. When we watched television it was a superhero who saved the day, and before them, cowboys. Superman, Davey Crockett, Wyatt Earp, Bat Masterson, Matt Dillon, Mighty Mouse—all the same. The great American hero. The individual fighting against evil, and winning, occasionally with his (almost never her) trusty sidekick, but always the hero at large.

In our own accomplishments the same pattern has emerged. Doing it yourself was always better than doing it with others. Excelling and competing are themes as American as apple pie.

So how does this conflict with our desire for diversity? How do we create a greater sense of community in our organizations and in society if we are so culturally driven to make it ourselves or, at best, with our "clan"?

This is not to say that there are not exceptions. The notion of the American hero certainly includes some references to people acting in collaboration, but far more to people acting on their own. This is true in those we call our business heroes as well. As Harvard professor turned U.S. secretary of labor Robert Reich wrote:

> The older and still dominant American myth involves two kinds of actors: entrepreneurial heroes and industrial drones—the inspired and the perspired.

In this myth, entrepreneurial heroes personify freedom and creativity. They come up with the Big Ideas and build the organizations—the Big Machines—that turn them into reality. They take the initiative, come up with the technological and organizational innovations; devise new solutions to old problems. They are the men and women who start vibrant new companies, and shake up staid old ones. To all endeavors they apply daring and imagination.[21]

Yet, if we look carefully, the myth begins to become a little harder to grasp. In virtually every case what we see is that these powerful individuals would have gone nowhere without a phalanx of support, those who helped them to the top, those who worked with them to supply their ideas, and even the historians who glorified them while forgetting others.

The point isn't that there was anything wrong with these people. The problem is that our tradition is bound and gagged to the notion of the solitary hero and, like all traditions, it has a way of propagating itself. The past becomes the future. And the tradition of the solitary hero by its nature struggles with the notion of diversity because diversity is, by its very essence, a phenomenon of the collective, and the collective of collectives. The "me" struggles with the "us."

It is in that context that we all exist in the communities of which we have become a part, on one hand looking for support, and on the other, schooled in only one fundamental tradition: that the pursuance of our individual goals will somehow magically benefit society as a whole. Is it any wonder that we have such a difficult time with collaboration? How can we trust it? We begin to engage in the conversation, and everything that we have ever been taught confronts us and yells, "Run!" It is a system that is designed to challenge the notion of trust.

The point of this is not condemnation. On the contrary, it is somewhat amusing when you think about it. Here we are, the products of a cultural narrative that has been spawned for generations. A proud tradition of individualism that is rich in our folklore and deeper in our psyche. It is at the very deepest heart of what it is to be an "American."

So when we begin to create a conversation about a diverse community, we are again like the Kalahari Bushman Xixo. Being given a Coke bottle, we don't know what to do with it. The discomfort it creates for us is almost unbearable. That is why we see the "turtling" effect that Putnam found in his study. And the irony is that the more we struggle and feel uncomfortable, the more we slip back into our natural pattern, the pattern of least resistance, the pattern of individualism. We see community as a concept. We even speak about it in hallowed terms. But when it comes to living it, it is no more real than the statue of Lincoln in the Lincoln Memorial is actually Lincoln. Our conversation is a symbol of something we long to have that eludes our grasp. The main problem with this is that the person we have been raised to become—the rugged individualist that we have all been taught to emulate—can no longer win the game.

So what has the legacy of separateness left for us? We grow up inside of this conversation. We are apart, but at the same time we are fundamentally connected. We know that the message of our culture is one of individualism, separation, and competitiveness. And even if the ethnic culture that we originally came from has a different set of values, we are taught quickly that to be successful here you have to adopt these. We are instructed from the time we are very young that we survive based on our individual talents, skills, and other traits, *even though we are told that teamwork and relationship are important.* Herein lies a fundamental dichotomy to our existence. The very things we are told are a contradiction to our life experience. We know that we "should" share our toys. We know that we "should" be good team players. We know that we "should" support everybody around us and make him or her better people, better neighbors, and better co-workers. Yet at a very basic level, all of our feelings and our skills are oriented toward being separate and succeeding separately.

What this has created in us is a sort of cognitive dissonance: a sense that what we want, aspire to, and achieve is not right. There are moments when people fully own their inheritance, but rarely out in the open. In Oliver Stone's film *Wall Street* Michael Douglas plays such a character. His Gordon Gekko extols the virtue of greed. "Greed," he says, "is good!" And yet he is the villain. So how has this left us? We are at once driven, and at the same time critical of the very thing we are driven toward. At once self-reliant and independent, yet at the same time perpetually lonely. This phenomenon leaves us incomplete, like half of a puzzle, missing the satisfaction and joy that comes from true wholeness but driven in the wrong direction to find the other piece. It is like we are wandering in the desert *away from the water.*

The phenomenon plays itself out in our organizations. How could it not? Our organizational cultures are nothing if not the amalgamation of the dynamics we all bring. We bring our incomplete selves, searching for completion but hopelessly lost, into an environment that is supposed to provide the "other half." Yet what we find, of course, is more of the same: more frustration, more resignation and hopelessness, more of our own lost sense of self. Some of us are fortunate enough to work in environments that are the exception, but for the overwhelming majority, work is something you do to afford to live your life. If you have any doubt, ask any ten people what they would do if they won the lottery.

In fact, consider that the U.S. Department of Health and Human Services recently conducted a study in which it uncovered an extremely interesting and frightening fact. In Western industrialized society there is one day of the week on which people die more than any other, and they do so by a large margin. That day is Monday. And the most fatal single hour of the week is Monday morning between eight and nine. Our work environments are becoming not only unmanageable but also unlivable.

The sense of isolation, the resignation and the hopelessness, begins to shape our world. We make judgments and assessments about people that we do not see as judgments but as *the truth*. We often see things at a moment without realizing what has gone into the development of that moment. What history has resulted in this behavior occurring at this moment in time? Our shortsightedness can blind us to the dynamics that are truly at work. We don't see things even when they're right in front of us.

I found this dynamic to be true a number of years ago when I had an opportunity to attend a gathering of a number of survivors of the Holocaust. Most of the people in the group were Jews who had survived the ordeal and had ghastly stories to tell about their experiences in ghettos, in concentration camps, or in hiding. The most fascinating story, though, was one that was told by an Austrian woman in her sixties who was not Jewish. She was being honored as a rescuer—someone who had risked her own safety to save Jewish children from being exterminated. However, her story about herself was not about heroism. Actually, she was quite critical of the time it took her to realize what was really going on.

> When I was a little girl, the Anschluss (the Nazi occupation of Austria) occurred and the Nazi and Austrian Fascists came to power. My earliest memories of Jews were that they were a dirty, dangerous people who lived behind barbed wire fences in certain parts of the city. When I would observe them I would see them going through garbage for food, looking dirty and in rags. They were always trying to grab at people, trying to get help. The honest truth is that they scared me. It wasn't until a number of years later that my priest educated me to what was really going on and I got involved in the underground. Then I learned that the Jews had not put themselves in that situation, that they had not chosen it. All I knew at the time was that they scared me, and when people spoke about their being taken away, I was relieved.[22]

Of course, this very phenomenon also is fed by our guilt. Many white Americans, for example, would rather not rehash the past experiences of Blacks because to do so can leave us feeling guilty or defensive. It is easier to say, "That was so long ago . . . let's move on," even though by any logic, it was not that long ago at all. Consider that any African American who is just fifty-five years old is very likely to have started school in a segregated school.

Our sense of loneliness forces us to attempt to create community. We feel it missing, and in one way or another we respond. Sometimes we create community constructively, by bringing people together for joy or a higher purpose.

And sometimes we create community destructively, by bringing people together for unprincipled or even evil reasons. But the people who came together to create the Holocaust and the people who came together to save the victims of the Holocaust *were all, to some degree, drawn by a sense of wanting to be a part of something bigger than themselves.* We may give up, hopeless and resigned, and attempt to function without it, but rarely are people successful in doing so. It can usually occur only through the development of a misanthropic worldview, which then allows us to withdraw by making everyone else not worth engaging with or, even worse, the source of all of our problems.

For the most part, the way we react is by attempting to link up somehow, somewhere, with somebody. We attempt to make these links but, ironically, can do it only by using the tools that we have—tools that have been forged in the fires of our loneliness—our egos, our individual desires, our competitiveness. We attempt to force our way into the good graces of people so that we can feel connected, but our way of forcing has no power in it and leaves us, instead of connected, more isolated than ever. These methods all inherently fail because the process they create is directly counter to the process they seek to create. They are tools of isolation and loneliness, and they create just that. It's like some kind of cosmic joke. The more we try to alleviate the suffering of our loneliness, the more we use tools that are the result of our loneliness, the more our loneliness is reinforced, and the more we suffer. As Robert N. Bellah and others wrote in *Habits of the Heart: Individualism and Commitment in American Life*:

> The inner tensions of American individualism add up to a classic case of ambivalence. We strongly assert the value of our self-reliance and autonomy. We deeply feel the emptiness of a life without sustaining social commitments. Yet we are hesitant to articulate our sense that we need one another as much as we need to stand alone, for fear that if we did we would lose our independence altogether. The tensions of our lives would be even greater if we did not, in fact, engage in practices that constantly limit the effects of an isolating individualism, even though we cannot articulate those practices nearly as well as we can the quest for autonomy.[23]

All of our life exists on a continuum of that story. This moment, this day, this behavior, this action, this statement, all are but a part of a chain of events, a historical narrative that has led up to what we now do and leads past to what we will do in the future. The historical narrative provides the background of understanding that gives us the world we see. Yet in our experience we live only in the moment, and in doing so may miss the essential nature of why things are happening the way they are happening. While we have no obligation to look into the historical narrative that has led us to where we are today, it is helpful in understanding both what is going on and how to address what is going on.

So in the next chapter, we look at the historical narrative that has given us the way we approach diversity, the paradigms it has left us with, and the new ones we have an opportunity to create.

CHAPTER 5

Uncovering the Background of Diversity

In true dialogue, both sides are willing to change.

Thich Nhat Hanh

There are no permanent allies. There are no permanent enemies. There are just the issues.

Saul Alinsky[1]

I have been discussing the phenomenon of background and how it gives us the world we see. I also have reflected on our particular background where the question of community and group identity is concerned. I now want to look at how both of these concepts have given us a particular way of looking at the issue of diversity and inclusion.

The background that we are exposed to contributes to the fact that human beings have a natural tendency to get into patterns of behavior that we're familiar with and then to stay in those patterns. We see things in a particular way, interpret them in a particular way, and make choices that are familiar within that particular way of thinking. The fascinating thing is that once we see things in a particularly fixed way, we can easily fall into a rut that gets so deep we cannot see any other way of doing things. We saw this phenomenon in action earlier in the case of the typewriter keyboard.

Our beliefs, *even those that we create ourselves*, become self-justifying and limiting. We commonly refer to these patterns as *paradigms*, a concept initially introduced by Thomas Kuhn in his landmark book, *The Structure of Scientific Revolutions*.[2] Kuhn suggested that new paradigms, those that create revolutionary ways of thinking, are fundamentally theoretical applications or ways of looking at the world that are "sufficiently unprecedented to attract an enduring group of adherents away from competing modes of scientific activity."[3] Kuhn actually was writing about paradigms as a phenomenon that occurred in science. In a later book, *The Essential Tension: Selected Studies in Scientific Tradition and Change*, he elaborated, "A paradigm is what members of a scientific community, and they alone, share."[4] In "hard" science, paradigms are somewhat definitive. For example, once we discovered that the Earth was a sphere, it became challenging, if not impossible, to make any credible argument that the world is flat.

Social sciences, of course, have historically been somewhat more controversial. Some sciences cross the border between "hard" and social sciences and, consequently, have a bit more historical deniability. In the earlier part of the twentieth century, eugenics, the notion that races of people had inherent abilities or lack thereof, was a concept widely agreed upon by scientists around the world. It wasn't until the Nazis took eugenics and used it as a justification for the nightmare of the Holocaust that people widely abandoned it. Yet it returned again in the 1960s, when William Shockley, the winner of the 1956 Nobel Prize in Physics for his work with transistors, created a furor with his assertions that, in fact, Blacks were inherently intellectually inferior to Whites. Eugenics still resurfaces in subtle and not-so-subtle arguments to justify racial disparities both within the United States and around the world. Of course, as we will explore later, these beliefs still exist unconsciously in many people, *without their even realizing it*, and impact many decisions that people make regarding diversity-related issues.

The key to our understanding of paradigms and the way they work on the human mind is that our belief systems are often so strong that even when we see something right in front of us, we may not realize the significance of the change. Psychology professor Daniel Simons of the University of Illinois, Urbana, has demonstrated this phenomenon countless times in his studies of visual awareness and inattentional blindness. His demonstrations show that people can miss obvious things, right in front of their face, when they are focused on something else.[5] You can get a sense of how this dynamic works right now by doing this little experiment:

Take about fifteen seconds to look around the room and see how many objects you can identify that are green . . . and then look back at the book.

Now close your eyes and see how many of the red objects in the room you can identify.

If you didn't cheat, you probably found that you "saw" very few red objects. Why? Because your field of vision was limited by your mind. You saw what you were looking to see, in this case consciously, and were not able to see other things even though they were right in front of you.

Simons reported that there is a surprising extent of this inattentional blindness in the inability of people to notice unusual events that are visually available when their attention is otherwise engaged. On the other hand, we see hundreds of examples every day of ways in which we selectively focus our attention on certain things rather than others. How many times have you noticed that things appear when they are things you are thinking a lot about at the moment? For example, if you or your partner were pregnant, did you notice how many pregnant women you saw? Or when you are thinking of buying a new car, how many times do you see cars like it on the road or in advertisements?

This phenomenon of selective attention is not only normal; it is fundamentally necessary for our survival. By counting the receptor cells of the sensory organs and the nerves from those cells to the brain, it has been estimated that at any given moment, the human mind is being exposed to eleven million pieces of information through our five senses of sight, hearing, smell, touch, and taste. The most liberal estimates are that we can consciously process forty pieces of information per second.[6] With the huge amount of data that we are exposed to and the limitations of what we can absorb, unless we were selective, consciously and unconsciously, our experience would be like trying to drink from an open fire hydrant. We would be drowned by information.

And so, as is depicted in figure 5.1, while we are exposed to these eleven million pieces of information, our brains are sorting and filtering all the time through our various perceptions, interpretations, preferences, and this mechanism of selective attention.

To some degree, we are aware of this filtering process, but largely we are not. When these factors remain unconscious to us, we are often (and often very habitually) responding and making decisions based on influences that we are not even aware of. So we become very adaptive to these limitations. We walk down a busy street and we do not see everything, but we see *what our mind thinks it needs to see*. We sit in a loud concert and talk to our friend next to us, even as the band plays at 150 decibels or more, and we are able to hear because *we hear what we need to hear*, or *what our mind thinks it needs to hear*. We "fill in the blanks" based on our experience and what fits our memory of the patterns in that experience. As an example, complete the following sentences:

Ca y u rea th s?

You a e not r adi g th s.

W at ar ou rea in ?

A huge majority of native English speakers will read these sentences relatively easily, even though they could very well be read many different ways, including as gibberish, with the insertion of different letters.[7] Why? Because we have seen the patterns of these words before and we automatically find the missing letters. We "fill in the blanks" like this all the time, when people who have known each other for a long time complete each other's sentences, for example. We make assumptions that things will be how they have been in the past.

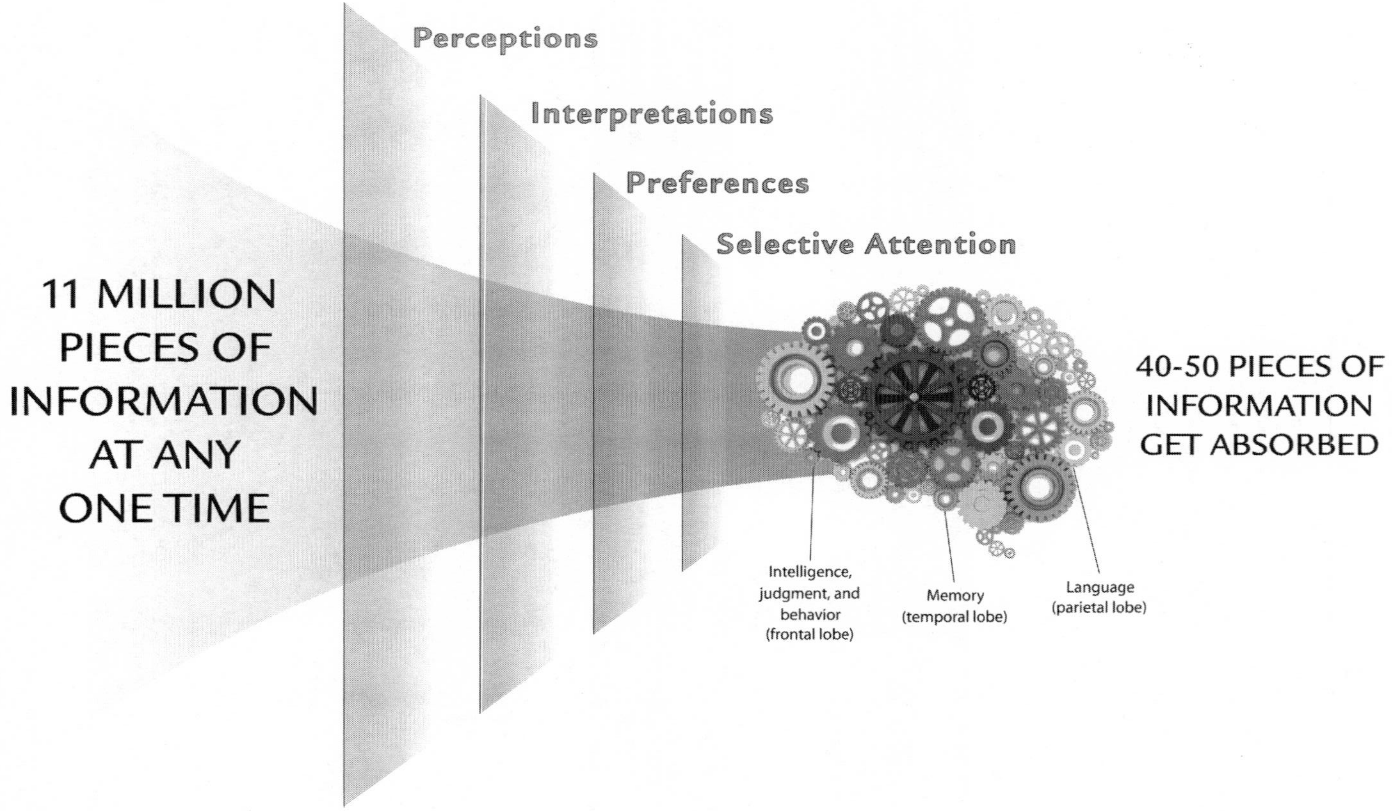

Perceptions

Interpretations

Preferences

Selective Attention

11 MILLION PIECES OF INFORMATION AT ANY ONE TIME

40-50 PIECES OF INFORMATION GET ABSORBED

Intelligence, judgment, and behavior (frontal lobe)

Memory (temporal lobe)

Language (parietal lobe)

Figure 5.1

In fact, this is fundamental to the way the human mind works. Richard Rorty describes this notion of the mind as a "knowing entity."[8] The human mind is capable of gaining *universal knowledge*, not simply the awareness of things as they occur. For example, as we look at a road stretching into the distance, the two sides coming together visually into a point, we *know* that they remain parallel because of the universal principle they represent, not because we have to drive all the way up the road to see whether they meet.

But sometimes this leads to mistakes, even tragic mistakes. One such mistake occurred on July 19, 2010, when Shirley Sherrod was forced to resign from her position as Georgia state director of rural development for the U.S. Department of Agriculture after a conservative blogger, Andrew Breitbart, excerpted for his website parts of Sherrod's address at a March 2010 National Association for the Advancement of Colored People (NAACP) event. The clip he posted was of Sherrod saying the following:

> The first time I was faced with having to help a white farmer save his farm, he took a long time talking. He was trying to show me he was superior to me. I know what he was doing. But he had come to me for help. What he didn't know—while he was taking all that time trying to show me he was superior to me—was I was trying to decide just how much help I was going to give him.
>
> I was struggling with the fact that so many black people have lost their farmland, and here I was faced with having to help a white person save their land. So, I didn't give him the full force of what I could do. I did enough so that when he—I assumed the Department of Agriculture had sent him to me, either that or the Georgia Department of Agriculture. And he needed to go back and report that I did try to help him.
>
> So I took him to a white lawyer that we had who had attended some of the training we had provided, 'cause Chapter 12 bankruptcy had just been enacted for the family farmer. So I figured if I take him to one of them that his own kind would take care of him.[9]

People reacted instantly to what seemed like a black U.S. government official stating that she had discriminated against a white family. The public reacted furiously. To the right, this was an example of black racism. Even liberals reacted. Sherrod's resignation was requested and quickly accepted. Days later, the remainder of Sherrod's statement became public knowledge. It turned out that what she had continued to say was this:

> Well, working with him made me see that it's really about those who have versus those who don't, you know. And they could be black, and they could be white, they could be Hispanic. And it made me

> realize then that I needed to work to help poor people—those who
> don't have access the way others have.[10]

In other words, Sherrod had clearly said the exact opposite of what she was being accused of saying. She was, instead, demonstrating an understanding that all people need to be treated equally.

How is it that so many people on both sides of the political spectrum went along with the misrepresentation? Breitbart had either consciously or unconsciously (we can only speculate on his motives) chosen a part of what Sherrod had said, but it so comfortably fit with what people could imagine that she might have said that people were comfortable filling in the blanks.

Maturana and Varela discovered this phenomenon in their research as well and postulated:

> What is observed are not things, properties, or relations of a world
> that exists "as such," but rather the results of distinctions made by the
> observer himself or herself. Consequently these results have no exis-
> tence whatever without someone's activity of distinguishing them.[11]

And the distinctions that have us "see" the world are the result of our traditions and our history:

> We live our field of vision . . . we are experiencing a world. But when
> we examine more closely how we get to know this world, we invari-
> ably find that we cannot separate our history of actions, both biologi-
> cal and social, from how this world appears to us. It is so obvious and
> close that it is very hard to see.[12]

In other words, as I stated earlier, we see the world not as it is, but as we are.

In the sense of what Simons, Rorty, Maturana, and Varela propose, the paradigm that we adhere to is actually a mental model of a "right" way of doing things or the "right things to see" that creates a lens through which we see certain things and don't see others. The alternative keyboard, or the Betamax video system, for example, and hundreds of other technologies that were not successful despite the fact that they were more effective, are not discarded because people do not believe they can be better, nor are they discarded because they have been shown not to be better. They are discarded because the lens through which we see "keyboards" *does not allow it to be seen as a real possibility, even though by any rational measure, it might be superior.* Using the "normal" keyboard or video player becomes a meme in our culture. It is the way we do things around here.

It is important to recognize that our tendency to stay within our comfort zone is a natural human trait. History is filled with countless examples of our struggles with new ideas and new ways of doing things. Some are legendary. For instance, do you remember this man?

Dick Fosbury won the Olympic gold medal in the high jump in 1968, clearing the bar at 7' 4.25" using (at the time) an unorthodox method of jumping. Nowadays this jumping style would not appear abnormal at all. That is just the point. Up until the 1968 Olympics, high jumpers around the world all used the same basic method for jumping. Called the Western Roll, it involved jumpers running to approach the bar, next throwing their lead leg over the bar as if straddling it, and then following with the rest of their body. Fosbury learned the Western Roll like most of his peers, as a high school student in Medford, Oregon. The problem was that he wasn't very good at it. As a result of his disappointing performance, he began experimenting and ended up with this method, later called the Fosbury Flop. His high school coach, upon seeing him jump for the first time, was reported to have said, "I don't want any circus act on my track team"; yet he was soon convinced since Fosbury's performance improved dramatically.

Even after his high school performance improved, his college coach tried to get him to change back to the then-traditional method of jumping, giving in only after seeing the results it produced. When Fosbury reached the Olympics, he was greeted with wonder. One journalist wrote:

> The high jump [competition] provided a sensation of a special and totally unexpected kind. Dick Fosbury, USA, showed an astonished world a brand-new way to jump better and higher. He invented and perfected it himself and there's an indication that many jumpers, novices and world class alike, will begin copying what has been named the "Fosbury Flop." It isn't easy to describe in words . . . one has to see it in action. Fosbury's new Olympic record speaks a clear language. This flop is no flop.[13]

In fact, Fosbury's innovation radically changed the sport of high jumping. After Fosbury won the Olympic gold medal in Mexico City, the American coach, Payton Jordan, commented, "Kids imitate champions. If they try to imitate Fosbury, he'll wipe out an entire generation of high jumpers because they all will have broken necks." Twelve years later, thirteen of the sixteen finalists in the Olympic high jump were using the Fosbury Flop, but there were no broken necks. In addition, the world record in the sport began to grow at a pace twice that which had been recorded before Fosbury introduced his innovation.

What does an Olympic high jumper have to do with this book? With diversity? The reason that Dick Fosbury's innovation was initially treated with such resistance wasn't because people didn't think it would work. The reason was that nobody would, or perhaps could, even bother to consider whether it would work because they were so comfortable with the way they had always done things in the past. The Western Roll was "the way we do things around here."

In most cases we don't even know why we do things "the way we do them around here." We just know that we feel more comfortable, more familiar, and less fearful doing things in ways in which we are used to doing things, even if the reason for doing it that way is invisible to us. Sometimes our cultural patterns of behavior have resulted from conscious strategies of the past, and sometimes they have evolved rather unconsciously. This impacts how quickly people are willing to adopt new ways of engaging as a result of the changing demographics and diversity needs of the workforce, the workplace, and the marketplace. I also would maintain that our societal and organizational approach to diversity has been frustrated by a number of limiting paradigms, many seemingly "obvious" and some "well intended." Some were more necessary in the past than they are today, and some are even partially true, but our mostly rigid adherence to these paradigms has been a major factor in frustrating our success. Most of them have resulted from the fact that the diversity reality has changed, but our basic conversation about it has not.

When the diversity movement really kicked into gear in the mid-1960s, white men overwhelmingly dominated the workforce. In fact, in 1965, it was estimated that 64 percent of the American workforce were white men, a majority so dominant that anybody outside of this group was generally referred to by the monolithic moniker "women and minorities."[14] And the term was often spoken as a single word, much as a child says the letters "L-M-N-O-P" in the alphabet.

These statistics were actually highly inaccurate because there were far more white women and men and women of color in the workforce, but their jobs were not, in those days, classified as "real jobs" (e.g., domestic labor, day labor, child care, and so forth). In any case, the U.S. Department of Labor defined the workforce in this way, and these numbers also were reflected in most corporate environments.

Inside of this imbalance, the roles of each group became somewhat clearly, even if unconsciously, defined inside of an "us/them" paradigm (the "us" or "them," of course, being defined by whichever group you saw yourself as a part of). The majority tended to support the status quo, which included a great deal of both conscious and unconscious biased attitudes toward members of the other groups. As of 1965, many of these attitudes were still codified into restrictive laws or covenants or were in the process of being changed. As change emerged, it occurred either as a threat to that status quo and was often resisted or was often responded to with a lack of awareness ("What problem?").

On the other hand, white women and men and women of color (as well as other groups) were being marginalized by the system that was in place. The major orientation from people in these groups, or those "allies" in the dominant group that supported them, was to right the wrongs of the past, to eliminate the existing limitations to opportunities and roles, and to be seen outside of their perceived monolithic identity. Their main focus was in being treated justly and "getting in" to the system.

This "us/them" paradigm was an inherent part of the diversity conversation and, as we will discuss, remains so today. It was built on a particular energetic relationship. As the civil rights movement and related activities expanded across the country, the energy became more and more aggressively oriented toward change. That is why so many of us who were involved in the movement at that time use the terminology that we "fought in the civil rights movement." It was a fight. Doors needed to be broken down. Barriers had to be eliminated.

At first, the attempts to change the system were relatively easily suppressed. But the stronger and more aggressive the attempt at change, the stronger the resistance developed to that change, in some cases consciously and in some cases less so. The two polar sides, the "us" and the "them" may seem completely disconnected, but one cannot exist without the other.

This is the fundamental basis of the dualistic nature of the mind. Things often exist in our awareness only in contradiction to things that are "not them." There needs to be no mention of "day" unless there is a night to distinguish it. No "cold" without "hot," and so on. We do not research a cure for cancer unless there is a cancer to be cured.

Tension seeks resolution in nature. We can see it when we view a pendulum that swings back and forth, one side pulling until it brings the pendulum back into another direction. The same is true when we pull back the bow to shoot an arrow. In that case, we use the tension to launch the arrow forward. The tension needs to be relieved, and in the relief, a counterbalancing energy occurs. Hence Newton's third law of motion: for every action there is an equal and opposite reaction. If the tension is created in the right place and in the right direction, it can launch change as surely as the bow launched the arrow. That is why some of history's great breakthroughs were stimulated by events that were exactly opposite. The civil rights legislation of the 1960s, for example, was stimulated by terrible events that occurred in opposition to civil rights: the 1963 16th Street Baptist Church bombing in Birmingham, Alabama, in which four children—Addie Mae Collins, Carole Robertson, Cynthia Wesley, and Denise McLair—were murdered, and the killing of three civil rights workers—James Chaney, Andrew Goodman, and Michael Schwerner—that same year in Philadelphia, Mississippi, along with similar horrors, had a huge impact on waking up the country to the need for the legislation.

The challenge is that the existence of this kind of tension between some objects can create a form of conflict that doesn't resolve itself but rather continues back and forth, like a pendulum that never settles, and can be very destructive. In societies or organizations this may occur as the result of two strongly held points of view. The one that dictates a particular choice today will usually find itself losing another tomorrow, and the group involved gets caught in a terminal cycle of competing actions and reactions.

At some level, we develop ego identification with our belief systems, particularly when they have been related to actions that we have taken and are related to our sense of success, safety, or normalcy. The more we identify with our role, the more it becomes who we are, the more our survival will depend on it, and the more rigid we become. The identity of a reformer needs something to reform. A codependency is created between those who are trying to create change and those who are resisting it. Without realizing it, one side of the conversation is engaged so deeply by the other side that a *conversational network of contention* forms, an ongoing discourse that is stuck in a repetitive cycle of "I'm right, you're wrong!" And the more we become identified with our "right," the more important we perceive the issue is, the more righteous both sides become. And the more righteous we become, the less flexible we become and, as a result, the less able to see or hear the other side's point of view. But of course, we don't see it as a position or a belief at all. To us it is the truth.

Our fundamental way of thinking is that if there are sides, we have to choose one. And by choosing one, we (including myself) define both the one we choose and the other as good or bad. There is nothing wrong with that in principle. Every person living in a civil society has to have some sense of what is good and bad or right and wrong. The challenge is how attached we get to those points of view. Being attached to our position on a subject or issue is limiting as a method of creating true transformation because it locks us into the system that has created the tension with which we must deal. That is at the heart of the conversational network of contention that we all live in. What most of us see as an alternative to this approach is compromise, which diminishes both points of view; debate, which puts them at war for the purpose of one winning and the other losing; and apathy, which simply distances us from caring.

It is easy to see how this has happened in our political system. Imagine two candidates debating. One makes a statement about health care, and the other responds, "I have to say that was brilliant. You clearly understand these issues better than I do. I still think that overall I would make the best president, but if I am elected I certainly hope you will work with me on that issue." The next day the newspapers would have a field day. Beyond the individuals in it, the system itself calls for conflict, for the "us/them" to continue, and we can all get caught up in it.

In fact, our political discourse seems almost hopelessly locked in this thoughtless kind of discourse. How many Americans, if we really tell the truth to ourselves, have a tendency to believe or not believe certain things or agree or disagree with a proposal as soon as we hear whether it was sponsored by Democrats or Republicans? How often do we justify or minimize what our candidate says that is questionable but take umbrage to a similar comment on the part of the other candidate?

The more one side pushes, the more the other side responds, either overtly or in a passive-aggressive fashion. And, of course, when we are compulsively and habitually looking through the lens of contention, we find more and more things to contend. Without even realizing it, our identities become consumed by our role in the contention, and we become dependent on the other side to exist.

Think about some of our most aggressive proponents of diversity. One example that I like to use is that of Reverend Al Sharpton because he epitomizes, in a way, people who are willing to confront racial problems when they exist. The issue is not whether you like Reverend Sharpton or not. It is just that he is indisputably someone who represents the particular energy of change that I am talking about. Now consider this: What would happen to Reverend Sharpton if there were no racial problems? How much interest would there be in his radio show? Without intention, his very identity might need the very thing he has spent his life fighting against!

> "The 'conversational network of contention' is a reality and challenge for us all. Even in the lesbian, gay, bisexual and transgender community, which has found itself at the receiving end of the so-called 'God, guns and gays' culture wars, we see on a regular basis how members of our community can slip into this divisive mindset about each other. For example, some gay people don't want to include the 'T' in the LGBT or refuse to believe that bisexuality is not an identity crisis. All of this points to an inextricable reality: We have a lot of work to do, starting with ourselves."
>
> Cuc Vu
> Chief Diversity Officer
> The Human Rights Campaign

If we are not careful, diversity practitioners can fall into the same trap. Even though we often say that we are "trying to put ourselves out of business," as long as this paradigm maintains itself we can unconsciously believe that our identities and our livelihoods depend upon there being diversity "problems" to solve. So, lo and behold, when we are asked to look at an organization, what do we find? The very problems that sustain our existence! If people tell us about their success, our tendency might be to point out how far they still have to go *without being willing to fully acknowledge that success*. It is a powerful self-perpetuating cycle.

Where organizational diversity dynamics are concerned, the realities have evolved significantly during the course of the past four decades. There have been dramatic increases in the workforce numbers of white women, people of color, people with disabilities, huge numbers of immigrants, as well as large numbers of gay, lesbian, bisexual, and transgender workers who are now more open about their sexual orientation than they were forty years ago. Because of these increases, the dominant group of native-born, straight, able-bodied white men is far less than a majority of the American workforce. In addition, other groups, rather than being monolithically identified, are identifying more with their own group definitions. Only 40 to 42 percent of the workforce remains in the white, male, native-born, straight group, while the majority are in the other groups.

Of course this is not to suggest that this breakdown represents access to power, influence, or inclusion in organizations. It does not. An inordinate preponderance of white men still occupies senior leadership positions in major organizations, and the dominant group still has much more access to power, influence, and inclusion than others do. Partly as a result of that, and partly because old patterns die hard, the old paradigm has maintained itself, and thus, the old "us/them" paradigm persists, only with a lot more distinct groups of "us" (or "them," depending upon what side of the equation you find yourself). And so the conversational network of contention continues.

The challenge is that we have been "fighting the diversity battle" for so long that the "us/them" paradigm feels like the natural way to approach things. It has become "the way things are" about diversity. As with politics, as soon as an issue emerges, our all-too-instinctive tendency is to immediately choose whose side we're on and pick who's right and who's wrong. In fact, the "us/them" paradigm of diversity is such a pervasive background of understanding for diversity that it even affects people within their own groups.

A classic example of this occurred on July 16, 2009, when Henry Louis "Skip" Gates Jr., professor and director of the W. E. B. DuBois Institute for African and African American Studies at Harvard University, was arrested after an altercation with police while trying to break into his own house after his key did not work. America woke up the next morning to find this noted scholar's mug shot plastered all over the news.

By noon that day, tens of millions of Americans already "knew" what had happened, including President Barack Obama, who famously said, "Cambridge police acted stupidly in arresting somebody when there was already proof that they were in their own home."[15]

The opinions covered two generally predictable reactions: "Once again an African American man is treated harshly by a white police officer, obviously racially motivated" (which, I must admit, was my first reaction), or "Once again a white police officer, doing his job, is accused of racism just because the perpetrator is black!" The incredible thing is, none of us knew what happened that night. All of our judgments were automatic assumptions based on the historical conversational network of contention. This is not to suggest that Dr. Gates was not treated inappropriately or, for that matter, that people didn't make inappropriate assumptions about the police officers. But what was most noteworthy was how quickly we automatically assumed as much based on our previous experience. We saw the road going into the horizon and *knew* that it would remain parallel.

So as we have more diversity, we now have more diversity conflicts, both between and within different groups: religious or political differences between Whites; conflicts between African Americans and Caribbean or African-born Blacks; conflicts between Latinos from different countries; or conflicts between gays, lesbians, and transgendered people. The point is that the conversational network of contention is such a pervasive background in the diversity conversation that it is almost impossible to have a diversity issue without an almost automatic sense of contentiousness, of some "us/them."

In many cases it is patently irrational because the conflicts are between people who have far more in common than areas of difference, yet the issue is not the content of the disagreement; it is that our memes for conducting discourse about diversity are so habitually framed in the conversational network of contention that we can't see our way out of it. It is like the proverbial water to the fish. It is the paradigm we have for addressing diversity. But do we have it, or does it have us?

I am reminded of an old folk tale I once heard:

> Once upon a time there was a monkey who was very fond of cherries. One day he saw a delicious-looking cherry, and came down from his tree to get it. But the fruit turned out to be in a clear glass bottle. After some experimentation, the monkey found that he could get hold of the cherry by putting his hand into the bottle by way of the neck. As soon as he had done so, he closed his hand over the cherry, but then he found that he could not withdraw his fist holding the cherry, because it was larger than the internal dimension of the neck.
>
> Now all this was deliberate, because the cherry in the bottle was a trap laid by a monkey-hunter who knew how monkeys think. The hunter, hearing the monkey whimpering, came along and the monkey tried to run away. But because his hand was, as he thought, stuck in the bottle, he could not move fast enough to escape.
>
> But, as he thought, he still had hold of the cherry. The hunter picked him up. A moment later he tapped the monkey sharply on the elbow, making him suddenly relax his hold on the fruit.
>
> The monkey was free, but he was captured. The hunter had used the cherry and the bottle, but he still had them in hand.[16]

A question naturally arises from the story. When the monkey's hand was "stuck" in the bottle, did the monkey have the cherry, or did the cherry have the monkey? Perhaps we might ask ourselves the same question. Do we have diversity discussions, or do they have us? Our relationship with our belief systems is like that, too. We accept a belief in our life, often without realizing that we are stuck because it appears to us as "the truth" rather than as a belief we have accepted. That belief then begins to shape the world we see. It creates a particular perspective, which, as Maturana and Varela indicated, creates a world for us to observe consistent with that belief. It may be a belief about a certain kind of person, or a certain business process, or perhaps something that we "know" is true about our organization or our management. There is nothing wrong with believing something strongly. But when we don't see the belief *as a belief* and instead see it as truth, we stop listening and start justifying matters. Regardless of what the particular belief is, at that moment we are as trapped by that belief as the monkey is by the cherry, and our ability to free ourselves is not much better.

The landscape is changing all the time. In reality, we now have a much more complex web of relationships that exist and are interacting with one another every day in many ways.

On a day-by-day, person-to-person basis, any of these issues can be affected by diversity. There are limitless interrelational issues that might emerge, especially as our view of diversity expands, as we discuss in the next chapter. However, I want to be clear that the presence of other interrelational dynamics between groups does not change the fact that there are historic contexts around some issues that are distinct and need to be addressed distinctly. Race, gender, and sexual orientation, for example, have a particular history that impacts them in ways that other distinctions of diversity do not. In fact, each area is distinct in the way it has to be addressed.

Nor does it change the fact that members of the dominant groups are still affected in their opportunities and ways of being by the way the system has developed. I am not suggesting that every interaction is the same, simply that a vast complexity of them needs to be addressed but is not adequately addressed within the old paradigm. In addition, even though on a broad scale certain groups have historic issues that they have been dealing with for years, when it comes to individual interactions, almost any diversity issue can have an impact.

All of us have the potential of being stuck in our thinking about others, even if we have been victims of discrimination ourselves. As I suggested earlier in this book, do you know anybody who doesn't have something going on with somebody?

This background of the *conversational network of contention*, then, is the lens through which we see and react to diversity. Our pathway to shifting that dynamic starts with gaining a better understanding about ourselves and in realizing that we, like everybody else, have the capacity for blindness about our own biases. Doing so requires two fundamental shifts in orientation.

The first is to develop a much greater capacity to observe ourselves and our own thinking. Generally, this is not something easy for us to do. We are usually oriented toward looking at what is going on with "the other." We are like the detective, searching around out there with a flashlight, looking for what's wrong. What we must learn to do is to turn that flashlight on ourselves so that we can watch ourselves doing the looking.[17] In psychological terms, we become the aware observer of ourselves. We may still have our reactions or points of view, but in seeing them in this way, we tend to be less attached to these reactions or viewpoints. We can see them *as points of view.*

Watching ourselves in action also can allow us to more easily see the other's point of view *as a point of view.* Once again, it may not mean that we start agreeing with that person, but it may mean that we can be more inquisitive about why the person thinks that way, rather than simply declaring that the person is wrong.

If we begin to develop this capacity, we move into a level of mastery that I call "sitting in the third chair," the ability to view the conflict from both sides, even when we are a part of it. We explore this later in the book.

For now, I want to take a deeper look at the three streams of thinking that I introduced at the end of chapter 2, paradigms that have been created by the history of our relationship with diversity and have dominated the diversity movement for many years. I believe these are paradigms that will limit us as we move forward unless we learn to adapt them to the needs of the twenty-first century.

CHAPTER 6

Paradigm Shift 1

TRANSFORMING CULTURAL COMPETENCY INTO COMPETITIVE ADVANTAGE

> Culture is the collective programming of the mind, which distinguishes the members of one group from another. If the mind is the hardware, culture is the software.
>
> Geert Hofstede[1]

> Culture is what's left when you've forgotten everything you've learned.
>
> Roger Wilkens

Historically, the diversity conversation has emerged from a U.S.-based historical model. That model has largely been built on seeing diversity as a social justice issue. However, more and more we see culture as a distinction that crosses a wide range of identity differences, both domestic and across the globe. In order to deal with this evolution, we will need to develop a much higher level of cultural competency.

In global commerce, the concept of cultural competency is rapidly gaining traction.[2] Yet amid the eagerness to embrace new worldviews, confusion exists. Do organizational leaders really understand what cultural competency means and how it can be leveraged to increase participation, performance, and profit? Cultural competency has become a major focus in fields including sales, medicine, education, law, professional services, and nonprofit management. In this chapter, I want to clearly define and outline cultural competency in the context of business and commerce.

It is necessary to distinguish cultural competency from traditional definitions of culture and how culture gives us the world we see. Doing so helps us move beyond seeing cultural competency as simply a set of tips and techniques for dealing with different kinds of people. More importantly, by understanding what cultural competency is, we can more effectively strive to promote a better understanding of the way culture impacts our belief, our behaviors, and the decisions all humans make every day in the course of making a living and living a life.

Understanding what we do can often be secondary to understanding why we do what we do. Simply put, cultural competency is the individual and organizational ability to have and utilize policies, appropriately trained and skilled employees, and specialized resources to systematically anticipate, recognize, and respond to the varying expectations of clients, customers, and co-workers of diverse backgrounds.

A casual observer would find hundreds of examples of cultural interactions in the business world. In this chapter, I examine some of those manifestations of culture, along with distinctions that are critical tools for navigating the journey toward becoming culturally competent. I also detail why this relatively new knowledge is crucial to bottom-line success in today's business environment.

My interest in diversity took on a more expansive focus more than fifteen years ago. I was engaged in a culture change effort at a Michigan hospital when one of the internal diversity facilitators we had trained, a woman named Bonnie Jacobs, discovered a pattern with Vietnamese women becoming dehydrated during the labor, birth, and aftercare process. Bonnie was both curious and confused as to why these women became dehydrated at such a high frequency. Nobody from the obstetrics and gynecology department had an explanation. But after some research, we found that it was a cultural, and not a biological, phenomenon.

In Vietnamese culture, birthing is viewed as a "cold" time that depletes the body of warmth. In traditional practice, Vietnamese women in labor are careful not to drink cold water or eat ice chips, as they would further deprive the body of heat. The issue can be simply resolved by a nurse asking the patient what temperature water they want. But most nurses don't know to ask the question. As a result, patients become dehydrated, which extends their hospital stay (and the costs associated with it), affects their health, and delays lactation, therefore impacting the attachment of mother to baby. That, in and of itself, was striking enough, but the question I was left with was "How many other ways does culture impact us?" That question led me into a focused study of cultural competency.

In an increasingly evolving global economy, cultural competence may be the single most important quality required to lead and inspire employees toward innovation and quality customer service. Cultural competency demands that we evaluate and change the ways we think and interact with one another in significant ways. And in order to be able to develop that competency, we have to be willing to explore how the background through which we see the world may be distinct from the background through which our fellow employees, customers, and the communities that we work with see the world.

Only by examining how we see the world can we begin to develop a more robust understanding of the world as it appears to others. I believe that awareness of shared fundamentals of human nature is what truly provides the groundwork for meaningful cultural competency.

Cultural competency matters greatly in a world with dissolving borders and dramatically changing demographics, technologies, and economies. I identified some of the trends that affect this in chapter 1, but consider these facts as well:

- In 1955, seventy-five of the one hundred largest industrial businesses in the world were in the United States. By 1996, there were only twenty-four. It is thought that by 2037, the number will drop to eight.
- Almost 12 percent of documented United States residents were born outside of this country, the highest recorded percentage of such persons since the nineteenth century.
- The more than one billion Internet devices in use worldwide create opportunities to network socially and commercially with people in places we have never visited and may never visit. Yet we can still do business with these people, study with them, and even make them our friends. Hundreds of millions of people worldwide live and work outside their country of origin.
- The share of the world's population that lives in the traditional Western world (Europe, the United States, and Canada) has dropped from 33 percent in 1913 to less than 17 percent today. By 2050, that number is expected to be less than 12 percent.
- Only five of the world's sixty most populated cities are in the United States or Europe: New York, London, Los Angeles, Berlin, and Madrid.
- The West's portion of the global gross domestic product dropped from a high of 70 percent in 1950 to less than 50 percent in 2009.
- The proportion of the world that lives in urban areas and is thus thought more likely to interact cross-culturally is predicted to rise from less than 30 percent in 1950 to more than 70 percent in 2050.

The net combined result of these powerful trends? Mass communication, immigration patterns, and demographic movement have radically altered our sense of the world, making it seem smaller and, to borrow Thomas Friedman's vernacular, "flatter."[3] As such, the whole world now resides in the midst of our businesses, communities, and homes.

Given these facts, what does all of this mean to all of us and our businesses? Just think about these questions:

- How do customers and employees from different cultures interact with your business?
- Do distinct customers from different cultures have specific needs from your business?

- Are there products or services that are specifically needed or not needed by particular cultural or diverse groups?
- Do employees understand differences in beliefs, behavior, and communication styles among people of different demographic groups, both among one another and with customers?
- Do customers from different cultures have different expectations regarding interaction with your employees?
- Are there normal business activities that might be considered offensive or confusing to particular cultures?

Answers to these questions provide clues to help determine our degree of cultural competence, both as individuals and as organizations. The impact of some of these trends occurs on a macro level. For example, Western countries with diminishing numbers of workers have to take a different approach to increasing productivity than countries such as China and India, which have massive numbers of bodies that can be used to increase productivity. Efficiency, incremental productivity enhancement, and other subtle ways to increase performance have to be used in order to compete in the global marketplace.

The ability of organizations to be inclusive of people and traditions from multiple and overlapping cultures is a key to growth, profitability, and productivity in the twenty-first century. But the raw truth is that too many businesses and organizations have not yet begun to seriously contemplate these questions, and they continue this neglect at their own peril. Additionally, the changes in the size and composition of the world's workforce make cultural competency a domestic concern as well as a worldwide one.

"The professional development of our employees at Freddie Mac makes us stronger as a team, as individuals, and as a partner across the communities we serve. Diversity and inclusion training that raises cultural awareness and builds skills is a cornerstone of our development program. Our training strengthens the skills that our employees use to forge strong relationships and positively impact our internal and external work environment. Enhancing and expanding our cultural competence facilitates our mission-driven efforts and allows us to better understand, respond to, and support our diverse communities across America."

John Stickeler
Senior Diversity Officer
Office of Diversity and Inclusion
Freddie Mac

The economic power of the American consumer is being harnessed by the rapidly growing power of our counterparts in emerging markets. Corporations understand and appreciate the explosive growth of spending power among previously marginalized groups and are marketing products and services in new sectors. Organizations have flattened their organizational hierarchies and structures in a deliberate effort to engage mixed work groups and teams to accomplish key tasks.

The good news is that many organizations are more heterogeneous than ever before, the result of direct efforts to give opportunity to women and people from historically marginalized categories in the post–civil rights era, and also of the globalization of business and increase in immigration. Bringing a variety of perspectives and talents to teamwork while simultaneously ensuring the ability of individuals to maximize potential and minimize friction on teams is a major challenge facing the world of business and commerce.

The challenge, as I stated earlier, is that although diversity and inclusion have become standard corporate language, relatively few organizations have truly embraced the kind of organizational culture development that it takes to create true cultural competency. While active, full-throated resistance is seen much less frequently than in the past, in too many places it has become acceptable to use the excuses of budget limitations, time constraints, and the illusion of a merit-based organizational culture to resist exploration of deeper cultural differences.

In addition, many companies who operate on a global scale see a difference between the way U.S.-based employees see the issue versus those who come from other parts of the world and are not governed by either the social-justice paradigm of the U.S.-based model or the requisite patterns of political correctness or corrective methodologies. Even the word *diversity* may not fit for some who prefer *multiculturalism* or other terminologies.

These challenges not only impinge upon the advancement and participation of certain groups, resulting in many barriers to full participation for those who remain in the shadows of organizational life, but also cost organizations millions of dollars in productivity, innovation, and market share. In addition, the understanding and appreciation of the need for cultural intelligence as a true competency is often eclipsed by the concern about diversity "problems."

I do not encourage organizations to become blind to fundamental human differences. Rather than ignoring or overlooking differences, I believe differences should be recognized and mined as untapped strengths. In spite of this resistance and reluctance, my role as an advocate of inclusion is to shine a bright light into these shadows and continually highlight the return on investment of building a culturally competent organization.

I am firmly committed to systematically helping organizations manage diversity and become culturally competent. This is accomplished by partnering with organizations as they move through the continuous process of growing awareness, increasing knowledge, and enhancing skills. The increase of cultural competency is a long-term developmental practice. It is not a skill set that can be acquired after a single training event. But cultural competency is a skill set that can pay powerful dividends to individuals and businesses worldwide.

I also believe that everyone's contribution matters. For more than twenty years, my firm has partnered with a wide array of organizations to unleash the untapped potential of people, performance, and profit. Moving toward full inclusion necessarily requires the elimination of exclusionary practices, but more importantly, it requires a systemic integration of culturally competent practices into all facets of our personal and professional lives and into organizational structures and normative behaviors.

In my view, cultural competency is not a fixed concept.[4] Rather, it is a dynamic developmental process that requires personal and organizational commitment and evolves and unfolds over time, trial and error, and unpredictable business and political environments. Individuals and organizations are located at various levels of awareness, knowledge, and skills along the cultural competence continuum.

It is my belief that understanding the nature of our cultural influences is critical to understanding what gives each of us meaning in our lives. Our cultures are at the heart of the development of our core values. The challenge is that the amalgamation of culture that many people have experienced over the past several generations has often left people with a sense of disconnection from their core values.

Humans share many basic similarities that should be a source to understanding our common bond. However, differences arising from cultural factors including nationality, ethnicity, acculturation, language, religion, gender, sexual orientation, and age, as well as those attributed to family of origin and individual experiences, all affect the beliefs, behaviors, and expectations of co-workers, customers, and communities that are engaged by organizations.

These differences also create enormous opportunities to better understand the needs of our markets and the potential for providing products and services that dramatically outstrip the limitations of those created by a homogeneous group, as the research from both Scott Page[5] and James Surowiecki[6] (noted in chapter 1) indicates.

Of course, these benefits can be realized only if we develop the skills and capacity to harness the transformative power of cultural competence within organizations. If not, evidence also indicates that a diverse group can have a higher probability of conflict if individual members' differences and talents are not respected and utilized. Yet the integration of younger workers and increasing numbers of women, immigrants, and people of color has created cultural challenges in many organizations.

As an example, research from a comprehensive multisite employee survey revealed that during the course of one year, 61 percent of employee respondents reported witnessing diversity-related acts of incivility, disrespect, and/or discrimination at work.[7]

These actions resulted in a decrease in productivity, unexcused absenteeism, and greater rate of turnover. Incivility and disrespect are not just examples of bad behavior but are factors that can cost businesses significant amounts of both time and money. This same survey found a number of costs: 22 percent of the employee respondents decreased their work efforts, 10 percent decreased the amount of time they spent at work, 53 percent lost work time due to worry about the incident and potential future repercussions, and 12 percent actually changed jobs in order to get away from the person or persons responsible for the difficulty.

In 2007, the U.S. Bureau of Labor estimated voluntary turnover rate to be approximately 24 percent and that documented turnover replacement cost is one to three times the salary of a vacant position.[8] Imagine what those numbers add up to in bottom-line expenses for a large company. On a purely economic basis, the changing demographics of the workforce and the marketplace require all organizations to develop a better understanding of the people they are hiring and working with, as well as those to whom they are selling their services. When I look at the steady stream of numbers like this, I find it ironic that some people even question the ROI of addressing diversity issues.

"At the Food Lion supermarket company, a correct recognition of the importance of the Latino market led to business success. Food Lion is being smart about tailoring our appeal to Latino customers and employees. In stores serving large populations of Latino customers, we have significantly bulked up selections of dry goods such as beans, tortillas and spices, and the stores also carry cuts of meat and produce items popular with Hispanic shoppers. In addition, we have added Spanish-language signage to improve the customer experience and communicate how much we value their business. Employees at many of our stores also undergo training both in the Spanish language and Hispanic culture. At Food Lion, our commitment to being culturally competent is reflected not only in our values, but in our day-to-day operations."

Eric Watson
Vice President of Diversity and Inclusion
Delhaize America (Food Lion's parent company)

The ability to communicate to the marketplace is another domain in which our awareness, knowledge, and skills about culture can prove either embarrassingly inept or lucratively competent. Political literature is filled with examples of global marketing efforts or statements that not only failed to produce results but also caused problems for their proponents.

But the annals of business are chock-full of examples that went badly awry. The "Come alive, you're in the Pepsi generation" slogan was translated in China into language that actually meant "Pepsi brings your ancestors back from the grave!" Coors put its slogan, "Turn it loose," into Spanish, where it was read as "Suffer from diarrhea." Frank Perdue's chicken slogan, "It takes a strong man to make a tender chicken," was translated into Spanish as "It takes an aroused man to make a chicken affectionate." When Gerber started selling baby food in Africa, it used the same packaging as in the United States, with a baby on the label. Later it learned that in Africa, because of multiple languages, dialects, and illiteracy, companies routinely put pictures of ingredients on food labels. A bit unnecessarily awkward, don't you think?

These are only a small sampling of hundreds of examples of mistaken marketing campaigns that did not fail due to bad intentions or lack of effort but because of a lack of cultural competency. Lots of companies are multinational, but not all multinational companies practice cultural competency. The previous examples don't even include examples of colors, tastes, symbols, and other reasons why the product representations contributed to marketplace disappointment. On the other hand, many global corporations find their brands and business grow when they become more sensitive to the needs, language, and symbols of their target markets. Some examples include the following:

- Colgate-Palmolive, which does more than 75 percent of its business outside of the United States, reaps success by selling products that are culturally unique in their labeling, tastes, and purpose.
- McDonald's creates different store designs, products, names, and tastes in order to profitably conduct business in more than 120 countries around the world.
- Sodexo, employing four hundred thousand people in eighty countries worldwide, is supported by a strong global diversity and inclusion strategy.
- Starbucks Coffee Company teams with the nonprofit organization Conservation International to create coffee farms in developing countries that not only provide jobs but also support sustainability by creating an alternate economy that reduces deforestation.

I've long believed that cultural competency can be learned and developed. I also know it can lead to unprecedented growth and vastly improved productivity, morale, internal communication, leadership, and customer satisfaction. On the most basic level, culturally competent organizations help people better understand how cultural distinctions impact and enhance our ability to work with one another and serve diverse employees and customers. At the same time, increasing cultural intelligence in order to improve communication, enhance team performance, and seize opportunities in new markets relies upon the ability of organizations to confront important cultural challenges and opportunities that will only increase in the near future.

We have reached an important milestone in the evolution of the global marketplace. Not so long ago, American culture and U.S.-centric cultural values were both pervasive and dominant. The world is no longer as willing to accept U.S.-based advertising, organizational models untested in global markets, and goods and services that have not been vetted in multicultural markets. And when we look to the very predictable future, we can see that this trend is likely to continue.

Within the United States, because we have more people in the workforce and marketplace from more different places than ever before, the "melting pot" that we used to talk about has changed. More groups of people are maintaining their cultural patterns, forming more cultural subgroups than ever before, and continuing to speak their native languages, eat their native foods, and act in ways taught to them by their cultures. In short, they are homogenizing less than in the past, thus giving the melting pot many different meanings.

Given the vast demographic changes at work in the United States and around the world, recruiting a diverse group of people is necessary for many organizations. However, it is not the biggest or only challenge facing organizations right now. Perhaps even more critical than increasing overall participation by all possible workers is expanding opportunities in leadership, engagement, and decision-making so that organizations can become truly inclusive at every level. The goal is to ensure that people from all backgrounds are fully integrated, fully engaged, and fully empowered.

This phenomenon can be witnessed in many industries today, from retail to health care. For example, we know many doctors and nurses must respond to patients who come from dozens of different countries and present with needs that vary tremendously among groups. These needs are not only in the less direct areas of business competency (e.g., communication, family patterns, and so on) but also with regard to issues such as genetic differences that affect the ways drugs are metabolized by one group versus another.

It is no exaggeration to say that a culturally competent provider can mean the difference between a patient "making it" or "falling through the cracks." For example, Latina social worker "Josie" has a brother with schizophrenia who speaks only Spanish. When her brother failed to receive culturally competent care over a twenty-year period, he was hospitalized 162 times. When he finally did receive culturally competent care, he was hospitalized only once in fifteen years.[9]

Perhaps even more critical than increasing overall participation by all possible workers is expanding opportunities in leadership, engagement, and decision-making so that organizations can become truly inclusive at every level. Organizations are now clearly at the stage where they are beginning to include cultural differences in the way that they anticipate how they are going to interact with and treat people. In some sectors of the economy, there is no choice but to become culturally competent and culturally flexible.

Confronted with these challenges, how do we develop a better understanding of culture and its impact on how we see and experience the world around us? How does our cultural background give us the world we see?

Each of us tends to think we see things as they are, that we are objective, but as I discussed earlier, the world we see is a function of both our individual and cultural background. As Stephen R. Covey says in *The Seven Habits of Highly Effective People*, "We see the world, not as it is, but as we are, or, as we are conditioned to see it."[10]

What does it take to move us toward developing more culturally competent people and organizations? As discussed earlier, it is not enough to simply designate new behaviors. New behaviors sustain themselves only when there has been a transformational shift in the consciousness through which we see the thought or behavior we are trying to change. This is true whether it is our weight we seek to change or our ability to effectively engage with people from cultural backgrounds different from our own.

Transformation is built not on the surface behaviors we engage in, but on shifting the background framework through which we see the surface. Most of us have had circumstances in our life in which something happened, and seemingly out of the blue, our attitudes changed about things to which we had grown quite attached. The circumstance or issue we are dealing with looks completely different, and our interpretation of it is different. We see things in ways we never have before. A person who is committed to his job and community falls in love with somebody who lives somewhere else. In a matter of months, he leaves his job and moves his home. A person is given a promotion, and all of a sudden, the same behaviors that she engaged in with her co-workers previously are now unacceptable.

Have you ever visited Great Britain or another country where people drive on the left side of the road or, for that matter, visited the United States if you come from one of those countries? Many a tourist from countries like the United States, where traffic drives on the right side of the road, has narrowly escaped being crushed by a big bus or car when crossing the street. Why? In Great Britain, one must obey the signs to "look right, then look left." Since cars there drive on the "opposite" side of the road than most American tourists are accustomed to, safety requires practicing this critical street-crossing technique. Most Americans instinctively look left when crossing the street without ever thinking about it.

Looking left is a powerful habit that is deeply ingrained in the architecture of our automatic behavior. Many behaviors and thoughts related to culture are similar. If someone fails to make eye contact with us, we may think them untrustworthy rather than understand that their cultural background deems looking someone straight in the eyes to be disrespectful or too personal. When a person shakes our hand and it is not firm, we may think they are weak or not confident, while in some cultures a firm handshake may be interpreted as rude or as attempting to be too familiar with a stranger.

Background gives us what we see and what we do not see. Culture gives us the background through which we see the world. It frames what we see and what we don't by giving us certain distinct qualities and phenomena we notice that other people may not even see or may value less. And culture does it in a largely unconscious way.[11]

If we are Kalahari Bushmen, for example, and we hunt dung beetles to survive, we will see dung beetle tracks in the sand as boldly as black footprints across a white rug. For the rest of us, we are likely to see only sand. If we are an accountant, we may see and understand numbers and metrics that others do not. If we are a doctor, we look for certain things that others don't pay attention to at all. If we come from a particular country or ethnicity, we may pay closer attention to or notice something that somebody from a different country or ethnicity does not. This is the way our cultural background gives us the world we see.

I describe culture as a more or less enduring pattern of basic assumptions and mental models that a given group has invented, discovered, or developed in learning to cope with its internal and external influences. Culture informs the way its members respond in specific ways for a sustained period of time and has worked well enough to be considered valid, and therefore right to be taught to new members as the correct way to perceive, think, and feel in relation to these situations.[12]

Culture may occur distinctly in different people because of differences in social categories, such as race, ethnicity, gender, age, religion, sexual orientation, or physical abilities. Or it may show up as a difference in cognitive categories, such as education, training, class, experience, information, expertise, or personality. In reality, for most of us it is a combination of these distinctions, or a multiplicity of lenses. An elderly Indian, female doctor, for example, is responded to through an amalgamation of the way we respond to age, gender, race, ethnicity, education, class, and so on. We don't necessarily even know the impact of each, but there is an overall effect of the combination of all. They include all kinds of memes: trends, fads, or fashions. They are infused with different familiar symbols, artifacts, sounds, or images. Can any of us forget, for instance, certain phrases that have become part of our culture, such as "Where's the beef?"[13]

At a deeper level, memes represent expected and accepted behaviors. They represent behaviors that we reward or punish people for or that we value or invalidate people for demonstrating. Often this occurs in unconscious and irrational ways. The same behavior that is valued in one kind of person may be considered inappropriate in another, without our even realizing the contradiction.

For example, a male business leader who demonstrates "hard-nose, kick butt, and take names" behavior may be valued as somebody who "knows how to make things happen." But a woman who demonstrates that very same behavior may be seen as overbearing, aggressive, and unlikeable. The unconsciousness of this contradiction is critical to understand. It is not that most people say, "She shouldn't act that way . . . only men should act that way!" On the contrary, the very person making that assessment may argue for the importance of women in leadership. Such a person may say, "I have no problem with women leaders . . . it's just that she [the woman in question] is b@!#hy!" This paradox is often referred to as the "double bind." The same qualities that are valued in men are criticized when women demonstrate them in equal measure. Many people may like women who are warm and unthreatening but then also judge them as weak and not respect them as leaders.

Our learned expectations create a particular way that we interpret people and behavior. During the early stages of the 2008 presidential campaign I conducted an experiment. Over a three-week period, I tracked adjectives that were used to describe any of the (at the time) twenty candidates in the *Wall Street Journal*, the *Washington Post*, and the *New York Times*. Senator Hillary Clinton was described more than a dozen times as being either "cold" or "hard." Not once, in three newspapers over three weeks, were any of the nineteen male candidates described using those adjectives. Why? Because in many people's minds, women are *supposed to be* "soft and warm." The assessment appears in the context through which it is perceived.

Edward T. Hall has said, "Culture hides much more than it reveals, and strangely enough what it hides, it hides most effectively from its own participants. Years of study have convinced me that the real job is not to understand foreign culture, but to understand our own."

Just as our DNA contains tens of thousands of genes that combine to form our biology, our social identity is formed by a plethora of memes, which combine to give us the world we see and the way the world sees us. They may include a particular worldview, based on memes of morality and righteousness, the way we identify ourselves as groups, our sense of equity and fairness, our relationships with hierarchy and power, our biases, our perceptions and interpretations, and our value systems.

They may define how we see people and relationships through our expressions of emotions, deference to authority, sense of individual or collective identity, way of dealing with conflict, ways of saving face, or taboos. They certainly define our communication patterns: language, greetings, style of communication, gestures, eye contact, directness in addressing subjects, or our focus on content or context. And they may define hundreds or thousands of other patterns of behavior: how closely we stand to one another, our work styles, how competitive or cooperative we are, whether we are task or people oriented, how tolerant we are to change, how we feel about ourselves, and how we behave toward others. They take many forms, including the following:

Topical: Culture consists of everything on a list of topics or categories, such as social organization, religion, or economy.

Historical: Culture is social heritage or tradition that is passed on to future generations.

Behavioral: Culture is shared, learned human behavior, a way of life.

Normative: Culture is ideals, values, or rules for living.

Functional: Culture is the way humans solve problems of adapting to the environment or living together.

Mental: Culture is a complex of ideas or learned habits that inhibit impulses and distinguish people from animals.

Structural: Culture consists of patterned and interrelated ideas, symbols, or behaviors.

Symbolic: Culture is based on arbitrarily assigned meanings that are shared by a society.

While every person's memetic structure is designed ideally for survival in the person's own culture, when we come together we usually lose sight of its purpose. Instead, we judge one another's cultural memes as "good or bad," "right or wrong," "moral or immoral," and so on. How can we coexist more effectively and thrive in organizational cultures when we have so many differences in how we see the world and in what we see as "right?" That question is at the heart of the need for cultural competency.

The challenge to achieving cultural competency is that we often see different meme structures, different cultural models, not as "different" but as "wrong," "less competent," or even "evil." In doing so, we dismiss the actual social identity that has been formed by the other person's heritage, experience, and cultural memes, and turn it into a virtual social identity that exists only in relationship to our own. We are, in fact, stigmatizing the other individual by dehumanizing him or her and turning that person into a caricature that exists only as a projection of our judgments and interpretations of the person's actual social identity. As sociologist Erving Goffman has said:

> Society establishes the means of categorizing persons and the complement of attributes felt to be ordinary and natural for members of each of these categories. . . . When a stranger comes into our presence, then, first appearances are likely to enable us to anticipate his (or her) category and attributes, his (or her) "social identity" . . . evidence can arise of his (or her) possessing an attribute that makes him (or her) . . . of a less desirable kind—in the extreme, a person who is quite thoroughly bad, or dangerous, or weak. He (or she) is thus reduced in our minds from a whole . . . person to a tainted, discounted one. Such an attribute is a stigma, especially when its discrediting effect is very extensive. . . . It constitutes a special discrepancy between virtual and actual social identity.[14]

Even attributes such as accent can have an enormous impact on how people respond to one another. In 2010, Shiri Lev-Ari and Boaz Keysar of the University of Chicago revealed the results of a study regarding how people with non-native accents are perceived.[15] They found that people with non-native accents are perceived as "less credible" than those with native accents. People were less likely to believe simple information that the people with these accents shared than they were to believe the same information from native speakers. Even when people were made aware of this effect, they were able to correct it only in response to mild accents. Strong accents still had the same impact.

This dynamic can be true even within the same country. I remember a number of years ago working with a client in the Deep South, near the Mississippi Delta, who told me that her husband, who had grown up in that area, went on to get an advanced degree in physics from MIT. However, he returned to the South because he, in her words, "got tired of people treating him like he was less intelligent" because of his Southern accent. Simply put, culturally competent people and organizations both know and operate in accord with the understanding that human cultures, and the language and behaviors they engender, are not right/wrong, better/worse, or virtuous/immoral. Cultures are different. Cultural competency goes well beyond cultural awareness. It denotes an individual's ability to effectively interact with and among others whose values, behaviors, and environments are different from their own. This is done through a profound understanding of their own cultural background.

This doesn't mean that we don't have opinions or reactions to other cultures, styles, or ways of being. Of course we do. Strong ones. We can feel strongly that the memes of another culture are not memes that we would like to adhere to, *without labeling them as "wrong," "evil," or "bad."*

> "First, we have to accept that there will be differences in cultures; one cannot make a single-culture organization. But it is critical to build a uniform performance culture. By that, I mean how we think as one enterprise and set targets for the larger organization, how we go about realizing the group vision, including how we benchmark performance and identify sources of value and how we measure less tangible actions and behavior. These things are especially relevant now because there are no standard operating procedures for overcoming a global financial crisis. The Indian mind-set is generally not rigid and has significant empathy. We are generally enthusiastic about welcoming people from different geographies, with different languages, and are proud to be a truly global organization. The inclusiveness of the Indian mind-set helps in building a global business, especially when that mind-set is reinforced by a structured emphasis on profit and value creation for the stakeholders."
>
> Koushik Chatterjee
> Chief Financial Officer
> Tata Steel

It is a critical point of understanding to recognize that cultural competence is not an individual competence, nor is it simply cultural. As I stated earlier, cultural competence is an individual *and* organizational ability. The historic pattern of diversity and inclusion work has often created unintentional barriers to the acceptance of cultural competence as an organizational imperative.

Cultural competence requires awareness and sensitivity. However, because of the historical need to correct problematic diversity-related behavior, too many well-intentioned efforts have become mired in attempts to "blame and shame" and to find the "bad people" and fix the problem.

As a result, people and organizations can be defensive about the need for awareness and culture change. In order to attempt to avoid friction, many organizations skip important steps in their growth and seek to overlook and move beyond differences.

In order to be "politically correct," we may even avoid talking about cultural differences, as if our avoidance of them will make them disappear. There also is some dispute as to whether or not the identification of cultural patterns leads to stereotyping. "Isn't it true," people ask, "that every individual is different? Don't we run the risk of making false assumptions about people when we focus on their cultural backgrounds?"

There is an important difference between archetypes and stereotypes. If we assume that an individual's behavior is given by his or her group identity, then we are stereotyping. But if we recognize that certain patterns are archetypically "normal" in a particular culture, it may give us insight into how to best interact with people of that culture, and especially what questions to ask.

Consider the question, "Are men taller than women?" The answer, of course, is yes in virtually every population group in the world. Yet is every man taller than every woman? Obviously not. The two concepts are not exclusive. We can be aware of archetypical patterns and still be aware of and careful about individual differences.

Cultural competency emphasizes the idea of effectively operating in different cultural contexts and altering one's established practices and behaviors to reach different cultural groups. Traditional approaches to cultural knowledge, sensitivity, and awareness have often not included this concept. Although they imply understanding of cultural similarities and differences, they often have not included action or structural change.

My experience has been that some basic principles provide the foundation for the understanding and practice of cultural competency.

1. Defining culture broadly, rather than seeing it only through our own lens
2. Acknowledging and respecting customer and employee cultural beliefs
3. Recognizing complexity in language and image interpretation
4. Facilitating communication and learning between businesses and the communities they serve
5. Collaborating with our community and customer base in defining and addressing needs
6. Working closely with community and cultural groups in implementing programs and providing products and services that meet their needs
7. Developing more effective ways to hire and train staff
8. Making culturally competent behaviors the norm in our organizations
9. Improving communication, including an awareness of accent and language barriers
10. Motivating workers through the accurate cultural interpretation of desires and behaviors
11. Accurately evaluating culturally diverse applicants and employees through a better understanding of presentation styles, behaviors, and language facility

12. Increasing harmony and comfort in the workplace through an understanding of the motivations and perspectives of others[16]

Still, an organization may be quite diverse yet lack cultural competency. Cultural diversity refers to the diversity of representation in an organization or system. Cultural competency refers to the ability and aptitude of organizations and systems to function and perform effectively in cross-cultural situations. An organization that reflects and values its ethnic and cultural diversity will maximize productivity and work more effectively with culturally diverse stakeholders, clients, and communities.

Diversity and cultural competence are mutually inclusive, but they are not the same. In creating robust organizational structures, employers and employees must work in partnership to make cultural competence a core value. This commitment to cultural competency must fully saturate the organization at all levels, from talent development to strategic planning to board development. Organizations that enhance their diversity with cultural competency will increase both productivity and profit through their culturally diverse customers, colleagues, and communities.

Cultural competency requires organizations to

- have a defined set of values and principles and demonstrate behaviors, attitudes, policies, and structures that enable them to work effectively cross-culturally;
- have the capacity to value diversity, conduct self-assessment, manage the dynamics of difference, acquire and institutionalize cultural knowledge, and adapt to diversity and the cultural contexts of the customers and communities they serve; and
- incorporate the above in all aspects of policy making, administration, practice, and service delivery and systematically involve consumers, key stakeholders, and communities.[17]

Every organization has preferred cultural traits. Sometimes these are consciously chosen because we have determined that they will serve our purpose and comfort better, but more often they are unconscious manifestations of our historical experience (e.g., "appropriate" professional behavior or dress, ways to organize, extroversion versus introversion, and the value of task orientation versus people orientation). I believe that an organization's effectiveness is directly tied to the degree to which its cultural structure and memes are consciously chosen and reinforced.

Building an organization's diverse representation does not demand that we expand our worldview, although clearly this expansion allows the full benefit of that diversity. One powerful strategy for expanding that view, once the organization recognizes the diversity among its stakeholders, is to understand the concept of "cultural relativism." This means that an individual's beliefs and behaviors should be understood in terms of his or her own culture. This also includes the view that no culture is superior to any other culture, even if it is preferred, and that all cultures have positive attributes to contribute to organizations and society.

Conceptually, this is easy to understand. In everyday practice, it is not so easy to remain judgment-free when confronted with behaviors that are different from those we have been taught to value for our entire lives.

Inclusion and teamwork are increased when people understand that there is no single "right way" of acting and thinking. Right and wrong vary with cultural norms.

When cultural relativism is understood and practiced, the benefits of representational diversity are harvested through increased productivity, teamwork, and innovation. Benefits also accrue through minimizing worker alienation that can result from misunderstandings of etiquette, values, and behaviors; costly discrimination suits that arise from poor communication and worker alienation; unnecessary terminations that result from communication breakdowns and misinterpretation of employee behavior; managers' reluctance to hire and work with culturally diverse workers; and discrimination that can result from misinterpretations of the behaviors of others.

Societies, organizations, groups, and individuals all have cultures. Culture in an individual refers to the individual's beliefs, attitudes, behaviors, and values. Culture in an organization comprises shared principles, purposes, goals, norms, and processes. In organizations, we are always creating culture. The question we have to constantly ask ourselves is, "Are we creating it intentionally or unintentionally?"

I am sorry to say there is no one method for getting started on the journey toward cultural competency. There are many entry points. Yet during the more than twenty-five years I have spent creating organizational transformation in all kinds of organizations across the United States and around the world, I have found there is a basic framework that has been used successfully with a variety of organizations. In later chapters I describe a process for consciously creating the kind of culture you want to have in your organization.

Cultural competency requires a deeper level of understanding so that people can move fluidly from exposing their own cultural values and reactions to others and on to inquiry, paying attention to the automatic judgments all of us make. It also necessitates aligning diversity and inclusion systems and structures with desired outcomes and then regularly evaluating progress.

Patricia St. Onge, a member of the Haudenosaunee tribe, has said:

Paying attention to culture is considered by some to be among the "soft" skills that are often seen as less important than "hard" skills, such as fiscal management . . . and governance. We make the necessary investments, often with a combination of dedicated staff and outsourcing, for each of the "hard" functions. We recognize that it will be difficult for organizations to survive if these are neglected. For those of us who work to help organizations thrive over the long term, however, experience reveals that neglecting "soft" skills is equally dangerous.[18]

If one lesson has emerged during the time I have spent helping organizations achieve their missions, it is that systemwide commitments are important. Any organization is likely to have diversity and inclusion programs that are consistent with a wide variety of positive attributes and outcomes. The various programs may or may not be strongly connected to mission, may or may not be consistent with one another, and may depend on the personnel developing the initiatives. Such factors that affect program stability may lead to promises that are not honored throughout the organization and may present unclear diversity messages for employees or clients. For these reasons, adopting a systemic, mission-related commitment to cultural competency is an important goal. Systemwide commitments, supported by chief executive officers and executive champions, help lead organizations to exceptional accomplishments and mission enhancement.

The path toward cultural competency is not easily traveled. Even when an organization develops a culture where every employee understands and values the impact of culture and develops a high level of cultural flexibility and cultural intelligence, we may still be confronted with more culturally different types on a daily basis than we can ever possibly remember and manage all of the memes for. For example, one of my client hospitals had patients, guests, and staff from more than 120 countries last year!

To illustrate, most pharmaceutical companies have recognized that their customer profile is changing. Not only have they been doing segmented marketing to the consumer, they also recognize that the face of the physician is changing. Physician marketing is migrating from its focus on group-oriented sales to individually tailored sales approaches. Given the increase in the number of women physicians, attempts are made to engage them during the workday and not after hours or on weekends at events. Sales teams study the holidays and cultural norms of the increasingly foreign-born population of physicians and incorporate this into their relationship building.

I worked with one pharmaceutical company's sales force to integrate cultural competence as a tool to build their relationships. One salesperson reported back shortly after the course that he had made progress with a Chinese physician he had been trying to connect with for years by recognizing the Chinese New Year and building a relationship around the holiday activities.

I find that there are three ways to support employees in developing their cultural competency. A multifaceted approach includes increasing the following:

1. Awareness of the impact of cultural factors on employees' and customers' values, beliefs, and behaviors.
2. Knowledge of cultural issues and how they impact the specific ways people may react in the environment. For example, in hospitals, these may include disease incidence or prevalence among groups, ethnopharmacology, and historical factors that might shape health behaviors. In law firms, they would cover the ways various people may respond to questioning on the witness stand or choose juries. In retail, they would entail how customers from various backgrounds respond to positioning, marketing, strategy, and product composition.
3. Skill building that includes practical methods for engaging customers and co-workers in planning, innovating, problem solving, and transacting, as well as ways to communicate more effectively.

Organizations and the people inside them are at various stages along the cultural competence continuum. At the same time as the organization is becoming more culturally competent, consider what is happening on an individual level. Understanding where you are now and where you want to go will give you not only a roadmap but also a set of metrics to quantify progress toward stated goals.

I know that there are several factors that contribute to the individual development of cultural competency. Learning to be more aware of our cultural biases is one. Most of us are unconscious about how many of our core beliefs are cultural. We assume our "rights and wrongs" to be *the* "rights and wrongs." Cultural competency starts with a willingness to understand that our views may legitimately differ from others. We may still prefer them, but that doesn't make them "right."

Exposing yourself to cultural influences outside of your own is another. This can be through meeting people, reading literature, watching broadcast media, and going to cultural festivals, art galleries, or museums. The more we see people for who they are, the less we treat them like "what" they are.

Openly inquiring into the differences in the way people approach work and relationships is a third way. One of the challenges that our historic way of approaching diversity has left us with is a fear of "saying the wrong thing" or being "politically incorrect." Unfortunately, this sometimes suppresses us in engaging with one another. Become fascinated with culture and explore it with the people around you.

Trying new things is one more. Be willing to explore. Imagine your exposure to new cultures as if you were going to another country. Do research. Learn about it. Then wander out and try some new things. It doesn't have to become your "new normal," but it will expand your worldview.

For investments in cultural competency to remain productive and lasting, change must be generated from inside organizations. Without substantial buy-in to a new emphasis on more inclusive core beliefs and values, there will not be enough rich soil to plant the seeds of cultural competency. The first step toward cultural competency requires senior leadership to commit time, financial resources, and corporate priority to shape the organizational culture to reward respect and trust, develop role models, incubate new policies and practices, and create new forms of recognition and acknowledgment of the benefits of respecting differences among people, as well as to reach an increasingly diverse customer base.

Organizations that act defensively are on a clear path toward mediocrity. The combination of prolific mass communication, new immigration patterns, and dramatic demographic movement has radically altered the size and interaction of the world. These changes have brought the world into our businesses, our communities, and our homes. The continued advancement, and indeed, the very survival of businesses, organizations, and societies will depend in great measure upon our ability to be culturally competent and develop the capacity and the collective will to utilize an expanding global array of talents and aptitudes.

Today, organizations play as powerful a role as families and social groups do in shaping the identity of their members. Organizations play the role of an "imagined community" where people are united in common cause to promote and achieve group and individual goals. For all organizations, the benefits of bridging values are priceless. The costs of failing are devastating. Successful cross-cultural business means understanding people's worldviews. The challenge is to step out of what we know and into another frame of reference.

CHAPTER 7

Paradigm Shift 2

HOW CAN WE KNOW BIAS WHEN WE CAN'T EVEN SEE IT IN OURSELVES?

> To know what we do not know is the beginning of wisdom.
>
> Maha Sthavira Sangharakshita[1]

> People travel to wonder at the height of the mountains, at the huge waves of the seas, at the long course of the rivers, at the vast compass of the ocean, at the circular motion of the stars, and yet they pass by themselves without wondering.
>
> St. Augustine

In spring 2010, my son and daughter-in-law stayed with us for a few months with my two little granddaughters, Sloane and Penelope. One evening, just before dinner, Sloane came up to me and asked, "Can I have a cookie?" It being just before dinner, I told her it wasn't a good time to eat cookies, but she asked again. So, trying to be the dutiful grandfather, I sat her on my lap and with my best memories of "schoolteacher talk" explained to her why it wasn't a good idea for all of the appropriate reasons. When I was finished, I asked her, "Do you understand?" "Yes," she said. "Now, can I have a cookie?"

How many times have you had conversations like that about diversity with people in your organization? People sit there and tell you that they really believe in the business case or the equity case for diversity, but their behavior isn't in synch with their statements. Or, for that matter, how many times have you had conversations like that with yourself about something? You wake up in the morning and say, "Today is the day that I start eating right." Or stop smoking. Or exercise. And yet by noon that day you are eating that thing you know you should not, lighting up a cigarette, or saying, "I'll get to the gym tomorrow."

Where diversity and inclusion are concerned, this is often a frustration. People seem to understand but not act. We sometimes attribute disingenuousness to them, but the reality is that they probably are being honest when they say they believe in it. They could probably pass a lie detector test. It is just that believing in something doesn't automatically make it happen.

What we are encountering in circumstances like these is the power of the concealed mind to manage our behavior while the conscious mind believes something entirely different. I believe that understanding this phenomenon is at the heart of the need for another new way to look at diversity and inclusion: moving from our "us/them," "good person/bad person" paradigms into a better understanding of how people think.

The historical frame of reference has given us the need to create structures to monitor and change historically discriminatory behavior. Beginning in the 1960s, Equal Employment Opportunity (EEO) laws were passed to ensure that people were not discriminated against based on their group identity. At first, these laws applied mostly to race, but over the years they have been expanded to protect people's rights based on gender, appearance, age, physical or mental abilities or disabilities, and even, in some places, sexual orientation. While we might disagree about particular applications of EEO or related codes, most Americans generally agree that it is a good idea to ensure that people are not discriminated against because of who they are.

Affirmative action, the conscious attempt to increase the representation of previously underrepresented groups in our organizations, schools, and so on, on the other hand, remains more controversial. As I discussed in chapter 2, I believe this is largely because people have bought into several myths about it—that it is no longer necessary, that it is only for women and people of color, and that it is a relatively new phenomenon—none of which is true. We have affirmatively hired people throughout our country's history, and in some cases we need to affirmatively change the patterns of representation that such hiring has left us. The real question should be whether we are doing a good job of hiring people. But, as the old saying goes, "Never let the facts get in the way of a good story."

Yet these issues have become less significant in daily life, especially within organizations, than the far more subtle examples we see, such as the interview I described earlier. In fact, after twenty-five years of working on diversity and inclusion issues, I have come to believe that an overwhelmingly large number of the behaviors that are engaged in that differentially affect one group over another are not engaged in by people who are being willfully discriminatory. On the contrary, they are decisions made by people like you and me, good people who have no intention to discriminate and, in fact, could pass a lie detector test as to whether we are being fair and equitable. How does that happen?

I want to be clear that, having said that, I am not saying that we do not still need to be watchful about more overt forms of discriminatory behavior. There are still circumstances when we have to be vigilant to root out inappropriate or harmful behavior. People are out there who are willful and conscious in their discriminatory behavior. Still, if the larger proportion of people affected are those who are affected unconsciously, how can we understand more about the way we think so that we can move from figuring out who the good people and bad people are to get to a point where greater consciousness figures in our collective decision-making?

We have all seen images of robots throughout most of our lives. They have been a part of movies, cartoons, and television shows from *The Jetsons* to *Space Family Robinson* and countless others. Today, robotics is expanding dramatically. We see robots used for all kinds of things in business, production, science, space travel, and so on. I recently saw a film of a robot created by Toyota that can play the violin.

The question, though, is does the robot choose to play the violin?

We all know that the robot doesn't really "choose" anything. Whatever choices it makes are the result of programming. The robot is constructed from some metal or plastic or other materials, with motors and computer chips that are driven by certain algorithms that have it "choose" certain things in certain circumstances. But how different are we from robots?

We base our worldview on certain assumptions about the way we see and interact with the world. We believe that we operate from free choice and that we make those choices based on preferences we have that serve our interests. We believe, for the most part, that we are acting rationally (though we all have our moments!) and that our preferences and choices are relatively consistent over time. We also believe that we control our choices, and, therefore, we can be held accountable for the choices we make.[2] And all of this is based on the fundamental belief that we see the world as it is in reality.

If you think about it, our entire social and societal structure is based on these assumptions. It is why we hold employees, spouses, and even criminals responsible for their behavior. In fact, we would be hard pressed to imagine a societal structure at all if we didn't do that, at least to some degree.

At the same time, we know that certain people do not control their decisions or their behavior. That is why the courts sometimes find people "not guilty by reason of insanity." We all know that we do things routinely that are reflexive, automatic, and inherently not rational.

Yet my guess is that most of us would quickly cast aside the notion that we are robots. After all, we think for ourselves and make choices for ourselves, right? But what if we do so less than we realize? What if far more of our decision-making comes from our "programming," just like a robot? And what if that programming is so complex that it even convinces us that we, and not "it," are running the show?

One of the most pervasive and limiting paradigms of diversity and inclusion is the belief that bias is a bad thing and that in order to do diversity right, we must eliminate all bias; in fact, on a personal level, to be a *good person* you have to eliminate all bias. We have turned the word *bias* into a pejorative.

The problem with this paradigm is twofold. First, it demonstrates a lack of understanding of a reality. Human beings, at some level, need bias to survive. So are we biased? Of course we are biased. Every one of us has and exhibits bias. Toward things, people, circumstances, and groups. Secondly, because that's true, it virtually assures that on both collective and individual bases, we will never "do diversity right" because every human being has bias of one kind or another.

We have been told repeatedly that bias is bad and that we shouldn't have any at all. This is why we often collapse people's intent with the impact of their behavior. If we believe that good people don't have bias, then somebody who is biased must be bad and must have had intent to harm. But as we will discuss shortly, this is not necessarily true. On the other hand, out of our defensiveness, we may believe that not having conscious intent is enough to negate the negative impact of something we say or do. We get into an offensive/defensive posture because we don't have the capacity to look at the issue from anything other than the right/wrong perspective. Our historic attempts at diversity training have often reflected as much. We have tried to show people how wrong they are, thinking that would force them to change. The problem is that, as I've said, guilt may seem effective as a motivator, but in reality it is not. It leads to self-recrimination, which is destructive rather than constructive, and, of course, more times than not it simply leads to resistance, forced compliance, and often backlash. The key is not to move people toward guilt, but to move them toward responsibility, to help them develop an understanding of how the dynamics might be benefiting them or impacting them in ways that they haven't realized *and haven't always intended.*

Without that emphasis, we react defensively. Instead of understanding that it is normal to have biases, we feel bad and wrong for having them, and we are made to feel bad and wrong by the people who communicate such to us. This gets in the way of our taking responsibility and ownership for those biases and being able and willing to inquire into whether they are rational, whether they serve us, and whether they are fair to those at whom they are directed. Our inner critic, what Freud called the superego, may judge us harshly for having some of the thoughts we do about groups of people, for feeling uncomfortable, or afraid, or negative in any number of ways. We don't want to think of ourselves as bad people. And so, in reaction, our superego, our inner "Supreme Court," defends our reaction, justifies it, and explains why we are perfectly rational in feeling the way we do.

"Virtually *all* bias is unconscious bias. We have learned to trust women to be nurturing and men to be powerful, for example, in much the same way that Pavlov's puppies trusted ringing bells to predict the arrival of meat powder. If we had to think *consciously* about keeping our balance, digesting, breathing and perceiving the moon as a celestial sphere rather than a floating coin, we would all fall over, throw up, suffocate, and fail to appreciate the moon's majestic beauty. Being biased is how we get through life without evaluating everything afresh every time we experience it."

Brett Pelham
Program Officer, Social Psychology
National Science Foundation

The reality is, as the experience I had in Louisiana that I discussed earlier shows, good people develop bias. Bad people develop bias. *All* people develop bias. The question then becomes, how can we see it in others if we're not even willing to look at it in ourselves?

Think about it. How long would you stay alive if you didn't have a bias about large, fast-moving metal objects with wheels? You would probably be dead within minutes of walking outside of your house or office. We don't walk into the street and look at oncoming cars and say to ourselves, "Hmmm. I wonder what that is and I wonder what will happen when it gets here?" Of course not. We react, based on our history and what we have learned about cars. We react based on what our parents taught us when they held our hand when we were crossing the street.

We react similarly toward somebody who comes at us with a weapon raised. We have developed a clear bias against people who do things like that. It is a direct function of our desire to survive.

That is the purpose of the mind and the identities that we develop. They are constructions designed to keep us safe, to help us navigate the world. The mind is fundamentally designed to help us survive.

We go out in the world every day and make decisions about what is safe or not and what is appropriate or not. It is what psychologist Joseph LeDoux has suggested is an unconscious "danger detector" that determines whether or not something or someone is safe before we can even begin to consciously make a determination.[3] When the object, animal, or person is assessed to be dangerous, a fear response, which has been called "fight or flight," occurs. On a conscious level we may correct a mistake in this "danger detector" when we notice it, but often, of course, we simply begin to generate reasons for why it was accurate in the first place. We are generally convinced that our decisions are "rational," but in reality, most human decisions are made emotionally, *and then we collect or generate the facts to justify these decisions.* When we see something or someone who "feels" dangerous, we have already launched into action internally before we have even started "thinking." Our sense of comfort or discomfort has already been engaged.

The actual "fear alarm" occurs in the oldest part of our brain, the amygdala, often referred to as the "reptilian brain." The amygdala processes and maintains memories of our deepest emotional reactions, especially fear. It sounds the alarm when something frightens us, and then the higher brain functions respond. The limbic system, or anterior cingulate cortex, rationally tries to make decisions about the messages it receives from the amygdala, and the prefrontal brain, or neocortex, brings in perceptual awareness, thought, language, and consciousness to try to make sense of it all.

You might think of it these terms. Imagine you are asleep at night and an alarm goes off. You wake up with the feeling of the fear present in your body (amygdala response). All of us have had that unpleasant feeling. But most people don't instantly jump up and call the police. Most of us stop for a moment and try to figure out what's going on (the anterior cingulate cortex at work). We then make a decision what to do (the neocortex).

The challenge is that we often unconsciously hold on to the danger associated with certain people without questioning it *or even though we question it.* In fact, when we are confronted with evidence to the contrary of what we "feel," we often come up with explanations that justify it to ourselves. This mechanism is often called "refencing," a term that was originally coined by Gordon Allport. "When a fact cannot fit into a mental field, the exception is acknowledged, but the field is hastily fenced in again and not allowed to remain dangerously open."[4]

This is not an inherently negative trait, even though it has obvious potentially negative repercussions. It is a necessary one. We have all heard the axiom, "It is better to be safe than sorry," and to a large degree, that is true. If you sense something coming at your head, you duck. And if later you find out it was only a shadow of a bird flying by the window, better to have ducked and not needed to than to ignore the shadow and later find out it was a heavy object falling off the top shelf of the cabinet near you that hit you on the head!

Where people are concerned, these decisions are hardwired into us. At earlier times in our history, determining who, or what, was coming up the path may have been a life or death decision. If it was a hostile animal or a hostile tribe member, you might die. Our minds evolved to make these decisions very quickly. And our minds often responded before we even "thought about it."

The heuristics by which we make those decisions inherently include bias. Heuristics are "a method of solving a problem for which no formula exists, based on informal methods or experience, and employing a form of trial and error."[5] In other words, we are constantly testing whether one thing is like or different from another. It is one of the fundamental ways we develop the system of judgments that we use to traverse our daily paths. Without these kinds of judgments, generalizations, and, yes, biases, we would barely be able to function. The question "Is this safe?" would come up so many times every day, and what it would take to be safe would be so involved that we would be paralyzed most of the time.

Obviously, we know there are still plenty of cases in which people are very consciously biased, bigoted, prejudiced, and discriminating against others. All you have to do is read the newspapers and it is clear that this kind of ignorance still exists. I am by no means trying to minimize these issues, nor am I suggesting that we stop paying attention to them. Yet any understanding of human psychology shows that the overwhelming influence of unconscious patterns of bias outweighs those that are conscious, and often even justifies these patterns. And it is not just "those people" who have these patterns. It is all of us. In fact, while Freud and others have conjectured that the conscious is only the tip of the iceberg while the unconscious is the far larger piece under the surface, current research indicates that the conscious is more like a snowball on the tip of the iceberg.[6]

The challenge, of course, is that we tend to bury most of our bias in our unconscious. There are two main theories for why this happens. The first is the Freudian notion of the superego that I discussed earlier. Part of us consciously believes that we "shouldn't" have bias and so we silently convince ourselves that we don't. We robotically bury the parts of ourselves that we don't like to believe are there.

The second theory, social cognition theory, ties very closely into our conversation about culture in the previous chapter. Social cognition theory was first introduced in 1941 by N. E. Miller and J. Dollard[7] and then expanded, particularly by the American psychologist Julian Rotter[8] and the Canadian psychologist Albert Bandura[9] in the 1960s and 1970s. The social cognition approach speculates that we learn certain behaviors and standards by clear observation and then imitate them as we form our identities. Because we generally get positive reinforcement for the "right" behaviors, they begin to appear to us as "the right way to be."

My personal belief is that a combination of both of these theories may be at hand. We learn what is right from a cultural and social standpoint, and we also self-regulate how we see ourselves as "the right kind of person." Anything that conflicts on a conscious level gets discarded.

Yet if bias is normal, even necessary, it calls for a very different way to approach the subject of diversity. One of the foundational ideas that has existed behind diversity and inclusion work (almost since its inception) has been the eradication of bias. There is a good, rational reason for such thinking. If we are going to create a just and equitable society, and if we are going to create organizations where all can have access to their fair measure of success, it clearly is not consistent for some people to be discriminated against based on their identification with a particular group. To this end we have worked hard through societal measures, such as civil and human rights initiatives, to reduce or eliminate bias. We have put a lot of attention on who "gets it" about diversity, as if "getting it" were the answer. What we are really saying, in other words, is this: "If they were as (wise, noble, righteous, good, etc.) as we are, then they would 'get it' like we do!" Usually this idea has been based on the notion that people make choices to discriminate based on surface or underlying negative feelings toward some groups or feelings of superiority about their own. There is no doubt that this is often true. But what if, more times than not, people make choices that discriminate against one group and in favor of another *without even realizing that they are doing it,* and, perhaps even more strikingly, *against their own conscious belief that they are being unbiased in their decision-making?*

Consider this: Less than 15 percent of American men are more than six feet tall, yet almost 60 percent of corporate chief executive officers are more than six feet tall. Less than 4 percent of American men are more than six feet, two inches tall, yet more than 36 percent of corporate chief executive officers are over six feet, two inches tall.[10] Why does this happen? Clearly, corporate boards of directors do not, when they are conducting a search for a chief executive officer, send out a message to "get me a tall guy," and yet the numbers speak for themselves. In fact, when corrected for age and gender, an inch of height is worth approximately $789 per year in salary![11] Similar patterns are true for military generals and admirals, and even for presidents of the United States. The last man elected president whose height was below average was William McKinley, back in 1896, and he was ridiculed in the press as "a little boy."[12] Yet this factor is largely ignored. In analyzing the 2008 presidential race, I have seen little evidence of anybody mentioning the fact that Barack Obama is five inches taller than John McCain, even though historical consistency indicates this could have been an unconscious driver in some people's selection of President Obama.

Being six feet, five inches tall myself, I have throughout my life heard all of the descriptors that are attributed to tall people: "strong presence," "a sense of authority," "charismatic," "a strong demeanor," and so on. So when a person my height interviews in competition with a five-foot, six-inch tall person, the board doesn't choose the "tall person." They choose the "charismatic person" with "a strong presence" and "a sense of authority about him." In fact, the five-foot, six-inch man displaying the same characteristics may even have them held against him, with some saying, "He has a Napoleonic complex."[13]

This dynamic is actually not at all unusual. There are dozens of circumstances in which the same unconscious dynamic occurs. It is not that we choose one person over another (or, more distinctly, *one kind of person over another*). There may, in fact, be little conscious choice at all. Rather, as in the case of the tall executives, one person *feels* to us as "more" than another. We perceive the person that way. That perception is a function of the background understanding that each of us has that creates a filter through which we interpret what we see. The background that we discussed earlier is an ever-present phenomenon that all of us experience almost all of the time. As I suggested, let's say you become pregnant, or you are wondering if you or your partner is pregnant, and it seems like all of a sudden, everywhere you look there are pregnant women. You buy a new car or consider buying one, and everywhere you look you see that car or an advertisement for that car.

Is it coincidence? Does it just happen to be that all of a sudden these people or cars turn up around you? Of course not. The background attention that you have on the pregnancy or the car creates an alteration in your perceptive lens. It is one that allows you to see things that otherwise would have passed by right in front of you unnoticed or, alternatively, miss things that pass right in front of your face. Earlier I mentioned that Dr. Daniel Simons, a professor of psychology in the visual cognition and human performance division at the University of Illinois, has demonstrated this firsthand in numerous experiments where people cannot see a person or object that walks directly through their field of vision. This is because they are focused on something else in the image.[14] I often use one of Simons's tests with clients. Recently, working with a group of seventy-five people, I showed his film of a group of people tossing a basketball back and forth and asked the participants to count how many times the basketball passed hands. After the film was over, I asked the group what they saw. The numbers were shouted out: "14, 16, 12, 13!" I asked whether anybody had seen anything else in the film. Five or six people raised their hands and said, "The gorilla that walked across the screen." In fact, a person in a gorilla suit had walked directly through the group of people playing catch, but only a handful of the people had seen it. Why? *Because everyone else was focusing on the basketballs!* What else do we miss every day because we are focusing on other things?

Our perceptual lens enables us to see certain things and miss certain others. It filters the evidence that we collect, generally supporting our already-held viewpoints and disproving views with which we do not agree. Think about most political debates that you encounter. People from different sides take the same data and use it to prove completely contradictory points of view.

Where diversity is concerned, this creates hundreds of seemingly irrational circumstances every day in which people make choices that seem to make no sense and seem to be driven by only overt prejudice. Various studies have shown that heavier employees receive lower performance reviews; boys tend to be called on in school more often than girls; and the way people are dressed directly impacts the way they are responded to by others. We may create rational reasons for some of these decisions, but irrationality is in the background . . . and comes from the background.

To illustrate this further, I had a full knee replacement in 2003. My steel and titanium knee causes the airport's metal detector to go off when I go through security. As a result, I have to get scanned with the "wand" every time I fly (which is frequently). I began to sense that it was taking me longer to go through the security clearance when I was dressed in my casual clothes versus when I was dressed in my business clothing. So I tested my idea. It was a very simple test, one that probably wouldn't stand the rigor of the kind of testing protocols that some of the academics I will be discussing shortly use, but interesting nonetheless. I clocked fifty different experiences of each circumstance (in business clothing or casual) and found that, indeed, it took me 47 percent longer on average to go through the clearance when I was dressed casually. This, of course, is probably no surprise to anybody who has gone to a clothing store to go shopping in nice clothes versus going in jeans and a t-shirt. In our nice clothes it seems like we can't beat back the salespeople. In jeans, where are they? Do people consciously take longer to check travelers in jeans because they are more likely to be dangerous? Am I more likely to be dangerous dressed in jeans and a polo shirt as opposed to being dressed in a suit? Or do people tend to "see" me as less dangerous when I am dressed in a suit?

To be certain, in some cases people are hateful, hurtful, and consciously biased. Most of us know of some groups we feel uncomfortable with, even at the same time as we are castigating others for feeling uncomfortable with our own groups. I have yet to meet a person who is not biased against some group, *even if the reason for the bias is because the person thinks members of the group he or she doesn't feel comfortable with are biased!* These are conscious patterns of discrimination and are problematic, but, again, I believe they pale in comparison to the unconscious patterns that affect us every day.

The interesting thing is that while we assume that our decision-making process is (sometimes excessively) self-serving, the reality is that our reaction to bias is sometimes so irrational that it actually harms us. Yet we still do it. I was in Copenhagen in 2006 to give a keynote speech at the annual awards ceremony for the Danish Institute for Human Rights (Institut for Menneskerettigheder). The institute's director, Morten Kjaerum, told me about a conversation he had recently had with a right-wing anti-immigration activist. Surely, Kjaerum reasoned, the man had to admit that with an unemployment rate of (at that time) only 1.4 percent, the Danish economy would be in serious trouble if they were to curtail immigration. "Yes," the man acknowledged, "but if that is the way it has to be, that is the way it has to be. Denmark is for the Danes!" (And the Danes, in his mind, are white, as opposed to the ethnic and racial mix of the immigrants.) Even if it causes an economic collapse.

The reality is that we make these decisions every day in business, in hospitals, in our homes, when we're selling, and when we're shopping. Yale University law professor Ian Ayres has conducted many studies of this phenomenon. While at the University of Chicago Law School in the 1990s, Ayres conducted a study of car sales.[15] He hired thirty-eight testers—eighteen white males, seven white females, eight black females, and five black males—and sent them out to 242 Chicago-area car dealerships to bargain for cars. The testers were similar in all ways except for their race and gender. All of the testers were between twenty-four and twenty-eight years of age. All had three to four years of college experience. All were dressed in similar casual sportswear. All of them drove to the dealership in similar rented cars (so that the car salesman wouldn't make assumptions about how much they would spend for a car based on what they were driving). They all volunteered that they could self-finance the cars. All cited similar occupations and provided addresses in similar neighborhoods. All were subjectively ranked to be of "average" attractiveness. They were given a script to work from, so they approached the salespeople in the same way. In other words, the only discernible difference among them was their race and gender. They were not told that the test was intended to determine discriminatory patterns, nor did they know that others were going to be going to the same dealership.

The results were staggering. White male consumers were initially offered the cars at, on average, $725 over invoice price and were able to negotiate down to $418 over invoice price. White women were initially offered the same car by the same salesmen at $935 over invoice price, almost 30 percent more, and ended up with a price of $633, or 51 percent over invoice. Black women were initially offered the car at $1,195 over invoice price, which was almost 65 percent higher than the price given to white men, and they settled on an offer of $864, more than twice as high as that offered white men. Black men were offered the same car by the same salesmen at $1,687 over invoice, or *130 percent more than white men*, and a final price of $1,550, *almost four times the price that white men would have paid*.

However, the cause of this discrimination was not as clear. The interesting thing was that in interviews conducted after the test, the car salesmen apparently had little consciousness that they were making decisions based on race and/or gender. I have had a couple of car dealerships as clients and, I have to say, it is a very raw profession. A car salesman is pretty single-minded: spot a buyer, sell a car, and get higher commissions. It is a relatively straightforward formula. As one car salesman told me, "As far as I can see, the only color that matters is green. If Genghis Khan comes in here and wants to buy a car, and he has the money and can get somebody on board, I can't imagine that they wouldn't sell to him in a minute!"

So why the disparity? Car salesmen make microdeterminations, which make a big difference in their success. They determine who is likely to be the better bargainer, who is likely to know more about cars, who is likely to have easier access to funding, who is a real buyer—all, often, in a few seconds, and almost none of these determinations is based on any real data to substantiate matters. In fact, their thoughts are not usually even consciously articulated. "I guess I would have to say that I do it by feel," one car salesman told me. "Somebody walks in and I look at them and after more than twenty years of doing this, I know who is a buyer and who is not. In fact, every good salesman in here does."

For example, one of the common microdeterminations that a car salesman makes is to spot a "looker," somebody who is there to check out and maybe test drive the new models, but not with any real interest in purchasing a car. "Lookers" can be the bane of a car salesman's existence because they can take lots of time but produce no results. The common stereotype seems to be that Blacks are more likely to be "lookers" than Whites. Therefore, a salesman might either avoid them or give them a big, relatively non-negotiable price to get them to go away and allow the salesman to deal with a "real" buyer. The problem is that perception has no discernible basis in reality. I have not been able to find any study that shows that Blacks are "lookers" any more than Whites. In fact, anecdotal logic would suggest the opposite, that because of years of dealing with discriminatory behavior, African Americans may be less likely to assume that they would be able to test-drive the cars.

The background that the salesmen have about the way each of the different kinds of buyers shapes up in these and other categories defines how they will see that buyer, whether they consciously relate it to race or gender or not. The conscious choice that salesmen make is one part of the puzzle, but an even more striking one is the unconscious one. It appears that the black shoppers are perceived differently than the white ones in terms of their potential as buyers. In other words, when a white person comes into the showroom, a salesman sees a "buyer." When a black person comes in, a salesman may see a "looker." An interesting example of this was portrayed during the 1990s in a segment of the television news show *20/20*. In the segment, titled "True Colors," two men, one white and one black, are followed by a hidden camera as they attempt (among other things) to buy a car. The white "customer" is immediately approached by the salesman while the black "customer" is left standing around the car *for more than ten minutes* while the same salesman watches from the window and doesn't respond at all. Interestingly, in this case, the salesman himself was black. Why doesn't he respond? Most likely because one person was perceived as a potential sale and the other was perceived as a "looker" to him as well, based on being exposed to the same stereotypes as the white salesmen.[16]

Discriminatory practices, conscious or unconscious, occur not just in the hands of the providers of products and services, but among consumers as well. In a 2005 study, Ayres, along with Fred Vars and Nasser Zakariya, studied results of more than a thousand taxi rides in New Haven, Connecticut, and found patterns of discrimination that were directed by consumers toward the service provider.[17] Their study found that African American drivers were 80 percent more likely to receive no tip from a passenger than a white driver, in effect imposing a 6.6 percent "discrimination tax" on the African American driver. They also found that this disparity was not only the result of white discrimination toward black people. In fact, a greater percentage of Blacks refused to leave a tip than Whites.

These incidents occur every day and in numerous ways. I'll discuss some more examples in just a bit. But before that, let's take a minute to look at the way we experience these examples. Most people listen to examples like this and go in at least two different directions, assuming they react at all. One of them would be to try to justify the behavior of the salesmen (e.g., "Well, that's really not necessarily about race, it might just be good business!). The other may seem nobler but may be just as off base, and that is to demonize the salesmen. What if the salesmen simply are incapable of seeing the discriminatory behavior they are engaging in?

How do we know what is real anyway?

Consider a couple of experiments that I want to invite you to engage in as we look at this matter.

Look at the picture in figure 7.1 of the two tables and tell me which of the tops is bigger. Or would you say they are the same size? The same shape?

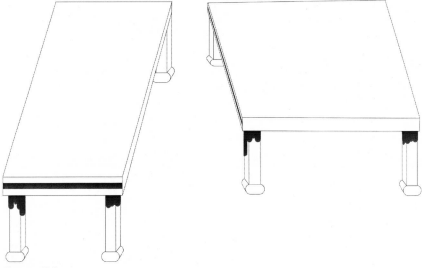

Figure 7.1

If you are like me, you would say obviously they are not the same shape. The one on the left is clearly narrower and longer than the one on the right. Or is it?

Take a piece of paper and either cut out or trace the tabletop on the left. Then put your cutout or tracing over the top of the tabletop on the right. Which is bigger? That's right, they are identical.

So do we see the world as it is?

This picture was created by Roger Shepard, a Stanford University professor and one of the creators of spatial relations research.[18] We all have seen some of these kinds of illusions over the years, in *Reader's Digest* or in e-mail exchanges, and we often refer to them as optical illusions. We would be more accurate in describing them as cognitive illusions because the illusory experience is not created by our eyes, but by our brain. As Shepard says,

> Because we are generally unaware that we are imposing a perceptual interpretation on the stimulus, we are generally unaware that our experience has an illusory aspect. The illusory aspect may only strike us after we are informed, for example, that the sizes or shapes of lines or areas that appear very unequal are, in fact identical in the picture.[19]

When we look at the picture, having no reason to assume that an illusion is at play, we don't even consider that we might be seeing something different from what is *obviously* right in front of us. The problem is that is not what is right in front of us at all.

I'm not going to get into the specifics about why we see the tables inaccurately because it would be a tangential conversation to my point. The point is that we make assumptions and determinations about what is real every moment of every day. If we "see" millions of pieces of information at any one time and can only process forty or fifty, as was discussed earlier, then we see certain things and miss others. And we see things in certain ways that fit into the background through which we process them in our minds. We see what we see, *and we believe that what we see is real.* Only occasionally do we realize how subjective those determinations are and how much they are impacted not by what is in front of us, but by *what we interpret is in front of us, seen through our own lens on the world.*

And, of course, we do the same thing with people as we did with the tables in the experiment. Our minds pick out the information that fits our existing narrative about "those kinds of people" and avoid the rest.

The challenge is that even knowing that, we may not be able to help ourselves. As Shepard says,

> Because the inferences about orientation, depth, and length are provided automatically by (our) underlying machinery, any knowledge or understanding of the illusion we may gain at the intellectual

level remains virtually powerless to diminish the magnitude of the illusion.[20]

Our perception, in other words, is so deeply buried in our "underlying machinery," our unconscious, that even knowing that it is there makes it difficult or impossible to see its impact on our thinking and on what we see as real. Think of it in practical terms. Let's say you start to shake somebody's hand. They respond with a soft handshake. My guess is that you are aware that in many parts of the world, people shake hands much more softly than we do in the United States. This is especially true in business environments, where it sometimes feels like a wrestling match to determine who has the strongest grip. However, even though you "know" as much, their handshake may feel "weak." You may apply a description such as "it feels like a wet fish." And you probably, without realizing it, attribute weakness to that person in other areas of the person's life. Knowing a plethora of reasons why somebody would shake hands that way doesn't change your visceral reaction to the handshake, does it? If we think about the various cultural dynamics we discussed in the previous chapter, we can see how problematic this becomes.

The associations we make based on these reactions are quite irrational. One of my law firm clients had an outing a couple of years ago in which many of the lawyers played golf together. One was a young associate who was in his second year out of a top law school. He was considered a real "comer" in the firm, having demonstrated a keen intellect and great work ethic. But he stank as a golfer. After he came back, people started to treat him differently. He was asked to participate less. People were subtly more critical of him. His mentor in the firm finally put together that the change had coincided with the young man's golf debacle, but only after hearing a number of partners make jokes about him. His golf clearly had nothing to do with his skill as a lawyer. But, of course, that is the rational mind speaking.

Now if all of this is about a silly illusion about a table, then who really cares? But what if it determines whether or not you will have to pay $1,500 more for your car? Or whether your tips as a cab driver will cover the rent this month? Or whether you get hired as an executive? Or how you are evaluated in your profession? It is becoming clearer and clearer how much these unconscious perceptions govern many of the most important decisions we make and have an effect on the lives of many people in many ways.

Sam Sommers, a professor of social psychology at Tufts University, has spent a good deal of time studying the composition of juries, a critical area where race discrimination has a dramatic impact on people's lives. Lawyers, of course, have the right to remove potential jurors from a jury through a process known as "peremptory challenge," which allows them to remove a juror for any reason other than race. Sommers, working with Harvard Business School professor

Michael Norton, found that race still plays a factor, if not so obviously. Sommers and Norton created two unappealing juror profiles and then asked a mixed group of college students, law students, and trial lawyers which people they would remove with a peremptory challenge. The results were dramatic. When test subjects were informed that the first juror was black and the second white, 77 percent chose to exclude the first juror. When they were told that the first juror was white and the second one black, the majority (54 percent) again chose to eliminate the black juror. Yet less than 10 percent of the subjects acknowledged race was a factor.[21] Were they being "politically correct" or deceptive in their responses, or were they deceiving themselves?

Sommers and Norton also went on to investigate jury performance, especially with black defendants. Here they found fascinating results. Their findings, when working with mock juries made up of real jury pools, found that mixed-race juries were less likely to convict black defendants, not because of the presence of black jurors but *because of the white ones.* Their findings were that approximately one-third of white jurors on a racially mixed jury found the defendants guilty, compared with almost half on an all-white jury. During the deliberations, the all-white jurors were less likely to consider the role that race played in the allegations.

What about the defendants in the trial? Does that affect the outcome? You'd better believe it does. Jennifer Eberhardt, a Stanford University psychologist, has studied the connection between race and perceived crime and has found some significant correlations. For example, when exposed to objects that are described as "crime relevant" (e.g., handguns), perceivers tend to notice black faces more than white faces. Even more startling is that when exposed to pictures of the crime-relevant objects that have been "degraded," people seem to be able to identify the object more easily when they also are being exposed to a black face as opposed to a white one. The race-crime connection is so strong that it affects what we see.[22]

And it doesn't stop there. It goes right into the courtroom. It is already well documented that murderers of white people are much more likely to be put to death than murderers of black people.[23] Eberhardt and her colleagues also studied the impact of racial stereotyping and unconscious patterns of reaction to the death penalty itself. After collecting the photographs of black defendants who might be eligible for the death penalty in Philadelphia between 1979 and 1999, she presented two faces of those who had been convicted of killing white people to a group of people, without telling them that the photos were of convicted murderers. She asked them to rate each face based on how much it appeared to be stereotypically "black."

What she found was chilling. While 24 percent of those who were rated as less stereotypically black received a death sentence, 58 percent of those who had been rated as more stereotypically black had received the death sentence. In other words, people were more than twice as likely to be sentenced to be killed *simply because their skin color and features were perceived to be "blacker."*[24] And, once again, the people making these decisions *do not seem to realize that they are deciding based on racial characteristics. They don't know what they don't know.*

Researchers at Harvard, Yale, and the University of Washington have been studying this phenomenon for almost fifteen years. The Implicit Association Test (IAT) is a computer-based psychological test that evaluates preferences between different groups and gives direct feedback as to whether the user has any evidence of preferential bias to one group versus another. The IAT was originally created by two psychologists, Tony Greenwald, from the University of Washington, and Mahzarin Banaji, formerly at Yale University, now at Harvard University, and they have teamed up with a third, Brian Nosek from the University of Virginia. As a three-university consortium, Project Implicit has made the IAT available on the Internet for many years. The test is available for more than a dozen different groupings including race, age, gender, sexual orientation, and so on. If you haven't taken it, you should.[25]

Millions of people have taken the free test by visiting the Project Implicit website and, as a result, researchers now have an extraordinary amount of data to study about people's implicit reactions. One of the most striking findings is the clear connection between bias and generalized societal norms and values. It is clear from looking at some of the patterns of responses that we develop patterns of unconscious bias not only about others but about people like us as well. For example, the analysis of responses shows that 88 percent of white people have a prowhite or antiblack implicit bias. Nearly 83 percent of heterosexuals seem to favor straights over gays or lesbians, and more than two-thirds of non-Arabs or non-Muslims demonstrate bias against Arabs and/or Muslims. Similarly, people tend to favor Christians over Jews, the rich over the poor, and so on.[26]

These patterns of preferred perception of predominant sociocultural groups may be surprising to some of us who see ourselves as more liberal or egalitarian, but at some level they seem somewhat understandable. After all, is it really all that surprising that people would tend to unconsciously consider a group that they belong to, that most of their family belongs to, and that they have likely spent their lives living with, the preferential group?

However, when we look at the results among nondominant groups, we see a pattern that is somewhat revealing and even more disturbing. Many people in these nondominant groups, it appears, tend to internalize the same negative perceptions about their own group that members of dominant groups have about them, even if not quite to the same level. For example, approximately 48 percent of Blacks who were tested demonstrated a prowhite or antiblack implicit bias; 36 percent of Muslims tested anti-Muslim; and 38 percent of gays and lesbians similarly seemed to demonstrate a bias against people who shared their sexual orientation. This phenomenon, which we briefly discussed earlier, in reference to the African American car salesman, has been referred to as "internalized oppression." It is the tendency for members of a nondominant group to accept the characterization of them by the more dominant group and to internalize those values and assessments into their own sense of self.

There are, of course, famous examples of this phenomenon. Perhaps the best known is Dr. Kenneth Clark's 1947 experiment with young children and dolls that was cited as part of the research for the landmark *Brown vs. Board of Education of Topeka, Kansas* case, in which the U.S. Supreme Court outlawed school desegregation. Clark found that when presented with white and black dolls, most of the black children tested chose the white dolls, describing them in more positive terms. Interestingly, a sixteen-year-old student named Kiri Davis conducted the experiment again in 2004. Almost sixty years later, the results remained virtually the same.[27]

"The Implicit Association Test measures the thumbprint of the culture on our minds," says Banaji.[28] This is, I think, a perfect characterization of how the dynamic occurs. All of the stereotypical images, stories, and experiences that members of the dominant group hear about a nondominant group also are available to the nondominant group members, and so they incorporate those images into their self-perception. We'll talk more about this process in the next chapter.

As much as we can understand this process, it is hard to minimize the impact that it has on profoundly important aspects of our lives. A 2007 Harvard study shows that unconscious bias on the part of physicians impacts their decision-making relative to patient care *even more than explicit bias does*, contributing to a continued pattern of health disparities among people of color.[29] Researchers from Project Implicit and the Disparities Solution Center at Massachusetts General Hospital, Brigham and Women's Hospital, Beth Israel Deaconess Medical Center, and the Harvard Medical School gave a group of physicians a pretest on the Implicit Association Test in order to identify any discernible patterns of unconscious bias. They then tracked the physicians' evidence of unconscious patterns of race against the decisions the physicians were making about a particular treatment protocol known as thrombolysis (or the breakdown of blood clots by pharmacological means).

Their findings were that physicians in the study demonstrated *implicit* bias favoring Whites and *implicit* stereotypes of black persons as less cooperative with medical procedures and as less cooperative patients in general. As physicians' prowhite implicit bias increased, so did their likelihood of treating white patients and not treating black patients with thrombolysis. Physicians reported no *explicit* preference for white versus black patients or differences in cooperativeness. In fact, when confronted with the findings, many of the physicians were upset that they reacted in such fashions.

Some studies point directly to how these decisions affect business decisions. Researchers at the Massachusetts Institute of Technology and the University of Chicago discovered that even names could unconsciously impact people's decision-making.[30] They distributed five thousand résumés to 1,250 employers who were advertising employment opportunities. The résumés had a key distinction in them: some were mailed out with names that were determined to be "typically white," while others contained names that were "typically black." Every company was sent four resumes: one for a person from each race who was considered to have an "average" résumé and one for a person of each race who was considered "highly skilled." Pre-interviews with company human resources people had established that most of the companies were aggressively seeking diversity, *at least consciously*, a fact that seems more likely to have them lean toward somebody with a name that indicates they are black. Yet the results indicated something else was going on. Résumés with "typically white" names received 50 percent more callbacks than those with "typically black" names. There was another striking difference. While the highly skilled candidates with "typically white" names received more callbacks than the white candidates deemed to be of average skill, there was virtually no difference between the numbers of callbacks received by highly skilled versus average candidates with "typically black" names. Even more striking is the fact that candidates of average skill with "typically white" names received more callbacks than highly skilled candidates with "typically black" names.[31]

It is worth noting that, up to now, most of these studies referencing racial differences have been conducted between black and white test subjects because they have emerged from the historic struggle around race relations in the United States and because the difference is most glaring between these two groups. However, the same patterns seem to apply across other aspects of "the racial divide," depending largely on the particular location in which the study is taking place. We are beginning to see some of these patterns emerging more strongly in the reaction against the immigration of Hispanics and Latinos. A July 23, 2007, *Washington Post*–ABC News poll reported that while 12 percent of Americans still saw themselves as uncomfortable with the notion of an African American president, and 20 percent saw themselves uncomfortable with the notion of a woman president, 24 percent saw themselves as uncomfortable with the notion of a Hispanic president.

Our view of politics is dramatically affected by this phenomenon. San Diego State University researchers Thierry Devos and Travis Gaffud and the University of Chicago's Debbie Mas tested the unconscious association that we make between our notions of what an American is and what we think of certain people we encounter.[32] They began by comparing the reactions that people had to two actresses: Kate Winslet, the British-born actress best known for films like *Titanic* and *The Reader*, among others, and Lucy Liu, the American-born, Chinese American actress known for her various television and movie roles, including *Ally McBeal* and *Charlie's Angels*. Perhaps not surprisingly, more people "automatically" associated the Caucasian Winslet with being "more American" than the native-born Liu. They then explored the same dynamic with Hillary Clinton, John McCain, and Barack Obama and found that the same idea held true. In fact, many people even thought of former British prime minister Tony Blair as more American than President Obama. I guess it is a good thing for Obama that he was taller!

Similarly, Princeton University professors Charles C. Ballew II and Alexander Todorov found that we reflexively choose candidates based on appearance.[33] In fact, we do so in dramatic and quick fashion. The researchers showed test subjects pictures of competing candidates for the U.S. Senate and gubernatorial races in 2006 for less than one second and asked them to rate the candidates on competence and trustworthiness. Test subjects picked the winners of the gubernatorial elections 68.6 percent of the time and the winners of the Senate races 72 percent of the time. And they did this based on less than one second of exposure.

So to reference a point made earlier in this chapter, how different are we from robots? I could go on and on because there are hundreds of studies that demonstrate the same patterns: we make decisions every day, in every area of our life, that are built on subtle, unconscious programming that we have developed through exposure to various messages we receive during our lives. Clearly, it is challenging at times to know whether test participants have truly made these decisions unconsciously or whether "political correctness" has nudged them into saying as much, but the overwhelming amount of evidence, as well as the nature of the tests, would strongly indicate that the results seem compelling. It would make no sense, for example, for car salesmen to make decisions counter to their ability to sell cars, for lawyers to choose talent based on their golf game, or, for that matter, for a human resources director to make decisions counter to stated hiring goals. Or for us to pick our leaders by a glance. It is much more likely that unconscious beliefs are influencing the decision-making process.

But we also can see how this plays itself out. Consider what has been called the "birther movement," which encompasses the whole range of conspiracy theories about whether or not President Obama was actually born in this country and, therefore, is a legitimate president. When we look at this on the surface it is clearly not very rational. The president has released a certified birth certificate, and there is plenty of proof that he was born in Hawaii in 1961. However, the part of the concealed mind that associates him with being less American can be triggered by the attempts to discredit him in that way. Therefore, a charge that would normally be discounted has sticking power with some people.

These unconscious decisions affect every aspect of our lives and in ways that are invisible to us, as I describe in the interviewing example I gave a few chapters ago.

We make decisions largely in a way that is designed to confirm beliefs that we already possess. I refer to this phenomenon as "confirmational behavior."

Such behavior can occur in both positive and negative ways. It is especially influenced by widely held stereotypes. You can see this mental process depicted in figure 7.2. Imagine, for example, that we have a belief, either conscious or unconscious, that "Young Hispanic men are lazy." (I am obviously not suggesting that is an accurate stereotype, simply using it as an example of one that is widely held.) How do we manage that person? What actions are we likely to take? It is likely that we will have a tendency to watch him more closely, to micromanage him and his work. Are we more or less likely to invest in developing him? Are we more or less likely to put him on important assignments? Are we more or less likely to go out of our way to introduce him to significant players in the organization or to inform him about job opportunities? When he makes a mistake, are we more or less likely to accept his explanation? The answers, I would guess, are

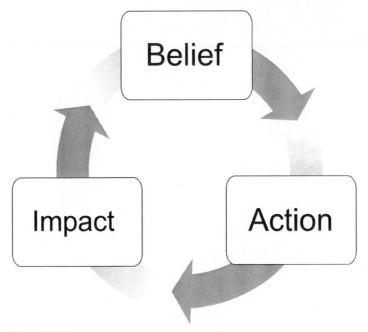

Figure 7.2

pretty apparent. As a result, how does the employee feel? My guess would be that the treatment would lead to his feeling frustrated and perhaps even angry. He would become resigned and probably lose motivation at some point, feeling like there is no way that he could win. He might leave, but, then again, having experienced the same kind of behavior in other places, he might be inclined to believe that this is "just the way it is" and stay while "going through the motions" on his job. In other words, he would behave in a way that would look "lazy" to us.

On the other hand, imagine an employee you really believe in, perhaps "John" in the interview I mentioned earlier. For some reason you believe in him and his skills. He reminds you of yourself when you were younger. How do you treat John? You show a real interest in his career. You introduce him to all of the right people. You make sure he gets the right job assignments. You invite him out to spend time with you in various ways. If people express concerns about him, what do you say? "Don't worry. He's a good kid. I'll talk to him and work it out." What's the result? John flourishes. In fact, two years later the announcement comes out that John has been appointed a director, the youngest person ever to receive such an appointment. And what is your response? "Boy, am I a good judge of talent or what?"

This dynamic has often been called the "Pygmalion effect," after George Bernard Shaw's play of the same name in which the street urchin, treated differently, becomes "My Fair Lady." In the original Greek myth, Pygmalion was a sculptor who carved a sculpture of a beautiful woman and then fell in love with the statue he had created. It has been proven time after time in experiments in which teachers are given different transcripts for the same student and treat them accordingly in ways that impact the student's performance.[34] Our beliefs about people lead to behaviors that become a self-fulfilling prophecy. And most of the time, it is unconscious.

We also are discovering that it is much more subtle and nonrational messaging than we ever realized. Lawrence Williams, an assistant professor of marketing at the University of Colorado in Boulder, and John Bargh, a professor of psychology at the Automaticity in Cognition, Motivation, and Emotion Laboratory at Yale University, have conducted a series of fascinating experiments about a phenomenon they refer to as "the priming effect." Williams and Bargh studied test subjects who were asked to conduct job interviews. Everything about the people they interviewed was as similar as possible except for the fact that some of the interviewers were given warm drinks while they were conducting the interviews and some cold drinks. Based on nothing more than that, the interviewers who were holding the warm drinks scored their interviewees higher than those holding the cold ones. They attributed a "warmer personality" to them.[35] Who knows why? Perhaps our messaging about people having a "cold heart" or a "warm smile" gets encoded, or perhaps it is because of the encoding that we make those assessments. Either way, the result is a nonrational way of conducting the interviews.

Mikki Hebl and Laura Mannix, two Rice University researchers, found that a similar dynamic was true when an interviewer was asked to walk out and meet his or her interview subject in a waiting area. If the interviewee was *sitting next to* somebody who was perceived to be obese, *they rated him or her lower in their interview scores.*[36]

In yet another study, Melissa Bateson, Daniel Nettle, and Gilbert Roberts, researchers at the Evolution and Behaviour Research Group, School of Biology and Psychology at the University of Newcastle-upon-Tyne in Great Britain, set up snack rooms in companies where people were asked to pay for their coffee, tea, and snacks on the "honor system." People were more honest when the note put on the wall had pictures of eyes looking at them rather than flowers.[37] You can see a sample of what these might have looked like in figures 7.3a and 7.3b. This is consistent with a study by Dan Arielly, the brilliant Massachusetts Institute of Technology behavioral economist, who found that students were more

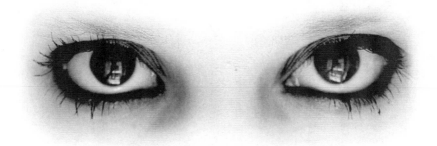

COFFEE CLUB

Prices:

Coffee (with or without milk): 50p
Tea (with or without milk): 30p
Milk only (in your own coffee or tea): 10p
Full cup of milk: 30p

Please put your money in the blue tin.

Thanks, Melissa

Figure 7.3a

COFFEE CLUB

Prices:

    Coffee (with or without milk): 50p
    Tea (with or without milk): 30p
    Milk only (in your own coffee or tea): 10p
    Full cup of milk: 30p

Please put your money in the blue tin.

Thanks, Melissa

Figure 7.3b

honest in grading themselves in tests when they had simply been asked to read the Ten Commandments before taking the test.[38]

So we know that these dynamics impact the way that we view other people, and it affects the way that we view ourselves. But does it also affect our performance as students or workers?

I'm afraid so.

A 1995 study by psychology professors Margaret Shih, Todd L. Pittinsky, and Nalini Ambady demonstrated as much.[39] A group of Asian American female undergraduates were asked to fill out a brief questionnaire and then participate in a math test that was drawn from the Canadian Math Competition. One-third of the groups were given a questionnaire that was referred to as "female identity salient." In other words, it was designed to activate the gender identity of the tester. The second group's questionnaire was designed to activate the cultural identity of the tester, and the third group's questionnaire was a control group that had no conscious focus.

Based on these different questionnaires, participants in the group that answered the "Asian salient" questionnaire preformed at the highest level, 54 percent, while the control group averaged 49 percent and the "female identity salient" group had only 42 percent. The positive stereotypes about Asians in math seem to have had an "encouraging" impact on the first group, while the negative stereotypes about women and math may have had a suppressing impact on the group that was focused on its gender identity.

These findings are not unusual. Claude Steele had demonstrated before that "stereotype threat" is sharply felt and hampers the performance of individuals, particularly African Americans, because of the preponderance of negative stereotypes in our culture about African Americans. If we believe that people believe bad things about us, we, in effect, perform down to the expectations that we perceive people have of us.[40]

Some of the most interesting work on this subject has been done by Amy Cuddy, a social psychologist at the Harvard Business School. Cuddy has distinguished two basic kinds of bias. One is based on how warmly we feel toward people and how inclined are we to like them, to be empathetic toward them, to see them as somebody we can personally relate to. The second is based on what we think of the person's competency.[41]

The impact of these patterns plays out in the way we react to different kinds of people. When Cuddy's team tested large groups, it found that some groups of people were related to as having both low warmth and low competence (poor Blacks, welfare recipients, and the homeless). However, other people were related to as high on one scale but low on another. In some cases, people relate to groups warmly but have a relatively low sense of their competence. This seems to be true of the elderly and the mentally and physically disabled. On the other hand, there are some groups whom most people do not relate to with warmth, but they do project a relatively high sense of competence (e.g., Jews, Asians, and wealthy people). And then, of course, there are those to whom a large percentage of people attribute both warmth *and* competence. This includes some that we might expect (e.g., Christians, Whites, and middle-class people) and one group that might surprise you—black professionals.

This may, in a way, explain some elements of "the Obama effect." In January 2007, when then–presidential candidate Joe Biden was asked about his rival candidate Barack Obama, he created a firestorm when he said, "I mean, you got the first mainstream African American who is articulate and bright and clean and a nice-looking guy." Biden added, "I mean, that's a storybook, man."[42] The use of the term *articulate* especially triggered a reaction because it is an "overqualifier" that African Americans have often heard. Why would he not be articulate? It reminds me of a friend who once described me as "generous for a Jew" and was surprised that I took offense!

But what was Biden really saying? In fact, he may have been speaking to the dynamic that Cuddy's studies revealed. Obama, he might well have been saying, is the kind of black person that mainstream America, and especially white people, "like to like." He is less culturally different, lighter skinned, and thus triggers less of a sense of "the other." The part of us that doesn't want to see ourselves as biased can feel good, either consciously or subconsciously, about liking Barack Obama.

But remember, these reactions are not rational, and not usually even visible to us. They can be quite automatic. Even, dare I say, robotic? And they result in our interpreting the same behavior in different ways. If you show most people a picture of a crying baby, for example, and tell them it is a girl, most of them will say that she's afraid. But if you show them the same picture and say he's a boy, they will say he's angry. It is a reflexive mechanism for figuring out what is going on around us that comes from our social programming.

I wrote earlier about how this plays out in corporate life. When we see a male leader who is willing to kick some tail to make things happen, we may not like him all that much, but we usually see him as a strong leader. When we see a woman, though, who acts in the same way, she often has a certain "B" word associated with her style. Such an attribution is even made by women, who, of course, have been trained within the same social programming as men. The fascinating thing is that it is not likely a person would say, "Sally shouldn't act that way . . . only men should!" In fact, the same person who derides Sally for her behavior might say something like, "I believe that we need women as leaders, it's just that Sally is a b*&@h!"

And again, all of this is driven by the amygdala, the fear center of the brain. It is constantly looking for the way we can be safe. Who is "okay" or even appealing, and who is threatening? Once somebody is deemed to be threatening, the mind then quickly searches for reasons to explain that threat.

Consider Hurricane Katrina. Almost as soon as the tragedy unfolded, race became an issue. A perspective. A way in which people could see, or not see, what was going on. (Remember Shepard's tables?) For many people, Hurricane Katrina was a tragedy, one that affected millions of people, but not necessarily or specifically a race issue. Others saw it as the quintessential race-related event.

USA Today conducted a survey about Hurricane Katrina in September 2005, approximately one month after the tragedy, and found significant differences between the ways that Blacks and Whites viewed the events surrounding the hurricane.

They asked several questions and compared black and white responses:

Do you think that George W. Bush does or does not care about black people?
Do you think the federal government was slow to rescue these people because many were poor?

Do you think the federal government was slow in rescuing these people because
   many of them were black?
Do you believe that people taking things from stores were motivated by criminal
   intent or by desperation?

Remembering that almost all of us had the same capability to watch the same
television news, read the newspapers, listen to the radio, makes it all the more
stunning that the differences between the responses was quite dramatic. We have
very different perceptions about what happened, and even how we saw things
as they were happening. One famous Associated Press report at the time of the
flooding showed two pictures of people taking groceries from a flooded store,
taken by separate news photographers on the same day.

The first photo shows a young black man pulling a bag of groceries that
he has taken from the flooded store. The caption reads, "A young man walks
through chest deep flood water after *looting* a grocery store in New Orleans."

The second shows two other people doing the same thing, except these two
people appear to be a bit older . . . and white. The caption that accompanied
that photo stated, "Two residents wade through chest-deep water after finding
bread and soda from a local grocery store."

I want to be very clear. I am not making any assumptions about the writers
of the two notations. I am not suggesting that they are racist, in the classic sense
that we think of it. I do not assume that they were hateful or hurtful in intent.
Nor do I know exactly what each saw. In many cases, what the people in both
photographs looked like they were doing as they approached the store may have
influenced it. Perhaps the fact that the second picture was taken by the foreign
press makes it less likely to slip into historically U.S. stereotyping. All of these
factors are sorted out by our unconscious.

But look at the difference. It is more than a word. One person is "looting"
the store and "walking" through the water, and the others are "wading" through
the water after "finding" bread and soda. It is not a stretch to sense that there is
casualness to one and heroism to the other.

Before we feel sanctimonious about this, consider that many of us would see
these pictures the same way. Why? Because what does the stereotype of a "looter"
look like? What do all the images that you have seen of looters look like? What
stereotype comes to mind when you think of "looter" in your mind?

Stanford University followed up on this theme about a year after Katrina
with a study that was gauged to determine how race might impact people's
treatment of Katrina victims.[43] Each participant in the study was exposed to a
story about a displaced victim of Hurricane Katrina. Each "victim's" story was
identical with a few exceptions. The victim's name was either Terry Miller or
Terry Medina. The victim might have been a parent, married, or single. The

victim was said to have either a blue-collar or white-collar job. Each story also had a picture attached to it.

In some cases, the same person's photograph was either lightened or darkened, so as a result, there was a total of thirty-six different photographs, one light and one dark, of eighteen people, including nine men and nine women.

Once again, the results were telling. There were 2,300 participants in the experiment. Participants were heavily self-identified as politically liberal and highly educated. Eighty-four percent had completed at least a bachelor's degree. They were asked to decide how much support the person in the story should get for how long.

Based on looking at essentially the same story with a different picture, people gave the black victims, on average, one month's less support than they did the others. White victims were given more than average support. Participants also gave more money to women than men and to white-collar workers over blue-collar workers. *All to people with the same story.*

For Blacks, Asians, and Latinos, their lighter-skinned pictures made more money than their darker-skinned ones. But for Whites, their darker-skinned pictures made more money than their lighter-skinned ones. I guess if you're white and are planning to be in a hurricane, it helps to have a good suntan!

These decisions are not rational. They make no sense. And they almost surely are not conscious. It makes no sense that when a May 2010 CNN/Opinion Research Corporation poll asked, "Do you think people who are openly gay should or should not be allowed to serve in the U.S. military?" some 78 percent of respondents said yes. But things changed when the question was "Do you think people who are homosexual should or should not be allowed to serve in the U.S. military?" Then, *11 percent fewer respondents responded in a positive fashion.* Don't most people these days know that "gay" and "homosexual" are synonymous?

I'm not trying to overwhelm you with all of these studies, and I understand if, at this point, you feel like you have been drinking from a fire hose. I do think it is critical for us to understand that these are not rare or aberrant studies. There are hundreds more where these came from, and even more anecdotal examples that we have all seen and experienced. This is how we function as human beings.

But does it really matter whether bias is conscious or unconscious? After all, the impact on the person whom the bias is against may be the same.

And are the people who feel these things, who act this way in all of the areas of life . . . are they all bad people? Are *we* bad people, because surely we have our own blind spots as well? If we are not, how do we know who is?

And maybe the most important question of all is . . . can we do anything about it?

It is not clear to some whether we can ever reach some of our unconscious. As Timothy Wilson writes:

> It can thus be fruitless to try to examine the adaptive unconscious by looking inward. It is often better to deduce the nature of our hidden minds by looking outward at our behavior and how others react to us, and coming up with a good narrative. In essence, we must be like biographers of our own lives, distilling our behavior and feelings into a meaningful and effective narrative.[44]

And having that capability to observe oneself requires consciousness. That is why I believe it is so important to begin to shift the "good person/bad person" paradigm that we have developed around diversity and inclusion work. If we continue to treat all examples of bias as if they were happening because people are "bad," then we miss the fundamental truth that all of these studies reveal. And that is that this is the way the human mind works. Yet I believe that our diversity efforts have generally been based on the notion that bias is fundamentally a flaw in the nature of people, and that it is a flaw that needs to be corrected. However, what if bias is a normal human condition? What if human beings have an innate tendency to make quick assumptions about others that is driven by a basic survival tendency? As Banaji says:

> Such mental shortcuts probably helped our ancestors survive. It was more important when they encountered a snake in the jungle to leap back swiftly than to deduce whether the snake belonged to a poisonous species. The same mental shortcuts in the urban jungles of the twenty-first century are what cause people to form unwelcome stereotypes about other people. People revert to the shortcuts simply because they require less effort. . . . Mind bugs operate without us being conscious of them. They are not special things that happen in our heart because we are evil.[45]

What does that mean about the way we approach issues of bias? If when we see disparate or inappropriate behavior we assume malice, as we historically have, we may have a hard time reaching the person involved if they *have no conscious sense that they have done anything wrong*. In fact, their natural tendency might be to defend against what occurs to them as an unfair or unfounded attack. However, if we can begin to help people understand how they see the world the way they do, *and if we can realize that we too have to understand the way we see the world*, a whole new world of possibility opens up in terms of our ability to understand one another and to live and work together.

In fact, there are ways to begin to understand our own unconscious tendencies toward bias and the ways it impacts us. There are ways to begin to change both our beliefs and our behaviors. It starts with our ability to "unconceal" that which has been previously *concealed by its obviousness*. This is so present to us that it is like the proverbial "water to the fish and air to the bird." It starts with our ability to develop an awareness of why we see the world the way we do. What is our particular perceptive lens designed to filter?

So how do we develop our perceptive lens? How did we become the "way we are" about diversity?

CHAPTER 8

Memes, Myself, and I

UNDERSTANDING PERCEPTUAL IDENTITY

People are always speculating: why am I as I am? To understand . . . any person, his or her whole life, from birth, must be reviewed. All our experiences fuse into our personalities. Everything that ever happened to us is an ingredient.

Malcolm X[1]

Most people are other people. Their thoughts are someone else's opinions, their lives a mimicry, their passions a quotation.

Oscar Wilde[2]

The power of the concealed mind to determine our attitudes about even our deepest beliefs is profound. We tend to think that we are being quite thoughtful and rational about our decisions. Yet when we look closely, we often trick ourselves into believing we are being rational when we actually are being quite visceral in our reactions. We can be quite robotic. We think we see something or somebody, evaluate it or them, and then determine how we feel. Yet it appears that the process is not that rational at all. In fact, most times we viscerally feel the person or circumstance and then, in microseconds, find things to justify those feelings.

But where do those filters come from? Why do we see certain things and react to certain things while we don't even notice others? I call this phenomenon *perceptual identity* because the way we see ourselves seems to play a major role in determining how we see other people and circumstances. But where does this perceptual identity originate?

We all have multiple identities as part of our persona. At any given time, one of those elements might be foremost. For example, somebody may be aware all of the time that she belongs to a particular religious group, but she might be especially aware of that part of her identity on or around a given religious holiday. It's not that she didn't have that identity at the other times. It is just that she wasn't thinking about it as much.

The fact that we are not particularly focused on an element of our identity does not mean it is irrelevant in our world. As we saw in the previous chapter, it may still be an unconscious driver in the way we perceive the world. In addition, other people may be relating to us as a member of a particular group, even if we are not especially conscious about it ourselves. For example, I might be identified as a white male by people around me to whom it might mean more or trigger a stronger reaction than it does to me, either positively or negatively. It's not that I don't know that I am a white male, but I just may not be as aware of the impact of being a white male.

Our sense of our own identities and those of the people we encounter comes as a result of the *cultural narrative* that we have lived in. This cultural narrative is the collections of history, story, and experiences that we and people like us have had that shape our feelings and expectations about the world. Some are obvious, such as the incidents we remember. Others, like the subtle values that we have been taught or the subtle experiences we have had, may not be so obvious but still may contribute to shaping how we see the world and other people. It is important to realize that we are shaped by the experiences of people like us almost as much as we are by our own experiences. In fact, the experiences of others might have an effect on our experiences. For instance, if your parents grow up telling you that "you really can't trust *those* people," you may be hesitant, distant, and untrusting of people like that before they ever have a chance with you. The stereotypes that you have developed or that they have developed about you may define your mutual relationships. On the other hand, those same comments may lead you in the exact opposite direction in reaction to your parents' comments. If your parents seem too judgmental to you, as a "correction" you may be particularly interested in proving them wrong by looking for the good qualities in "people like that." In either case, we are reacting to the parental messages, though in two diametrically opposed directions.

Our cultural narratives are influenced significantly by the integration of various "collective identities" we develop as a result of the groups to which we belong. I use this term to refer to an identity that is a general thematic way of looking at oneself or being looked at by others as a result of the history, experiences, and such of others in my same group. In other words, "people like me." While we tend to think of ourselves as individuals, most of the ways we look at the world are actually shaped by an integration of our individual experiences and these various group experiences.

Every human being has an individual personality or identity. At the same time, people see themselves and are seen by the world as a function of their group or collective identity. Whether it is our gender, race, sexual orientation, age, profession, or other characteristics, we see ourselves as a combination of who we are as an individual and who we are as a member of these groups to which we belong. In referring to the collective identity, I mean to imply that our group identities are bigger than ourselves. They are identities that reflect the collective experiences of a group, including that group's history. While they affect us personally, they are not personal phenomenon. As wet as we might become in a rainstorm, the storm is nonetheless not a personal rainstorm.

How do our collective identities become formed?

We are born without any strongly defined or articulated sense of identity. There is a "self" present, but developmental psychologists have hypothesized for years that while there may be rudimentary notions of personality present in infants, for the most part they do not even see themselves as separate individuals. George Herbert Mead referred to this as the "disidentified self [as you can see depicted in the center of the diagram in figure 8.1] . . . a sense of existence without a clear sense of 'who I am.'"[3]

IDENTITY

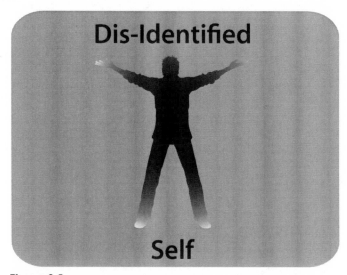

Figure 8.1

I remember being in the hospital with my twin granddaughters, Hannah and Mayah, the day after they were born. I was holding them in my hands and it occurred to me, at that moment, that they had no idea they are girls rather than boys. They had no idea that they are of mixed race (their mom is Indian). They had no idea that they came from two different religious backgrounds (we call them Hind-Jews). Yet all of those things will contribute to shaping their life experiences.

Over time, the identity begins to develop. There are several aspects of the development of what becomes our personality.

Cultural Learning

As we discussed in chapter 7, culture is the most foundational part of the background through which we see the world. You can see this depicted as the top "lens" in figure 8.2.

As we grow up, we are trained to believe certain things and act in certain ways based on the customs and mores, the memes, of the ethnic or group cultures to which we belong. This teaching may relate to aspects of culture as simple and obvious as our language, the kinds of food we eat or clothes we wear, or it may refer to behavior traits, such as gestures and greetings, and so on. In its more subtle form, our cultural learning also affects our system of values, wants, and needs. It also affects our sense of time, comfort with conformity, the importance we place on structure and planning, as well as our way of being in relationships and our open-

Figure 8.2

ness to those relationships along with our reactions to authority, and more. All of this results in the cultural archetypes I described earlier. The norms of the cultures we grow up in influence these and many more attributes of our personality and behavior in untold ways. Anthropologists have talked extensively about how this "cultural learning" gives us one significant element of our worldview.

For example, people from many cultures may show deference to authority by avoiding eye contact, and relationships may be valued over all other things. In 1999, I was hired by the Atlanta Braves major league baseball team to help them deal with an incident that occurred when Jeff Pearlman, a journalist with *Sports Illustrated*, interviewed one of their pitchers, John Rocker.[4] In the interview Rocker made a number of comments that were perceived to be offensive by a wide range of groups. As a result, he was suspended for a period of time at the beginning of the season. Team president John Schuerholz hired me to help deal with the situation, including conducting what was to be the first diversity training ever for a major league baseball team.

During the training, one of the players told a story. He had been raised in Venezuela, where he was taught that the way you show respect for an adult authority figure is by averting your eyes when you speak with them. To look them directly in the eyes, he was taught, would be considered insolent or disrespectful. This, again, is a pattern that occurs in many parts of the world.

When he was seventeen years old, the player was signed to his first professional baseball contract and sent to Idaho to his first minor league team. On the first day, the manager of the team came over to speak with him, and, of course, the player did exactly what he had been taught to do his entire life. He averted his eyes. At that moment the manager aggressively told the player, "Damn it, look at me when I'm talking to you!"

"I didn't know quite what to do," the player recalled. "When I looked at him it was almost like I could feel my father about to slap me from Venezuela!"

Cultures and cultural conflicts show up in many ways.

Of course, as we grow up into this cultural discourse, we don't see it as a worldview at all. We see it as "the right way" to be and act. It becomes one of the lenses through which we see the world. As a result, we see the world as we are but relate to the world in a way that suggests that the world *is* the way we see it—like the blue contact lenses I referred to earlier. Inherently, others who have come from other cultural discourses, who see the world as a "different color," are often seen as being or acting not differently, but wrong.

How does all of this play out in the workplace? Consider two people working together. One, Carmen, comes from a culture where she was taught that family is the most important value. The other, John, was raised in a family that values the "Protestant work ethic." His first responsibility, he was taught, is to work hard and take care of his family's needs. They are working together on a deadline. Both have children who play on a soccer team together and have a game that evening. As five o'clock comes, Carmen begins packing her things to go to the game, fully planning to continue working later that night when she gets home. John is incensed and says, "You can't leave now!" He feels bad about missing the game, but he feels he has to get the work done. Carmen is clearly not committed, in his eyes. Of course, in her view, he is a workaholic.

How many times have you seen people make similar judgments about each other?

Stop for a minute and ask yourself: What did you learn from your culture? How do the things you learned impact you at work? What are the things you do that conflict with the memes that others demonstrate from their cultures? How do you feel when you encounter those conflicts?

Most of these things are, as we discussed, under the surface. Yet they are affecting us in how we see people around us all of the time.

Historic Group Learning and Cultural Narrative

The second aspect of the development of identity comes in the formation of our historic group learning (depicted as the bottom lens in figure 8.3) and the cultural

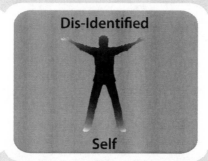

Figure 8.3

narrative that forms from the experiences we have had (and to an even greater degree, that people *like us* have had) because we are members of a particular group.

For example, a woman does not have to have been sexually assaulted in order to be concerned about her well-being and safety around men in certain circumstances. She may still have a reaction to comments, jokes, situations, and more that reflect a generic sense of danger to women, based on the experiences that other women, *most of whom she doesn't even know*, have had with men in certain situations. Similarly, people from nondominant groups of race, religion, ethnicity, or sexual orientation, as well as a host of other groups, may be aware of and/or sensitive to particular behavior or language that reflects on the history of difficulties that their groups have had *without having had experienced those difficulties themselves.*

We often see this in relationship to language. Our reaction to the "n-word," for example, is historical. When somebody hears the word spoken, it evokes a history of circumstances in which some people have been diminished, oppressed, or even killed because of their race. African Americans need not have had any of those experiences themselves to react to the word. Nor do some white people who also may react because of their group identity, or sometimes guilt, about the other side of the circumstance. The word evokes the experiences of people like them throughout history.

These dynamics are especially influenced by how strongly we identify with our dominant or nondominant group identities. Dominant societal groups[5] see the world more as individuals than by group identity. White people, for example, will archetypically tend to be less aware of racial dynamics than people of color. A similar dynamic is true around issues of gender. Women will notice gender dynamics more than men. It is not necessarily that the person doesn't care or is insensitive to these issues, but rather is a function of what has to show up on someone's radar screen in order for the person to survive in the world. When you are "the other," understanding the dominant group is critical to survival. Dominant group members, on the other hand, tend to see themselves more as individuals. They are less threatened by the "mainstream" culture because it is their culture. A white person may not pay a lot of attention to race until he is in a group in which he is the only white person. Then he may feel like he's never felt whiter in his life!

Dominant group members will tend to see their culture, language, values, and so on as "the" culture, language, values, and so on, and often find the culture of the nondominant group to be inferior, less than, or even humorous. Dominance also can result in a sense of transparent entitlement. Things may happen around us that we don't even notice, in which we are benefiting from our dominant group identity. As a tall white man I see this all the time. People seem to assume I am a leader in groups that I'm in. For instance, when I enter a restaurant with friends, I am usually the person addressed by the greeter.

Dominant group members may react to this by exhibiting guilt and demonstrating dysfunctional rescuing. I can give you a great illustration of what I mean. A number of years ago I had a regular coaching relationship with the chief executive officer of one of my client companies, a white man. He had an African American administrative assistant who had been with him for about six months. One day I asked him how he liked working with her and he said, "She's really good at the job, but the problem I have is that she shows up ten to fifteen minutes late two or three times every week. The other administrative folks complain about it all the time."

I encouraged him to speak to her about it and he replied, "I don't want to make a big deal about it. It's kind of sensitive . . . you know?"

I had an opportunity to talk with the administrative assistant a few days later and I asked her how she liked her job. Her response was classic. "I love it," she said. "I feel like I can do it well, and people here are very flexible. I can't get my son to day care until a certain time each morning so sometimes I'm a few minutes late, but everybody's cool about it."

She had no idea. In the meantime, people were creating a whole story about her that affected how she was seen professionally. After I spoke to the chief executive officer, it took about ten minutes to work out a solution. She simply started her day fifteen minutes later and took a shorter lunch break. Everybody was happy. But how many times have you seen people shy away from a conversation they obviously have to have because they are afraid it might end up being perceived to be about race?

Sometimes people in dominant groups are so blind to this phenomenon that we may deny differences between people. We literally don't even notice patterns that are obvious. We also may not even notice members of nondominant groups. Women often report that they will make a suggestion at a business meeting, which nobody responds to, only to have a man make the same suggestion and have it be enthusiastically welcomed. And, as a result of discomfort, dominant group members may simply avoid contact with members of nondominant groups and even be offended and get defensive when their culture is made visible. All of these behaviors happen every day, without people even realizing they are impacting the way they are acting and perceiving things in their surroundings.

Of course, similar opposite, yet complementary patterns can affect members of nondominant groups. Nondominant group members may focus more on their group identities and issues related to them and become defensive about issues relating to their group. For example, many American Jews may have mixed feelings about something that Israel does and feel free to debate it among other Jews, but may feel the need to defend Israel when they are among non-Jews. Nondominant group members also may internalize the dominant group view about them, creating the sense of internalized oppression that was discussed earlier.

Some nondominant group members may attempt to adopt the culture of the dominant group by trying to look, act, and be like them, but others may desire separation from the dominant group or rebel against the dominant culture and its systems and structures. Both of these behaviors can result from the same stimulus: the sense that being "who I am" is not acceptable to the dominant group. Some may become resigned, destructive, or self-destructive and drop out. However, others may develop pride in their own culture as an alternative to the promotion of the dominant culture. All of these dynamics are deeply influenced by our personal sense of our group identity and the societal experience of how our group is treated.

Talk a moment and ask yourself: What have you seen or been told about "people like you"? What messages did you pick up? What other groups do you notice you have strong reactions to, positively or negatively? What specific behaviors trigger your group association? What specific things that others do do you react to because of your historic group experience?

Individual Learning and Narrative

On the other hand, there are circumstances that we all have encountered in which we have noticed that we are different. We may have faced discrimination, prejudice, or hatred because of our race, ethnicity, religious affiliation, gender, or sexual orientation, or we simply noticed that we are different in some way from people around us and that our difference can be felt in a positive or negative sense (depicted as the right-hand lens in figure 8.4).

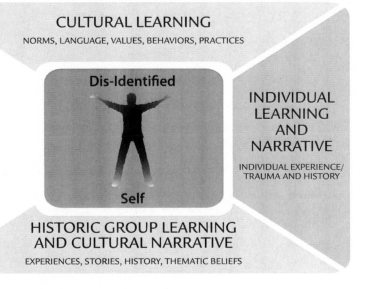

Figure 8.4

These experiences create a particular narrative about our role in the world and influence whom we can trust, what we need to watch out for, where it is safe, where it is dangerous, and what we need to do to survive. If somebody has grown up in an environment in which she was subject to specific incidents of anti-Semitism, she might be particularly sensitive to times when she feels excluded for being Jewish. She may, for example, be especially sensitive being in a work environment in which Christmas decorations are put up. The symbols and artifacts that she is exposed to (the Christmas decorations, for example) "trigger" a reaction that recalls her previous experiences.

We also can project our personal experiences into more generalized observations. The first experience you have with a Korean, for instance, can become your experience of "Koreans." There is nothing remarkable about this awareness. We all know that we pick up learning based on experiences. Can you sing? If you are like more than half the people asked that question, you might have said, "No." But how old were you when you realized you could not sing? Most people say it was when they were very young. The reality, though, is that an overwhelming percentage of people could easily learn to sing with just a little instruction and a bit of practice. Why can't we sing? Because we believe we can't, and we then engage in actions that reinforce that belief (e.g., not practicing).

Once again, take a moment and ask yourself: Can you recall a time when you felt different from people around you? See if you can remember a specific incident. How did it feel? What did you make up about it? Did you create any "rules" as to things to watch out for in the future because of experiences like that one?

Social and Institutional Learning, History, and Narrative

Finally, we have parts of our identity that are defined by the role we play in society and the institutions and identities that we affiliate with over the course of our lives. (See the left-hand lens in figure 8.5.) Lawyers, for example, have a particular identity in this society. Their thinking is trained by a particular learning process. The knowledge they have and the information and processes they are exposed to gives them a particular view of the world. Others also see them in a particular way and, often, a lawyer's reactions may be influenced by that identity. For example, a "lawyer joke" may cause a different reaction in a lawyer than it does in somebody else. The same may be true for people who work in particular companies, who live in particular cities, or who join particular organizations. People who have been in the military, for example, are often strongly affected by that experience. We all have identities that we affiliate with over the course of our lives. The more active and involved we are in the world, the more identities we have with which to affiliate.

IDENTITY

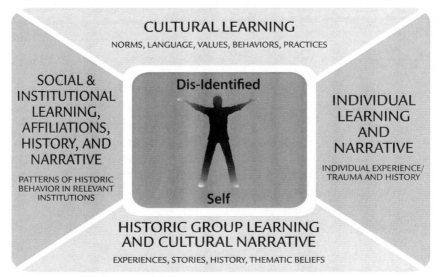

CULTURAL LEARNING
NORMS, LANGUAGE, VALUES, BEHAVIORS, PRACTICES

SOCIAL &
INSTITUTIONAL
LEARNING,
AFFILIATIONS,
HISTORY, AND
NARRATIVE

PATTERNS OF HISTORIC
BEHAVIOR IN RELEVANT
INSTITUTIONS

Dis-Identified

Self

INDIVIDUAL
LEARNING
AND
NARRATIVE

INDIVIDUAL EXPERIENCE/
TRAUMA AND HISTORY

HISTORIC GROUP LEARNING
AND CULTURAL NARRATIVE
EXPERIENCES, STORIES, HISTORY, THEMATIC BELIEFS

Figure 8.5

It is critical to recognize that only rarely are our reactions definitively attributable to one of these influences versus another. Most of the time, they incorporate some combination of the various influences on our lives. And *none apply to all people from a particular group*. Archetypical patterns exist, yet people from a group may feel very different about the same things. This is critical, because the assumption that all people from a particular group necessarily feel a particular way will inevitably lead to stereotyping. However, there are patterns in the reactions and behaviors of certain people, depending on these various aspects of their identities, that are worthy of understanding.

Ask yourself: What groups have you been affiliated with that have shaped your view of the world? How have they influenced you? How do you react to other groups? How might their affiliations give them a different worldview from yours?

Development of "Identity"

Who we are as individuals, our individual personalities, are then created through a combination of cultural learning, historical group learning, individual experiences, and societal and institutional learning. This learning has given us a particular lens through which we see the world and through which we react and respond to the world. The "identity" that we manifest is a combination of all of these forms of learning.

All of these experiences shape, over time, the way we are in the world. We make determinations about what we believe, the values that we hold dear, and the kind of people we feel safe around. We determine the "right" way to act, to talk, and to make it in life. We learn "appropriate" ways of communicating with the people whom we need to interact with, and so on.

As is depicted in figure 8.6, our identity is made up of these various outgrowths of our experiences: our worldview, mannerisms, attitudes, beliefs, biases, affinities, emotions, values, and behaviors. In addition, these experiences give us a particular sense of how we see ourselves in the world. They help create the image that we have of ourselves and the way we define ourselves. They also contribute to our developing a particular sense of entitlement. If we see, for instance, many role models of our race or gender who are successful in all walks of life—leadership, politics, professions, and business—we grow up believing that these things are possible for us, and in some cases expecting that they are so. If we do not see the same opportunities, then we more likely may feel that our possibilities are limited and begin to internalize those limitations.

The totality of all of the influences that we are exposed to creates our way of seeing the world and being seen by the world. They shape our reactions to certain stimuli and often explain why certain people react to an occurrence in one way while somebody else reacts to that same occurrence in a completely different way. That is why we see the world not as it is but as we are. To some degree, all of our reactions are based on our individual experiences. But to a larger degree, they are a reflection not only of our individual experiences but also of the experiences of the groups of which we are a part.

For the most part, we begin to see this "identity" not as a learned set of beliefs, attitudes, and reactions, as it truly is, but instead as "the way we are." A self that is identified with this personality replaces our disidentified self. The challenge in this identification is that we lose our sense of perspective and our sense of the ability to understand others, and more importantly, to change ourselves. If we *are* a certain way, it is likely that we see that as the right way, or at the very least an inevitable way that we are likely to behave. And if the way that we *are* is consistent with the dominant norms of our culture, then it clearly *is* the *right* way to live. We forget that this way of looking at the world is what we have learned, and that others have learned worldviews different from our own, hence our unconscious biases develop in our concealed mind. In fact, we reinforce our sense of "who we are" by choosing relationships and activities that fortify it. At some point it is comfortable enough to become habitual. It is somewhat like when we go out sledding on a fresh hill of snow. The first time down the hill we carve out a path. It is a bit slower, usually. Then we climb back up the hill and

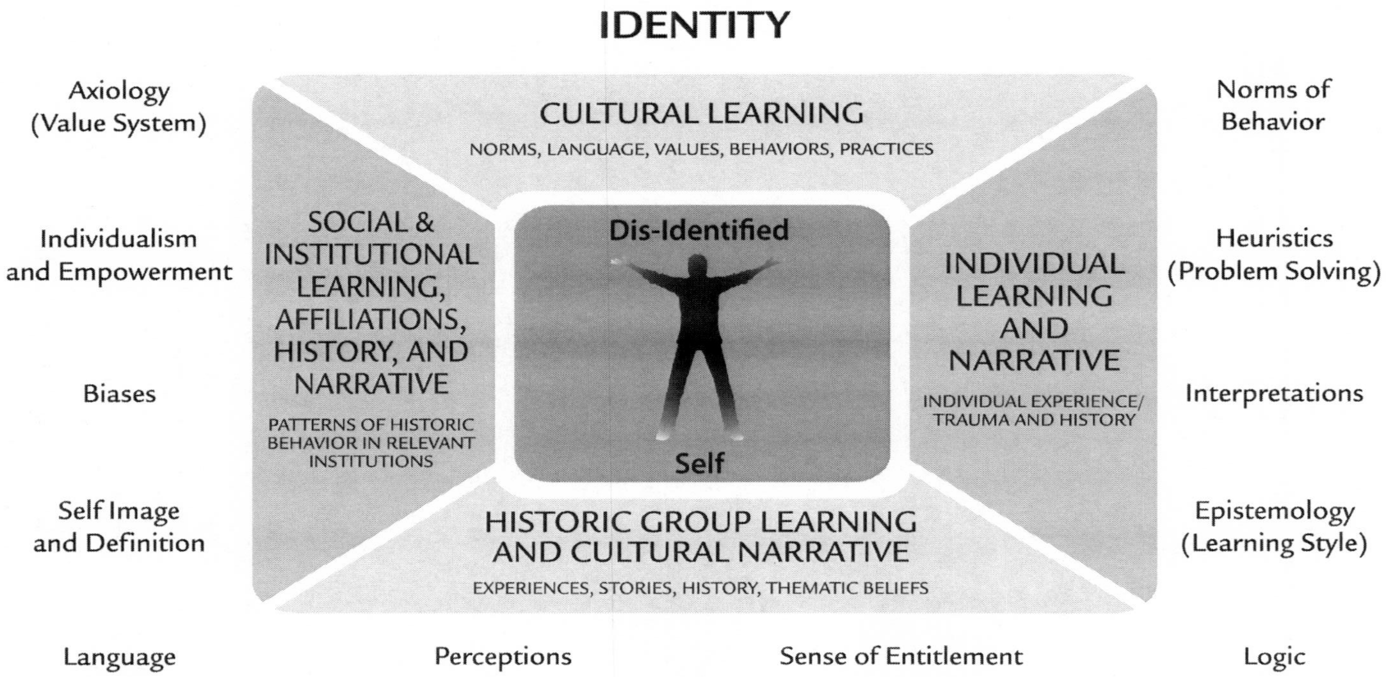

IDENTITY

Norms of Behavior

Heuristics (Problem Solving)

Interpretations

Epistemology (Learning Style)

Logic

CULTURAL LEARNING
NORMS, LANGUAGE, VALUES, BEHAVIORS, PRACTICES

INDIVIDUAL LEARNING AND NARRATIVE
INDIVIDUAL EXPERIENCE/ TRAUMA AND HISTORY

Dis-Identified

Self

SOCIAL & INSTITUTIONAL LEARNING, AFFILIATIONS, HISTORY, AND NARRATIVE
PATTERNS OF HISTORIC BEHAVIOR IN RELEVANT INSTITUTIONS

HISTORIC GROUP LEARNING AND CULTURAL NARRATIVE
EXPERIENCES, STORIES, HISTORY, THEMATIC BELIEFS

Sense of Entitlement

Perceptions

Axiology (Value System)

Individualism and Empowerment

Biases

Self Image and Definition

Language

Figure 8.6

go down that same path. Pretty soon that path gets slicker and slicker. It is the "best" path for us to go on. It is "our" path.

In the workplace environment these different worldviews clash. We encounter people who have come from different cultural backgrounds, with different group learning, different individual experiences, and different institutional learning. We expect their values, behaviors, and so on to be the same as ours and often even assume that they are the same as ours, and we can become judgmental when they are not. In reality, when we take the time to inquire with each other where our perspectives came from, we often find that had we been raised within the cultural narrative that they grew up with, our view would not differ much from their view.

So let's look at how these dimensions play themselves out. When somebody stands in front of you for the first time, before he even speaks or before you have learned anything about him, you "know" certain things about him, mostly based on the things you have learned from your cultural narrative. Another way of putting it is that you may project certain qualities onto this person, depending upon your experience with, or what you have learned about, people like him. You may see his race, his gender, his relative age, the way he is dressed, his hairstyle, whether or not he is wearing a wedding ring, his body size and shape, and so on, and make assumptions. These are some of the person's group identities, and in all of these cases, you probably have some sense, positive or negative, about the group and your experience with it or the experience that others like you have had with people like that person. Along with this you also may have expectations about what that person is thinking and feeling and about how he may act.

Let me give you a more specific example. Let's say that John, a white male, age forty-five, meets Sally, a forty-year-old African American woman. They do not interact in their first meeting only as John and Sally. Actually, they have not gotten a chance yet to experience who "John" or "Sally" really are at all. What they see, usually, is "white man" and "black woman," and what they actually experience at that moment are the feelings that they have associated with that other group. Sally, if she is like many black women, may have a conversation about white men that is something like "I want to be sure I can trust him." Why? Not because of John specifically. She doesn't even know John. She has that reaction because the history of African American women's relationship with white men, part of her cultural narrative, may have left her with that question. As discussed earlier, it is critical that we understand that this is a cultural conversation, not a "personal" reaction, even though it may affect John and Sally personally.

Similarly, John may approach Sally with his own reaction. The voice in his head may be saying something like "I hope she doesn't think I'm a racist!" Again, his reaction has little to do with Sally, whom he doesn't know, but with all of the black women he believes have felt that way about him or other white men in the past. Their competing cultural narratives may have created somewhat conflicting behaviors. One way that John might react to his concern that Sally not think he is a racist is to become overly deferential, to "try too hard." He might look for the right things to say, or avoid saying others. In his awkwardness he might throw out a comment that seems patronizing, such as "Hey, did you see [Chris Rock or Jesse Jackson] on TV last night?" In reacting to him, Sally may be convinced, given his awkwardness, that he cannot be trusted, and the cycle once again perpetuates itself. The harder he tries to reach her in this way, the more she feels guarded.

When people remain focused on their group identities it is very difficult—in fact almost impossible—to create a real sense of connection and trust.

Our individual identities, on the other hand, are the parts of us that are unique and special to us: they contain our values, our personality, our personal histories, and the things that define us as unique individuals. While they may have evolved as a combination of our various collective identities, they have, nevertheless, become the way we see ourselves as individuals. We know that at the same time we have group identities that are important to us and define who we are, but our individual identities distinguish our uniqueness. They may, in fact, make us different from the norm of people in groups like ours in the way we think, feel, or act.

Most people know somebody who is in a different group than they are for whom their group identity is no longer much of an issue, even though it still exists; a man and a woman who work together, for example, who know and trust each other as individuals, may have little concern about their gender difference. People of different age groups, different religions, even different races, have individual relationships where their group identity is not a barrier.

Yet, at the same time, we can experience trigger behaviors that remind us of the differences. A comment, the use of a word, or a gesture can make one of us remember that the other person is a member of another group, and the perpetrator may not have any idea that he or she caused that shift! I may be triggered by something when I am talking to you that you do not notice at all. An excellent example of this is an incident that occurred several years ago, when a white department head in the Washington, D.C., government used the term *niggardly* in a conversation with his African American employees.[6] Even though the term has nothing to do with race (*The American Heritage Dictionary*'s definition is "Unwilling to part with anything; stingy"), the use of the term to an African American audience triggered an emotional reaction that went beyond the intent.

We also can be stimulated to focus on our group identities more by events or influences totally outside of our relationship but that frame our relationship in a particular context. Many people noticed, for example, that after the trial of the policemen accused of the Rodney King beating, or during the O. J. Simpson trial, Blacks and Whites who had worked comfortably together up to that time experienced some awkwardness with one another. Why? They were not likely involved with either circumstance directly. However, the incidents that were occurring *outside of their relationship* framed their interaction in a way that had them become conscious of their particular group identities. We saw that earlier in the studies that were done after Hurricane Katrina. Such occurrences are neither bad nor good. They occur because it is simply the way we function with one another as human beings.

When we consider these dynamics, we can begin to understand why we find ourselves in some of the more confusing, confronting situations that we do. Why, for example, does the same exact question, in the same circumstance, trigger a completely different reaction in two different people? Take the man who asks his male colleague whether he would mind getting him a cup of coffee. No problem. But the same man, in the same circumstance, makes the same request of a female colleague, and it is, perhaps, considered "sexist." She may say something like "I'm not a waitress!" Why? Because the cultural narratives and collective identities of men and women are different. To the woman, the whole history of women being expected to get coffee for men in the workplace occurs along with the request. To the man making the request, it is the same thing he asked his male colleague. What's the issue?

So we can see that the influence of these cultural narratives on our identities can influence us in our reactions to others. And they can shift depending upon changing circumstances. An African American woman with a disability, for instance, might in one situation focus on her disability, in another circumstance focus on her gender, and at yet another time focus on her race.

We may move from one level of identity to another at any given time. Perhaps somebody says something, or we have an experience, or something is going on in the world around us. Whatever triggers the shift, all of the identities are always present. For a time, we tried as a culture to believe that we could move closer to a universal or community identity by ignoring our differences and suggesting that we are all the same. In the 1960s, they wrote songs about such thinking. But we have learned that the only way to really get there is not by avoiding the differences but by understanding them and how they impact us. The more we learn about the different cultural narratives of the people we work with, live with, and interact with, the more likely we are to be able to treat them as people. It is a seeming contradiction that our knowledge of our differences can be what makes us appreciate and be able to focus on our sameness.

This brings us back to our own individual identities. We often hear people say, "I just want to be treated as an individual." And, in fact, most of us do. However, the reality is that who we are as an individual is an integration of all of our collective and individual experiences. It is the unique way that we have processed all of our group *and* individual learning. Even as a unique individual, we have many aspects of ourselves, and, indeed, our fundamental sense of ourselves, that are a part of the groups to which we belong.

Why does all of this even matter? It matters because this awareness offers us the potential for a richer, fuller way of being with one another. If we really understand this, we have a much greater chance to listen to one another, not with judgment, but with true understanding, and out of that understanding, find ways to work together with greater respect and more effectiveness.

But how do we get there?

CHAPTER 9

Developing Diversity Mastery

UNDERSTANDING YOUR WIRING

> I have one major rule: Everybody is right. More specifi-
> cally, everybody, including me, has some important pieces
> of truth, and all of those pieces need to be honored, cher-
> ished, and included in a more gracious, spacious, and com-
> passionate embrace. To Freudians I say, "Have you looked
> at Buddhism?" To Buddhists I say, "Have you studied
> Freud?" To liberals I say, "Have you thought about how
> important some conservative ideas are?" To conservatives I
> say, "Can you perhaps include a more liberal perspective?"
> And so on, and so on, and so on.
>
> Ken Wilber[1]

> The curious paradox is that when I accept myself just as I
> am, then I can change.
>
> Carl Rogers

So how do we address our own unconscious? By definition, we can't see it, and
some psychologists believe that means we cannot inherently do anything about
it. My experience has been that some things we may never be able to see about
ourselves, but others we can influence.

It is especially challenging for many of us who strongly identify with being
progressive on these issues. Our identity can be so tied into our view of ourselves
and our values that it may be hard to see that underneath those values are beliefs
within our concealed mind that are very different. It takes a lot of courage and
humility to confront this probability.

People can be consciously committed to egalitarianism and deliberately
work to behave without prejudice, yet still possess hidden negative prejudices

171

or stereotypes. When encountering a person for the first time, our brains automatically make note of detectable human differences. But if we are hardwired to discriminate, are we doomed? The answer is a resounding no.

An awareness of unconscious bias allows and requires us to fundamentally rethink the way we approach leadership, training, and organizational policy and culture on a number of levels. Organizations have focused a great deal of attention on trying to find ways for people, especially those in the dominant groups, to "get" diversity. The challenge is that "getting it," on a conscious level, may have little or no impact on our unconscious beliefs and, more importantly, behavior. In fact, thinking that we "get it" may blind us to the fact that these dynamics are at play. Our knowledge of unconscious bias makes several things abundantly clear:

- The limiting patterns of unconscious behavior are not restricted to members of any one group. *All of us have them*, and effective managers and business leaders particularly have to focus on our own assumptions and biases if we expect to have the moral authority to guide others in acknowledging and confronting theirs. We may have them about other groups or even about groups to which we belong.
- A person who behaves in a noninclusive or even discriminatory way does not have to be motivated by negative intent. When we approach people who view themselves as good individuals trying to do the right thing as if they "should have known better," we are likely to be met with resistance. If we approach them with an assumption of innocence in intent, but with an emphasis on the impact of their behavior, we are more likely to reach them effectively and win their willing attention.
- Finally, we cannot solely rely on any sense of subjective determinations of attitude, either individually or collectively, to determine whether our organizations are functioning in inclusive ways. Our conscious attitudes may have little to do with our success in producing results. We have to create objective measurements that give us individual and collective feedback on our performance if we are to create organizations that are truly inclusive.

Researchers have long believed that because implicit associations develop early in our lives, and because we are often unaware of their influence, they may be virtually impervious to change. But recent work suggests that we can reshape our implicit attitudes and beliefs—or at least curb their effects on our behavior.

Seeing targeted groups in more favorable social contexts can help thwart biased attitudes. In laboratory studies, seeing a black face with a church as a background instead of a dilapidated street corner, considering familiar examples of admired Blacks, and reading about Arab Muslims' positive contributions to society all weaken people's implicit racial and ethnic biases. In other words, changes in external stimuli, many of which lie outside our control, can teach our brains to make new, more positive associations.

But an even more obvious tactic is to confront such biases head-on with conscious effort. And some evidence suggests willpower can work. People who report a strong personal motivation to be nonprejudiced tend to harbor less implicit bias. And some studies indicate that people who are good at using logic and willpower to control their more primitive urges, such as people who meditate regularly, exhibit less implicit bias. Brain research suggests that the people who are best at inhibiting implicit stereotypes are those who are especially skilled at detecting mismatches between their intentions and their actions. Again, what virtually everybody agrees is that the willingness to admit the bias to yourself is the first step.

"Early in my work as a diversity and inclusion leader I realized that it was significantly easier to get people to open up about their biases if I first shared my struggles with, as the song goes, 'The Woman in the Mirror.'

"When I shared what it was like to see and then address my discomfort with people with disabilities or acknowledged how the unconscious misconceptions passed on to me by my family and culture impacted my actions, I could see that it allowed others in the room to feel safe and to look at how they were affected by their biases and assumptions. My belief, that it's harder to judge others harshly when you realize that biases live in all of us, has made me a much better D&I leader."

Rosalyn Taylor O'Neale
Vice President and Chief Diversity & Inclusion Officer
Campbell Soup Company

Nine Steps You Can Take to Manage Unconscious Bias

Regardless of your position in an organization or society at large, everyone can take practical and meaningful steps to reduce the influence of unconscious bias on decision-making.[2] Review the steps below, which are designated for either individuals or for people who manage others, and pick two or three that speak to you directly.

1. Tell the Truth to Yourself

   Remember that *all* human beings have unconscious preferences and biases, which is completely normal, and that those preferences and biases impact most, if not all, of the decisions we make, *including those regarding people.* Be willing to honestly admit your biases.

Table 9.1

Individual Exploration	Manager Exploration
What groups make you most uncomfortable (appearance/racial/cultural/religious)?	Does your team attract a certain type?
Notice the business situations you are in when you feel most uncomfortable.	Does your team "type" exclude any groups?
What kinds of people make you most nervous? Are these personal traits or group traits?	Is your top leadership engaged in exploring unconscious bias as a corporate goal?
What kind of people do you try your hardest to please? What characteristics do they share?	Are there patterns among the kinds of groups that are successful in gaining contracts in your supply chain?

2. Notice What Influences Your Decisions

   Remember: Unconscious preferences and biases can influence your decision-making in both negative *and positive* ways. In making people decisions, ask yourself, "How might my perceptions or biases be influencing my decisions?" Moreover, be open to the possibility that those influences could be present in your decision-making.

Table 9.2

Individual Exploration	Manager Exploration
Consider several of your last major decisions. How were they influenced by your feelings about others?	Do you often rely on your "gut" or intuition to make major decisions?
Do you take extra time during times of stress to ensure you make a fair decision?	Do you seek additional objective data to balance your decisions?
If you are feeling nervous in a social situation do you ask yourself, "What am I reacting to?"	Do you have a pattern of surrounding yourself with people who have made a good first impression on you? What was that impression based upon?
	Do you give yourself enough time to ensure that your decisions are free from impulse and reaction?

3. Gather Data about Yourself

The Implicit Association Test (IAT, www.implicit.harvard.edu) can help you identify your unconscious preferences. (*We all have them: see item 1.*) Some researchers say that the IAT and similar tests/tools have arguably revolutionized the study of prejudice. Taking one or more of the IATs is a free, voluntary activity that you can do at home on your own computer. You can make a personal note of your results for future reference.

Table 9.3

Individual Exploration	Manager Exploration
The IAT is only a window into what you have been taught. What has most influenced your thinking and feelings about other groups? The IAT is a snapshot of our "wiring" in time, not a reflection of whether we are good or bad people. What results seem most accurate or off-the-mark to you? Why?	What are the greatest influences on your belief systems (parents/school/friends/media)? Do you know your biggest blind spots? Who is empowered to give you painful insights without fearing consequences? How often is your team empowered to give you feedback that might be controversial or make you uncomfortable?

4. Stretch Your Comfort Zone

If you discover that you may have negatively biased tendencies in relation to a particular group, make a conscious effort to learn more about that group and, where you can, expose yourself to positive images and other input related to the group in question.

Table 9.4

Individual Exploration	Manager Exploration
Do your hobbies or home activities regularly expose you to diverse people and groups? Do you attend local cultural festivals, eat at ethnic restaurants, and go online to research the origins of interesting new cultures?	How do you encourage multiculturalism within your work team? Do you make conscious efforts and choices to include a broad array of people in your decision-making process?

5. Stimulate Your Curiosity about Others

When you interact with a person who is part of a group with which you have had little interaction, be aware that you may be especially susceptible to stereotyping, which could lead to false and, perhaps, negative assumptions about that person. Make a conscious effort to learn more about that individual as well as his or her group, recognizing that interaction with one person does not predict or explain his or her group norms.

Table 9.5

Individual Exploration	Manager Exploration
Are you aware of situations in which you are reluctant to share cultural information about yourself? What are they? How can you communicate this information to others to increase your comfort?	In what ways are you sensitive, oversensitive, or not sensitive enough to issues of privacy on your team?
Do you attempt to build relationships with your colleagues who are different from you? Have you shared with them about your background and perspectives? Is this welcomed or resisted? Why? Have you asked them how they prefer to be approached?	Are you willing to model appropriate kinds of sharing before asking others to do so? What do you do in the team environment to create new contexts for understanding, safe space for sharing, and opportunities to demonstrate respect and tolerance?

6. Expand Your Constellation of Input
   When appropriate, get input from people representing other groups or points of view during your decision-making process. That said, when you do, even if the other party agrees with your decision, do not assume that your decision wasn't influenced by your preferences or biases. Even if the person you engaged for input comes from a different group, that person's preferences or biases could still be very similar to your own.
7. Create Your Own Metrics/Understand Your Own Patterns
   Keep track of the decisions you make. Review your decision-making history to see whether there are any patterns that may not have been apparent to you (e.g., similarities in the persons you hire or select for stretch assignments, and

Table 9.6

Individual Exploration	Manager Exploration
Can you discern a pattern of inclusion/exclusion, both with yourself, and from others?	Do you surround yourself with people who only tend to agree with you?
Do you feel underutilized professionally? Are there ways that you can communicate your abilities and talents to decision-makers?	Do you make decisions more often based on business information or personal interpretations?

so forth). Patterns don't automatically indicate bias, but if you see a pattern, it would be wise to examine it further. Consult your human resources representative for additional guidance.

8. Be Open, Seek Feedback

    One of the best ways to bring your concealed beliefs and how they impact your behavior into visibility is to request peer feedback as to any potential patterns of preference that they might see. Most of us are nervous about doing so. We are inherently afraid of what we might hear. But are we better off with them thinking it and not telling us? At least if people bring these behaviors to our attention, we can do something about them.

Table 9.7

Individual Exploration	Manager Exploration
How do you respond to feedback from particular individuals? Do you notice that you ask one kind of person for feedback, and not another? What can you learn about yourself from this?	Do you provide regular avenues for gathering data and feedback on team performance? Have you ever conducted an anonymous 360-degree review to allow feedback from your team?

9. Turn the Flashlight on Yourself

    Don't be afraid to question yourself. And if other people question your decisions, instead of reacting defensively, *practice active listening* when they share their concerns, and *be willing to act on that feedback as appropriate.*

Unconscious patterns have an enormous impact on both our individual behavior and on organizational behavior. Only when we find the courage and curiosity to engage in a seemingly contradictory path—consciously becoming aware of and addressing something that is, by nature, concealed—can we begin to see more clearly into our blind spots. As Viktor Frankl wrote, "Between stimulus and response, there is a space. In that space lies our freedom and power to choose our response. In our response lies our growth and freedom."[3]

Awareness and growth does not happen overnight. Increasing our diversity, inclusiveness, and cultural competency requires us to undertake a long journey of continuously challenging our perceptions and slowing down our impulse to judge instantaneously and reactively. Ultimately, the result will be greater opportunity for all with more engaged individuals and more profitable organizations.

CHAPTER 10

"It's the System, Stupid!"

PARADIGM SHIFT 3: MOVING FROM EVENTS TO CULTURE-BASED SYSTEMS CHANGE

> Nature uses only the longest threads to weave her patterns, so that each small piece of her fabric reveals the organization of the entire tapestry.
>
> Richard P. Feynman

> This we know; all things are connected like the blood that unites us.
> We do not weave the web of life; we are merely a strand in it.
> Whatever we do to the web, we do to ourselves.
>
> Chief Seattle[1]

A number of years ago, I was working with a client that conducted a major renovation of one of its largest facilities. The building was completely redone, not just aesthetically, but also in terms of some of the basic operating functions. As winter came, they began to notice a rise in the use of gas heat. It wasn't particularly distressing because their overall utility costs were still down, but it was nonetheless perplexing. The situation persisted for a couple of months until one day they quite accidentally stumbled across the cause of the higher heating costs.

As part of their effort to increase their operational efficiency, the designers had put in place a number of energy-efficient strategies. They put motion sensors in the rooms, which automatically shut off lights when the rooms had been idle for a certain period of time. They put in a greater number of fluorescent and compact fluorescent lightbulbs to replace standard lightbulbs, and so required far less wattage. But what they hadn't considered was the fact that the old lightbulbs were helping heat the building during the winter!

In this case, the net gain was still greater than the net loss, but nonetheless this is a good example of how systems work. We are often affecting things by our actions, and we do not always realize we are making such impacts.

All too often in our diversity efforts, we are oriented toward finding the things that we can do rather than really working to understand the system that is in place and the ways that various aspects of that system affect one another. We do diversity recruiting and conduct training programs. We hold Black History Month or Women's History Month celebrations, and we have "International Food Day" in the cafeteria. We hear about best practices that our colleagues are using, and we replicate these practices. All of these things can be helpful and are definitely well intentioned. They often are the result of the reality that most diversity efforts are woefully underfunded and diversity leaders have to do the best they can with limited resources.

But these things, on their own, rarely, if ever, change the culture of an organization. This kind of event and activity orientation affects a system much in the way a short-term diet induces weight gain. We see an immediate "bump" in interest in diversity, but quickly enough, we revert to our old ways of doing things. Robert Allen used to compare this with the act of pushing one's hand into a foam pillow. As long as you hold it there, the pillow is indented, but as soon as you remove your hand, the pillow pops back into place. That is why it is so important to create environments that fundamentally change the way people relate if we are to get the most out of our people, and if people are to have the best chance to participate in their organizations. That is the *organizational community* that I described earlier.

The question of how to create sustainable change is one that organizations of all kinds have struggled with for years. Our challenge in creating cultures that will be sustainably more diverse, inclusive, and culturally competent is nothing new. But how do we avoid the tendency to think that simply conducting the right activities can create change? What is required is an understanding of how systems work and of how to create culture-based systems change.

Systems thinking requires us to understand that everything we do in an organization is part of a flow of activities that are interacting and influencing one another, often in ways that we don't even realize. One of my clients and friends, Eric Watson, vice president of diversity and inclusion, Delhaize America (Food Lion's parent company), described how systems impact us in ways that we don't realize:

> We always face the challenge of how to provide for communities in low income, depressed markets in our service areas. Often we noticed that these stores have the same staffing budgets and market size as our other stores, but they produce less and are lower quality performers. We often were very judgmental of the management of

these stores. And since many of these stores were in communities of color, we began to wonder if the lack of performance was diversity related.

At some point we began to see that there were things influencing the dynamic that we didn't even consider. For example, we began to notice that the parking lots in these stores were a lot dirtier than in some of the other communities. At first we simply saw it as one more example of poor performance on the part of the store, but then we realized there were other forces at work. A lot of our customers were driving cars that were older and in poor repair. They just didn't have the money to invest in the cars. When they parked their cars in our parking lots, they would leak oil and fluids, staining the parking lots. However, this became more than an aesthetic issue because the shoppers who came into the store were, of course, walking through the parking lot and because the parking lot was so dirty, they were tracking more dirt and oil into the stores. As a result, the stores required far more labor hours to clean than some of our other stores. Because labor costs are fixed by a formula based on store income, this also meant there were fewer labor hours available for cleaning the parking lot, which created a perpetual problem. But that wasn't all.

The drain on labor hours also meant that there were fewer labor hours available to stock the store's shelves with product. This resulted in a lower level of readiness for business, thus lowering both sales and profit. In addition, in lower income communities, people tend to shop more often. When you have very limited money, you tend to want to keep as much of it available as you can, so you do more small shopping trips rather than big ones. This meant that there was far more store traffic for the same amount of sales as our other stores, and even more dirt being tracked in, requiring even more labor for cleanup.

The circumstances and the system at play made it simply impossible for the stores to compete with some of the others using the same performance criteria.[2]

Complex systems are very challenging to diagnose, especially when we are inside of the system. Our oversimplified view of diversity issues contributes to these problems because even though we know at some level that there are very complex manifestations of the way diversity impacts our organizations, we often, with the best of intentions, look to "solve problems" rather than change culture. Let me give you a couple of examples.

I have worked with many clients in the professional services industries: law firms, accounting firms, consulting firms, and so on. They all have had a commitment to increase their hiring and retention of white women and people of color. In many cases, clients have established mentoring programs for their younger associates in these groups to try to assist them in being successful in cultures where they belong to nondominant groups. These mentoring programs, some of which I helped to create, are very well done for all of the right reasons. Yet it seemed in many cases that fewer participants signed up for the programs than expected.

We began to talk with the young women and people of color in the organizations and found that their low enrollment was endemic of a culture-based systems issue. What message was being sent to the organization by the way these programs were established? When we began to explore that question we found that the organization was making its own meaning of the need for the programs. If young white men were brought in, they simply went into the system as it was established. But if women or people of color were brought in, *the inadvertent perception that was created was that they needed mentoring.* Inadvertently, the mentoring program that was created to assist in the development of this talent *was contributing to the conscious and unconscious belief that these associates weren't as qualified as the white men.* Since this is a relatively common conscious or unconscious belief anyway, *the attempt to resolve a concern was actually deepening the very concern that it was created to resolve.*

In another case, an organization wanted to encourage the development of women and people of color who were new associates. They instituted a policy where new hires were assigned to engagement managers by a structured process, rather than allowing the engagement managers to choose who they wanted to work with as they had done in the past. The intention was to encourage some of the engagement managers, who were mostly white men, to work with a more diverse group of associates and to give the associates more exposure. One of the new associates was a young man named Bob, who was assigned to an older white male engagement manager named Bill.

Bill was not thrilled. He reportedly said to a colleague, "Just what I need, an affirmative action hire when I need good people on this job!" And so Bill "made the best of a bad situation" and assigned Bob to low-level tasks. "Have him handle getting the report put together and the rest of you get the audit done," he allegedly said to other members of the team. Bob, a highly educated and talented young man, could see the writing on the wall. Within the year he left the organization and took a job with a competitor. And what do you think his "on the street" statements about the company were?

In both of these cases, there was inherent bias at play. But I'm not suggesting that we don't use programs like this at all. What I have come to believe is that it is critical that we realize the way the system works so that we can address these issues.

In an earlier chapter, I talked about the fact that structure creates behavior in organizations. Organizational structures are a reflection of the core cultures of the organization, and cultures are a function of several different aspects that dramatically impact the way members of that organization see the world. They send clear messages about what kinds of beliefs and behaviors are accepted, expected, and rewarded, and they communicate what is required to be a successful member of the culture. Usually they exist because they are perceived to have been successful, and so they are consciously taught to new employees as they enter the system. They are, in the simplest sense, "the way we do things around here."

We mostly notice the outward manifestations of culture in organizations as the behaviors, symbols, and "artifacts" through which the culture is expressed. These external manifestations are important. They give people signals about the culture's values. And they also often symbolize success, so the people who are successful can become very attached to these manifestations. Sometimes they represent a history that was reflective of oppressive times for some members of the organization. One organization that I worked with was committed to creating a greater sense of diversity and inclusion, as their senior leadership team was mostly white men, almost all of whom had "grown up" in the organization. They had offices on the top floor of their ten-story building, and a separate elevator would whisk them up in the morning and down in the evening, not stopping on any other floors.

All of the leaders were fully involved in the process, participating in education programs and coaching, talking to stakeholder groups, and meeting with employee resource groups that had been created for various distinct identity groups. They were clearly engaged. Yet when the question of the "executive elevator" was brought up, they were intransigent. For the larger population, of course, the elevator was a symbol of old times. It was a hierarchical separation between those who were in power and those who were not.

The interesting thing was that all of the leaders had good reasons the elevator should still function. "It gets me to my office faster," was the most popular one. But when I went up and timed it and showed them that even stopping on each floor took a total of only a couple of extra minutes, they would find more reasons. For the leaders, their access to the elevator was representative of what they had achieved after years of working hard. It represented the "gold ring" they had sought. Eventually the elevator was opened, and to a surprisingly strong positive reaction in the organization, but that did not happen until the leaders were helped to realize why they were *really* holding on to the elevator.

"The vanguard corporations of today—those that are on the leading edge of both performance and organizational innovation—have learned to manage and capitalize on the connective tissue of systems thinking. Their cultures, policies and processes adapt readily to reflect this need to *manage* interdependence. They understand that sustained long-term success today requires systematically aligning the voices and interests of all organizational stakeholders—Employees, Customers, Investors, Partners, Society and the Environment. It is no longer about focusing on shareholders alone (historically often at the expense of other stakeholders). It is about skillful stakeholder management. It is about building strong inclusive cultures based upon a deeper purpose that embeds the organization on the 'right side of society.' It is about building empowerment and embracing diversity. Those organizations that have successfully achieved this have been rewarded by higher creativity, productivity and organizational performance."

Shubhro Sen, PhD
Co-founder and Executive Director
Conscious Capitalism Institute

The challenge for all of us is that we get so deeply entrenched in the cultures that we are a part of that we don't even realize how much they are informing the way we do things. We look at young people, particularly teenagers, and it is very clear how much they are driven by peer influence. Yet adults are just as driven by the influence of the normative behaviors of our systems. Sometimes we don't even realize why we do the things we do. We easily go along with "the way we do things around here," even when it conflicts with what we see as our personal values. Entire organizations can become blind to themselves every bit as much as individuals can, and the systems within that organization serve to reinforce the "identity" of the organization as much as our personal behaviors reinforce our personal identities. In that sense, an organization can be as unconscious as an individual.

While there are times when individuals within an organization act in uniquely aberrant ways, more often it is the case that these individual behaviors that seem out of concert with the norms of the culture are actually connected in ways that we don't see. We often are failing to see that all individual behavior is part of the community, system, and culture that it lives in. It does not exist separately, but rather as a part of the whole that is being expressed. I used to see this many years ago, when I was teaching. In every class I seemed to have one child who stood out as "the difficult one." Try as I might, I seemed unable to reach that child. Invariably, I found myself thinking, "If only David were not here, this would be an easy class." Then one day my prayers were answered. David's mother had to change jobs, and he was transferred to another school. Much as I hate to admit it, I was thrilled, because now it would be such a great class. It took just about one week before Paula began to act just the way David had acted. As it was, there was something being expressed by David's behavior that had to be expressed by *somebody*.

On a societal level we can see the way these patterns form and are inextricably connected. As people are perceived to become more violent we, as a society, naturally react. We put more distance between ourselves and the people we have come to fear, sometimes based only on the way they look, or where they live, or the color of their skin. We withdraw to what seems like safety. We stay in separate neighborhoods, don't talk to each other on the streets. The more we withdraw, the less affiliation we have with each other, and the less safe we feel. Our disconnection, our tendency to create each other as strangers begins to engender more hostility, not less, and the opportunity for more, and not less, violence to occur.

It is a paradigm that we have all grown up in. Our interpretations of our experiences in the past define our future, and fear in the past defines protectiveness in the future. However, the more protective we become, the more we fear, the less we trust, the less safe we are, and the easier it becomes to attack.

We can see this phenomenon clearly in the way we run our organizations. One or two people are late, so we put in a time clock or a new tardiness policy. What's the reaction on people's part? Resentment, hostility, anger, frustration, less commitment, and sometimes outright rebellion. People may in fact come on time, but the quality of their work may drop off dramatically, resulting in a net loss for the company.

What we're often not seeing is that we all function as parts of the whole, and all of our behavior is an expression of the common, systemic issues that we confront. To some this sounds like hocus-pocus, but virtually all realms of science are beginning to establish that these kinds of connections are, indeed, detectable. The Swiss psychologist Carl Jung talked about a collective unconscious that links us to a common sense of humanity, but more recent research has begun to quite demonstrably establish this connection. In the biological sciences, it is often referred to as a morphic or morphogenic field, which is a connection that has been established between units of a certain group that creates a kind of "tuning in" to the overall sense of the group. In philosophy, it has been referred to as a "zeitgeist," or a general atmosphere that conveys a particular mood or ambience, or cultural, spiritual, or political climate. In quantum physics, it is referred to as "entanglement" or "nonlocal connection," a phenomenon that has been demonstrated to show that some quantum particles influence others without any apparent connection.

One of the more popular references to this connection was described as "The Hundredth Monkey," a description that comes from the observation of a pattern of behavior in nature:

> The Japanese monkey, *Macaca fuscata*, has been observed in the wild for a period of over thirty years. In 1952, on the island of Koshima, scientists were providing monkeys with sweet potatoes dropped in the sand. The monkeys liked the taste of the raw sweet potatoes, but they found the dirt unpleasant.
>
> An eighteen-month-old female named Imo found she could solve the problem by washing the potatoes in a nearby stream. She taught this trick to her mother. Her playmates also learned this new way and they taught their mothers, too.
>
> This cultural innovation was gradually picked up by various monkeys before the eyes of the scientists. Between 1952 and 1958, all the young monkeys learned to wash the sandy sweet potatoes to make them more palatable. Only the adults who imitated their children learned this social improvement. Other adults kept eating the dirty sweet potatoes. Then something startling took place. In the autumn of 1958, a certain number of Koshima monkeys were washing sweet potatoes—the exact number is not known. Let us suppose that when the sun rose one morning there were ninety-nine monkeys on Koshima Island who had learned to wash their sweet potatoes. Let's further suppose that later that morning, the hundredth monkey learned to wash potatoes. THEN IT HAPPENED!
>
> By the evening almost everyone in the tribe was washing sweet potatoes before eating them. The added energy of this hundredth monkey somehow created an ideological breakthrough! But notice. A most surprising thing observed by these scientists was that the habit of washing sweet potatoes then jumped over the sea. Colonies of monkeys on other islands and the mainland troop of monkeys at Takasakiyama began washing their sweet potatoes![3]

Call it what we will, but most of us have had a sense of it. We often refer to it as "something in the air." It can create a sense of a collective will in which an entire group colludes in acting a certain way in regard to a certain situation. We know that we have had the experience ourselves. We have, or notice that certain individuals have, a point of view about something. Several other people pick up the idea and soon some critical mass is achieved, although nobody quite knows how many or when it occurs, and all of a sudden it seems like *everybody* is thinking that way. It becomes a new meme. It happens regularly in what we call fads. Why, for example, did Cabbage Patch dolls or the other "it" toys become all the rage a number of years ago, long before most people had ever seen a commercial about the toys? We have our personal concerns at the same time as we adopt a set of cultural concerns that affect all of us, sometimes without a clear sense of how things happen.

In this age of technological communication, it happens faster than ever. Things can go from unknown to omnipresent overnight. On April 11, 2009, Susan Boyle, an obscure contestant on the television show *Britain's Got Talent*, sang a surprisingly moving version of the song "I Dreamed a Dream" from *Les Miserables*. Within two weeks, the YouTube video of the performance had been viewed more than 150 million times! The rapid proliferation of these occurrences has become so frequent that they have been called "technomemes." Another example took place on January 9, 2010, when, as the *Washington Post* reported:

> The world awoke Friday to discover that Davi's bra is black. Janet's is blue with bows. Kim's is pink. And Susan's is "decadent beige." Throughout the day, on Facebook pages across the globe, hundreds of thousands of women were freely, willingly, even gleefully sharing the color of the bras they were wearing—without really knowing exactly why they were doing so. It was no game to the people at the Susan G. Komen Breast Cancer Foundation, who were stunned to find themselves the beneficiaries of a web phenomenon they didn't begin to understand. At the start of Friday, they had exactly 135 fans on their Facebook page. By 5:30 in the evening, they had 135,000.[4]

Our current environment makes this sense of connection stronger than ever, yet while we share many of the same concerns with others around us, we often insist upon taking them personally. As I've stated, the fact that they do affect us personally does not make them a personal phenomenon.

As a result of our lack of consciousness about our connectedness, decisions are made personally, rather than from the perspective of our social systems. We decide based on our perception of the immediate impact of a decision on us but not on the basis of the overall systemic implications on other people and on our organization.

Decisions that are made without thinking from a systems perspective are fraught with potential potholes because our orientation toward "belonging" can lead us to be the proverbial "lemmings to the sea." Stanley Milgram demonstrated this with the experiments I described in chapter 4. It is the same dynamic that allowed the Nazis to be successful in turning arguably the most cultured civilization on the planet into a killing machine. It also allowed citizens of the United States to somehow justify and participate in slavery and the genocide of Native American Indians. How does this happen?

Hannah Arendt wrote of this phenomenon in her coverage of the Adolf Eichmann trial in Jerusalem in 1961. Arendt was sent by the *New Yorker* to cover the trial and fully expected to find Eichmann an evil man. After all, he had clearly been a major player in what most people would agree was one of the most significant crimes in history. However, what she found was very different. Eichmann was not only less frightening than she anticipated he would be, he was also strikingly unimpressive. She chose to subtitle her piece "A Report on the Banality of Evil" because he struck her as a bureaucrat who she felt was best described as "banal," which is defined by the dictionary as "unaffecting and drearily predictable." In her story, she described her experience of him in this way:

> Eichmann was not Iago, nor Macbeth, and nothing would have been farther from his mind than to determine with Richard III "to prove a villain." Except for an extraordinary diligence in looking out for his personal advancement, he had no motives at all. And this diligence in itself was in no way criminal; he certainly would never have murdered his superior in order to inherit his post. He *merely*, to put the matter colloquially, *never realized what he was doing.* . . . He was not stupid. It was sheer thoughtlessness—something by no means identical with stupidity—that predisposed him to become one of the greatest criminals of that period. And if this is "banal" and even funny, if with the best will in the world one cannot extract any diabolical or demonic profundity from Eichmann, that is still far from calling it commonplace. That such remoteness from reality and such thoughtlessness can wreak more havoc than all the evil instincts taken together which, perhaps, are inherent in man, that was, in fact, the lesson one could learn in Jerusalem.[5]

The "banality of evil" that Arendt describes is exactly the point. It is a serious mistake to assume a moral understanding of the motivation of people who sometimes are committing even the most horrendous of crimes. That is not to suggest that there is any excuse for the crimes, or that we should be any less committed to intervene, to discipline, or to find whatever way necessary to stop the behavior involved. However, we should know when the behavior is the function of an individual with a seemingly aberrant moral code *and when it is the result of a systemic shift in values, priorities and norms, which, in the context of those within the system, make perfect sense.*

I can almost hear, as I write these words, this being misinterpreted by some to sound like an apology for criminal behavior. It is not. It is a way to understand what motivates that behavior so that we can find a way to intervene in it.

It would be foolish for us to believe that these kinds of patterns exist everywhere in society but do not exist in our organizations. In fact, there is every reason to believe that the organization is the place where most of humankind's pathology plays itself out. After all, as an adult, where do we find our richest source of authority figures to rebel against? Where do we find the greatest demands on our time? Where do we feel the most powerless and the most like we are going through the motions at somebody else's whims? Probably in our work environment. Therefore, it is no surprise that people act out their inherent issues in the organizational environment. The good news is that our tendency to follow the crowd also can be a source of extraordinary good, as when millions of people contributed hundreds of millions of dollars to Haitian earthquake relief in 2010, even in the midst of a historic recession. Such giving became "the way we do things around here." It represents the power of a true sense of inclusive community that expands even past national borders.

Organizational cultures are communicated to us through the external behaviors of people and the symbols and artifacts that we see, but that is just what is on the surface. Like the proverbial iceberg, underneath the surface are ideology, schema, and mental models that define what we really believe and *feel* as an organization. Unfortunately, in most organizations we are not conscious of this connection. In fact, for the most part we don't experience a sense of community at all in our organizations. The reality is that too many people exist in organizations that belong to any number of parallel communities. People may work next to each other without experiencing any sense of connection or common purpose. Almost all of us have some people we work with who we relate to better than others, but the notion of the entire workforce as a community seems a pipe dream to most people.

How do we begin to identify the distinctions that allow us to understand our cultures better so that we can move them toward a greater sense of *organizational community*?

CHAPTER 11

The Eight Basic Principles of Organizational Community

> My hope is for us to come together not only embracing shared beliefs and values, but acknowledging our differences in ways that promote respect and appreciation. If we are to emerge from the long shadows that can engulf us, we must talk with each other, come to understand each other, and renew ourselves and our perceptions of each other.
>
> Alma Abdul-Hadi Jaddalah

Key Elements of Organizational Community

In order to gain a better understanding of what "success" looks like, I want to more clearly articulate a sense of what *organizational community* looks like. My experience has taught me there are key elements that exist when what I am calling *organizational community* is present.

These eight elements are present in concert with one another, forming the foundation for the way the organization is to function. None of these is sacrosanct. They are simply core elements that I believe provide the building blocks for developing strong, diverse, inclusive, and culturally competent organizational communities.

1. CLEAR VISION

The word *vision* has been overused to the point of becoming trite, yet when it is well defined and has clear objectives and goals associated with it, it is an essential part of effective *organizational community*. Numerous studies have shown that individuals who set clear goals for themselves produce greater results. The same is true for organizations. A clear picture of the future creates a beacon that drives the behavior of an organization. It helps shape decision-making and resource commitment and provides a benchmark to determine whether or not the organization is on a successful track. Without this clear picture of the future, organizations may be successful in the short term but are rarely so over time. Consider a well-known interchange from Lewis Carroll's classic *Alice's Adventures in Wonderland*, when Alice meets the Cheshire Cat:

> "Would you tell me please, which way I ought to go from here?" asks Alice. "That depends a good deal on where you want to get to," said the cat. "I don't much care where," said Alice. "Then it doesn't matter which way you go," said the cat.[1]

The vision keeps us focused and helps us stay on target. It includes the clear set of values that the organization holds dear. It also plays an additional role in creating *organizational community*. It serves as a source of inspiration and alignment for people within the organization. It gives people an opportunity to understand clearly where the organization is headed and determine whether they want to be a part of that future.

Yet, where our vision for a diverse and inclusive organization is concerned, we are terrified of "quotas." We resist speaking our clear commitment to a definable vision because we are afraid that we will encounter resistance in our attempts to change the representational structure of an organization, even when that representational structure clearly is out of balance with our societal, community, and, in most cases, customer demographics. In a business sense, there is no logic to this resistance, but as we have seen earlier and shall see in later chapters, this is not a rational reaction but a visceral one.

A well-thought-out, committed vision has power not only when people act consistently with it, but also when they do not. The chief executive officer of a major hospital I worked with recalled:

> When we developed the vision for our organization, it was clear to us that we had to build a way of working together in which we held each other much more accountable than we ever had done in the past. Everybody on our management team knew that this would be essential to our success. Yet even after we had established that, I found that people, myself included, seemed unable to make this transition. The difference, I began to realize, was that while before I would avoid confronting things that needed to be dealt with and hardly even notice it, I now found my lack of action so glaring that it was bothersome. The fact that we had "raised the bar" made the gap

between what we said we wanted and what we were doing so obvious
that we had to act on it. And we started to move.

This kind of reaction is particularly present in the most ingrained patterns of
organizational behavior, and in the most serious. There are things that we do
so regularly, have done for so long, or want so desperately to avoid confronting
(denial, after all, is not just a river in Egypt) that they become concealed by their
own obviousness, like the proverbial water to the fish—always present, always
influencing, yet less and less noticeable until they virtually disappear. As John
Gardner, the founder of Common Cause, once said:

> When organizations are not meeting that challenge of change, it is as
> a rule not because they can't solve their problems, but because they
> won't see their problems; not because they don't know their faults,
> but because they rationalize them as virtues or necessities.[2]

One of the most difficult questions that leaders confront is how bold they may
be in creating their vision of the organization. If the vision is too far out of people's
experience, it can live as a pipe dream, seemingly unattainable. On the other hand,
if it is not bold enough, it will not inspire and direct the organization. The key is
in establishing the right level of what Robert Fritz refers to as "creative tension."[3]

Creative tension is established when the people within an organization
have both a clear sense of the current culture of the organization and a clearly
established vision of the future. The tension between the two forces the organization to a point of action. This dynamic is as real in social movements as
it is in organizational change. As Dr. Martin Luther King Jr. once famously
wrote:

> You may well ask, "Why direct action? Why sit-ins, marches, etc.? Isn't
> negotiation a better path?" You are exactly right in your call for nego-
> tiation. Indeed, this is the purpose of direct action. Nonviolent direct
> action seeks to create such a crisis and establish such creative tension
> that a community that has constantly refused to negotiate is forced to
> confront the issue. It seeks so to dramatize the issue that it can no longer
> be ignored. I just referred to the creation of tension as a part of the work
> of the nonviolent resister. This may sound rather shocking. But I must
> confess that I am not afraid of the word tension. I have earnestly worked
> and preached against violent tension, but there is a type of constructive
> nonviolent tension that is necessary for growth. Just as Socrates felt it
> was necessary to create a tension in the mind so that individuals could
> rise from the bondage of myths and half-truths to the unfettered realm
> of creative analysis and objective appraisal, we must see the need to cre-
> ate the kind of tension in society that will help men to rise from the dark

depths of prejudice and racism to the majestic heights of understanding and brotherhood.[4]

Dr. King saw the tension not as something that needed to be tolerated for people to move forward, *but rather as something that is an essential part of people moving forward.* He also recognized that there are two fundamental components without which the tension cannot exist. People must have an uplifting view of the future that inspires them as well as a clearly defined sense of the current reality. He had a dream, but he also felt a critical need to educate people as to the current conditions that existed.

This relationship between the two is vital. If we look at most examples of dramatic change, on almost any level, we find that someone had a sense of a new possibility for the future that he or she was creating. In some cases, as with Dr. King, that future was clearly defined and articulated ("I have a dream"). In other cases, the articulation of the future may not have been so clear, but the vision was clearly present. It is an accurate understanding of the current reality that allows people to make the changes they have to make in order to move forward.

In my experience this is particularly important when building a culture focused on diversity and inclusion because so much of the work that has been done in this area has been about fixing what is, rather than about creating what might be. But creative tension cannot be generated from vision alone; it requires an accurate picture of current reality as well. Vision that is not grounded in a realistic understanding of current reality will more likely foster cynicism rather than creativity.

The role of the leader is to keep the organization focused on dealing with the current reality *in the context of the vision of the future.* This is an important distinction. Getting in and resolving the concerns that exist will have only minimal impact on the organization. Leaders must have their eyes on the kind of organization they are trying to create and evaluate every concern that occurs in the current reality against that vision in determining how to act.

Fixing the problems will not change the organization. In fact, it is likely to simply fill the leaders' plate with more problems to fix. This is why systems thinking becomes so important. If we are merely correcting problems, we have missed the inescapable observation that there is something that is *causing the problems that must be addressed.* Many leaders have gotten so good at fixing problems that a problem-free environment offers no satisfaction. Give them a good crisis, and they're on their way.

It is in changing the system, fundamentally altering the way people are relating and working together, that the problems will begin to shift.

It is the charge of leaders to create an image of the future for people within the organization, but total success is rarely realized if people are not engaged in the process themselves to some degree. When *organizational community* is present, people know what the organization is about, where it is headed, and what it will look like when they arrive.

What is the vision for your diversity effort? Is it clearly articulated throughout your organization or community group? Are people aligned on that vision? Does it connect directly to the "business" of the organization?

2. FINANCIAL SECURITY AND RESULTS

Organizations exist for a purpose. This purpose drives the formation, development, and day-to-day operation of any company, nonprofit, and so on. No process to transform the organization can hope to succeed unless it is driven by the desire for the organization to win, and organizations win by producing the results they are shooting for.

Financial security is of paramount importance to the existence of *organizational community*. Our own experience and historical evidence demonstrates clearly that community breaks down when people are financially insecure. On a societal level, recessions yield increases in crime, race-related incidents, suicide, and depression. Most great historical upheavals (e.g., the Russian Revolution, the rise of Nazism, the American Revolution, and our own Civil War) were motivated by some combination of either immediate or feared economic concerns. The rise of the Tea Party shortly after the financial crash of 2008 is no exception.

In corporations, which are in existence to make money, financial insecurity creates conflict in management and between management and workers. In addition, a sense of loyalty, energy, and commitment diminishes. Innovation slows to a halt. In every way, the stability and productivity of the company suffers.

The interesting thing is that these same dynamics also occur in institutions that are not profit driven. Nonprofit organizations often make the mistake of not keeping enough attention on their fiscal viability and, as a result, are unable to be as successful as they want and need to be in order to survive and achieve their missions. In addition, the very existence of some organizations has been threatened by a loss in credibility due to financial mismanagement.

For a vibrant sense of community to exist, people within the group have to experience a sense that they are now, or have a chance of being, successful in producing the results they have come together to address. There is no mystery to this idea. We want to be winners. We want to know that our efforts are making a difference in the areas to which we are directing our energies. This is why it is so important to be able to build the business case for diversity, inclusion, and cultural competency in a clear, concise, and viable way *that speaks to the concerns of the dominant cultures within the organization.* Unless we are able to accomplish this, we will generate at best only tepid agreement.

What are the compelling financial drivers of your diversity effort? Have you been able to establish the return on investment to your organization? Are there future diversity-related trends that may impact the organization financially?

3. COMMON VALUES AND BEHAVIOR NORMS

To feel safe and connected, we must have a sense that we share a common frame of reference with those around us. When we know that we have agreed-upon standards, we are freed to participate more fully with each other. *Organizational community* values should be clearly articulated and understood by all members of the organization. They provide assurance that there is an ethical code with which I can feel comfortable and by which I can agree to abide.

At the same time, hundreds of organizations have well-drawn-out, articulately written value statements that live as writing on a piece of paper on the wall because nobody has distinguished clear norms of behavior within the organization that coincide with those values.

Behavior norms are critical to the development of *organizational community*. They are the way things happen. They are the expected and accepted behaviors within an organization. They tell us, informally as well as formally, the way we should act and the way we can expect others to act. They may be positive or negative. History provides dramatic examples.

In the cases of the treatment of Native American Indians, African-born slaves, Jews in the Holocaust, or during the trial of Lieutenant William Calley Jr. for Vietnam War crimes, we have seen circumstances in which behavior that we would judge to be unacceptable by almost any societal standard became "normal," ordinary, and in many cases, accepted.

We see this in organizations every day. The staff meeting that everybody arrives at ten or fifteen minutes late. The pencils or pads of paper that everybody feels are okay to take home. The issues that never get discussed because, as one of my clients once told me, "We just don't talk about things like that around here and we don't even talk about the fact that we don't talk about it!"[5] Organizations are flooded with negative behaviors that become standard operating procedure. In fact, the power of normative influence is so strong that positive behavior becomes aberrant and begins to appear threatening.

A college friend of mine worked one summer during college as a substitute mail carrier, hired to fill in for regulars on their vacation. He liked the job because the demands were fairly light and he liked being outside every day. During the first week he found that as he became more comfortable with the job, he was finishing his route by lunchtime, approximately three hours before he was scheduled to go home, and fully two and one-half hours before he was due back at the post office. Wanting to please his supervisor, he reported back and asked where he might be of help. The next morning, one of the regular mail carriers physically pulled him aside and told him, in no uncertain terms, that the route took the full day to do. My friend informed the man that he had, in fact, covered the whole route. The reply surprised him: "I don't care how you do it, what errands you run, or where you take your nap, but from now on that route takes a full day. Understood?" My friend, a very quick learner, understood completely. He did a lot of reading that summer.

In most cases, the reaction is more subtle but nonetheless very clear. Most of us have also seen examples of positive norms in action. A fourth-year medical student reported:

> When I lived in our old neighborhood, and went to the local school, none of the kids really cared much about grades. The attention was much more focused on sports, or partying. It was hard to get into studying. In fact, if you studied too much you were likely to be considered a little "geeky." I got mostly B's with an occasional A or C. Then we moved and I switched to a new school. *Everybody* studied. The grades you got really had a lot to do with your social standing. People studied alone, or in groups. They even had study parties! One sure way to be seen as an outsider was to slip up on your grades. I almost immediately jumped to mostly A's with a few B's. Looking back at it now it's so obvious, but at the time I just kind of went along with the flow. The reality is that had I not switched schools, I probably wouldn't be in medical school today!

When *organizational community* is practiced, positive norms of behavior are congruent with the organization's values. They are discussed and aligned with by all people within the organization.

Are the values that support your diversity effort clearly established and articulated within the organization? Is it clear how diversity and inclusion are consistent with your organization's values? Are there clear behaviors associated with the diversity effort that people are held accountable for?

4. LEADERSHIP

Surely there have been few topics more broadly explored and invested in than organizational leadership. Books on the topic line the shelves of stores and fill pages of catalogs. Films, videos, and course after course teach the path to effective leadership. Yet somehow, again despite our best efforts, we end up not with a new paradigm of leadership but with some new skills that enable us, at best, to be a little better. This occurs in a changing and challenging environment where we desperately need to be and do *a lot* better.

To create breakthroughs in their organizations, leaders will have to create breakthroughs in their own ways of thinking and being. The challenge is especially

difficult because leaders, almost by definition, are people who have been successful in the old ways of doing things.

Leaders must demonstrate the ability to design and produce a new future,
create the power to use relationships in ways that enhance and sustain individuals and organizations, and possess the freedom to explore, investigate, develop,
and motivate. This is a challenge for leaders who have been trained that the way
to lead is to command and control. Within *organizational community*, leaders
learn to conquer fear and embrace change, and to see the past and present as a
stepping-stone to the future, not a limitation of it.

In the context of *organizational community*, leadership is demonstrated not
only in the titular heads of the organization but throughout the organization.
Employees are called to participate by demonstrating leadership in their areas
of influence and by accepting responsibility for the success of the organization.
A new relationship must be created between employees and their organizations. It is all too easy for employees to sit back and wait for the organization
to fix things or to be taken care of by someone else. Employees at all levels
must lead the way.

Is it clear what true diversity leadership looks like in your organization?

"After a thirty-year career in fast-growth retailing and over ten years
as a private equity investor I have always strived to create an inclusive culture that supports the community of the company I have
been associated with. As a leader I have used a simple but effective
guide (people, brand excellence, and profits) to align any community with a focus and power to create sustainable value creation.
Empowered people create long-lasting and successful brands, which
lead to maximizing profits.

"Empowering any organizational community starts with respect
and treating everyone with dignity, but the power comes from the
collective actions of the entire team to raise the bar for the organization every day. In any consumer-oriented environment with millions
of transactions and customer interactions, even if we are 90 percent
in our execution, the 10 percent in which we are less successful can
create havoc and likely not even be recognized by senior management. But if an organizational community feels empowered, appreciated, and recognized for its extra efforts, great things happen,
exceeding consumer and employee expectations and creating not
only great brands but also the most valuable businesses."

Henry Nasella
Cofounder and Partner
LNK Partners
Former President, Staples

5. COMMUNICATION

We classically think of communication as any number of things. How do we share information? How do people find out about things in our organization? What do they find out about? Do we speak clearly, professionally, and in a way that motivates? Are we effective listeners? How do we present ourselves?

All of these skills are important and valuable, yet for some reason no matter how many courses we put people through, we still don't seem able to create the kind of extraordinary breakthroughs that we want. What if communication was something far more? What if the people in our organizations could be provided with a toolbox of linguistic skills that enabled them to more effectively manage their daily interactions in a way that produced dramatically different results?

Are the people in your organization included in the conversations that affect them? Do they all get the information they need to do their jobs effectively? Are there some people who are more "in the loop" than others?

6. SERVICE

Every organization's success relies on its ability to serve somebody. A business needs to serve its clients. Governmental organizations need to serve their communities and other agencies. Hospitals need to serve patients, guests, physicians, and so on. Nonprofits need to serve their communities of focus as well as their boards of directors. The challenge is that too few organizations are clear about what that service looks like, what standards are in place, and how we measure that service.

Organizational communities are very service oriented. That requires both the focus and the information to meet the needs of community members. It also requires the cultural competence to know how different community members will respond to their service based on their racial, cultural, and ethnic or other distinct backgrounds.

How does the diversity of your organization impact its ability to serve its customers? Do you have a base of customers from different demographic groups with special needs? Are the people in your organization aware of how to serve their customers?

7. KNOWLEDGE SHARING

One of the great challenges in many organizations is a tendency toward a "need-to-know" orientation. We give people only a limited idea of what is going on, what decisions are based on, what concerns leadership has, and then we are surprised when rumor mills and misunderstandings flourish. My experience has been that the human mind abhors a vacuum, and when presented with a vacuum of information, we will try to fill it.

Within *organizational community* we have learned that transparency plays a critical role in keeping people engaged and helps them see how their personal area of responsibility affects the whole of the organization. People who think that their work makes a difference in the organization are inherently more invested. They are also more trusting, and, as my friend Dr. Leon Butler has said, trust is to human systems as energy is to physics and cells are to biology.

Of course, there are times when certain information cannot be shared, sometimes even for legal reasons. These times should be minimized as much as possible, but even then we can tell people *what we don't know* as a way of keeping them in the loop. Most of us have been on airplanes that were stuck on a runway while nobody tells us what's going on. We sit there stewing. Then at other times, the pilot or flight attendants occasionally tell us, "I haven't found anything out yet but I'll let you know as soon as I do," and our whole internal system calms. The same thing is true for companies even in the most tense of times.

A number of years ago I was working with two companies that were merging, helping them create synergy between their two cultures. In the case of mergers there are actual legal restrictions about what can be shared with employees. I was facilitating a meeting of about two hundred mid-level managers with one of the senior vice presidents of the company in which several people were complaining about not knowing what was going on when one manager said, "My boss tells us everything." The senior vice president and I looked at each other, wondering whether there were going to be concerns about information that had been improperly exposed and then made a point of approaching the manager after the meeting and asking him what he was talking about in specifics. "Every morning," he reported, "our manager brings us together for a huddle. He tells us everything he knows and everything he doesn't. Then we get on with our day."

He knew nothing more than anybody else, it turned out, but he was confident that he was "in the loop."

Is knowledge in your organization widely shared? Is there a sense of transparency that generates trust or a sense that only certain people know what's going on?

8. INCLUSIVENESS, COLLABORATION, AND CONFLICT

I believe that one of the great challenges we face in most of our organizations, and in fact on our planet, is the myth of separation. We act as if we are separate individuals, separate families, separate companies, cities, and countries. We seem to believe that what happens "to them" or "over there" is not our concern. This creates enormous breakdowns when our behavior impacts others or theirs affects ours in ways that we don't see. Worldwide health epidemics and financial breakdowns should teach us how untrue this is in reality. More than ever before we share a common destiny. I'm not talking about singing "Kumbaya" here. I'm talking about systems thinking.

That is another reason why diversity and inclusion are so important. Of course, people should be treated fairly and justly. Such treatment is an essential American value. But as Scott Page found in the research I cited earlier, inclusion also produces better results. I was in a strategy meeting once with the leadership team of one of my clients. We had been working for hours and had drawn diagrams on the board about the way that certain aspects of their business process worked. At lunchtime, one of the administrative team members brought in the lunch. While he was in the room he was looking at the board. "Any questions?" the chief executive officer asked, noticing him looking. "Yes," he responded, "why is this over here rather than over there?" Everybody in the room stopped. He had uncovered a possibility that nobody else had really thought about because they were so much a part of the system as it had been designed in the past.

I could cite hundreds of examples of breakthroughs that have come from sources other than we might expect. One good example is the invention of the octet truss, a structural framework that is widely used in modern architecture. It was invented by a remarkable twentieth-century engineer and futurist named R. Buckminster Fuller, who is probably best known for his invention of the geodesic dome. Fuller came up with the idea for the dome as a child. He was given toothpicks and half-dried peas to use as toys. Fuller was effectively blind as a child, until he received glasses some time later. As a result, he did not make the same assumptions that most of his classmates did, that things were generally cubic in shape. The other children built what they had seen. Fuller later said that he built what seemed strongest. As a result he stumbled across a system of alternating octehdra and tetrahedra, which would become the basis of his work and which would transform architecture.

Had Fuller had the same history of visual reference that his classmates had—that is, if he had been able to see the "right" way to build a structure—he probably would not have experimented at all. Instead, he was forced to explore and discover and, in doing so, created a possibility that had not yet been discovered.

If we accept the notion that inclusiveness and interdependence are healthy for an organization, than we also have to understand that it is not our nature to work and act that way. The individualistic mental models that our culture has been built on actually discourage people from collaborating as much as they encourage it.

Structure creates behavior in organizations. In organizational communities we build structures for collaboration. People are engaged in regular dialogue in which they inquire into areas of importance rather than simply being informed of such areas. Feedback practices are developed, and people are encouraged to give their input. One of the great fears that many leaders have is that if they ask employees for their opinions about things and then don't agree and do the opposite, employees will be upset. Of course, sometimes that can happen. However, my experience has been overwhelmingly the opposite. When employees are involved and engaged in decisions that impact them and are given the opportunity to collaboratively work on organizational challenges, and when they feel like their leaders are genuinely listening and take the time to explain their thinking and the motivation for their ultimate decisions, they usually are more comfortable and supportive of the decisions that are made. This is true even when they didn't agree with the original ideas.

How inclusive is your organization? Are wide ranges of viewpoints encouraged, or are people more likely told (verbally or not) that they should "mind their own business?" Is healthy conflict advocated or avoided?

Organizational leaders sometimes express concern that the mass of employees may come up with a different set of values than the ones the leaders will on their own—that the organization will have to compromise itself. My experience in working with groups like this gives me two responses.

First, if that is the case, it is revealing a significant undercurrent of disassociation with the organization that is best brought out to the surface and addressed. An organization in which employees are that out of touch with the basic values of its leadership is an organization in serious trouble far beyond its vision statement. The surfacing of this dissonance could be the very thing that is needed to get the underlying issues on the table and deal with them right away.

However, and this is the second response, my experience shows that this difference in values rarely occurs. In fact, in group after group, I find that when people are given the freedom to create the kind of organization they want to work in, when they are acknowledged by the process for being responsible for that creation, their efforts are rarely less than inspiring. People seem to choose to create a vision far beyond what most of the leaders would be willing to go after. They create values that are geared toward diversity, inclusion, quality, service, and relationship, and they do so with a spirit that is driven by the elation of having the opportunity to have a say in their own lives. While the voice of cynicism often appears, it is remarkable how consistently one is drawn to conclude that people who feel valued and included speak to the good and expansive in us far more than they do to our limitations.

If we look at times when employees act in destructive ways, it is almost always in situations when they feel powerless to impact the organization in a positive manner. If I have no voice, I will find one through poor-quality work, laziness, work stoppages, or subtle or not so subtle sabotage. The message is clear: "I will be noticed." Power shared does not have to be taken in negative forms.

One important aspect of this is creating a culture in which people develop the ability to engage in constructive conflict. In the early stages of *organizational community*, people will usually create what Scott Peck has referred to as pseudocommunity.[6] A patina of harmony is created that allows people the illusion that they are functioning as a community but is actually a commitment to avoid conflict and controversy. People who are enlivened by the positive nature of the relationships they have created are afraid to allow conflict and controversy into the picture because it is perceived that it might "spoil" everything. Unfortunately, this has the same impact as the Zen story about the man who tries to hold onto the butterfly that alights on his hand and crushes it in the process.

True community includes conflict. It allows for conflicts and controversy to be aired, engaged in, and resolved. When conflict is not aired, it festers. Because it has not been voiced it cannot be resolved, and because it is not resolved it quickly begins to undermine the essential practices and relationships of the organization. Bringing up issues is difficult but essential in order for community to exist. This requires both personal and group work. And it also requires clear boundaries that can create a container for constructive conflict to occur in.

As I said earlier, these are core principles, not commandments. You may have your own basic principles as well. I have found that organizations that follow these particular principles create environments that thrive.

The answer to the question of how we reinvent these patterns lies in a deeper understanding of the paradigms that have dominated our diversity efforts and in the background that drives the way we look at diversity.

Building Blocks of Culture

In my work, I've discovered that there are twelve distinctions that we might refer to as "building blocks" of culture in organizations. These can function as lenses, if you will, that allow us to get a better understanding of the culture of our organizations. These building blocks can be monitored and measured and help us understand the conscious and unconscious ways our organizations function. My experience has been that inquiring into these questions in and of itself begins to create a greater sense of clarity and alignment within an organization.

1. ORGANIZATIONAL FOCUS

Why does the organization exist? What is it meant to accomplish? What are its core values? How do diversity, inclusion, and cultural competency contribute to that?

These questions lead us to a deeper understanding of how an organization functions. The answers might be different for each organization. These questions ultimately define what the organization stands for and what it is doing. The answers, though, may not be found on the poster on the wall that some consultants and marketing people designed. They live in the willingness to tell the truth about what *really* drives the organization.

I often see organizations where leaders profess a commitment to diversity and inclusion, but it is nowhere to be found in their mission or value statements, and there is no clear explanation as to how it contributes to what they exist to accomplish. Bad idea!

Once people understand these answers, they lead to the following questions: How do members of the organizational community contribute to that kind of thinking? Where should the organization's attention and resources be directed right now? Where should they be in the future?

2. LEADERSHIP

How do the organization's leaders reinforce the direction and mood of the organization? Where do they miss out on opportunities to do as much? What behaviors do we expect from the organization's leaders? How do they demonstrate their commitment to diversity, inclusion, and cultural competency? What are the strengths of leaders in the organization? What are their weaknesses? How do leaders relate to one another? Are the leaders in the organization admired as role models?

Leaders are critical to establishing an inclusive organizational culture. Members of the organizational community watch their leaders to determine what the organization is *really* about. When there is dissonance between leadership behavior and the stated organizational purpose, there is no question which has more weight. We can be reminded of Ralph Waldo Emerson's famous saying: "Who you are speaks so loudly I can't hear a word you're saying."

It also is important to get a sense of the less formal leadership of the organization. Who are the people who have influence? Who are the people who are celebrated within the organization: internal and external "she-roes" and heroes? And who are the skeptics: the people who can, and will, derail the initiative unless they are brought into the tent?

I once had a conversation with the chief financial officer of a client hospital. He was directly responsible for more than three hundred people and saw the diversity efforts as "touchy-feely BS." I told him that I understood his concern and thought it would be really helpful for him to come to the diversity task force meeting and share it. At first he declined, saying, "They don't care what I think." I responded, "Are you sure?" His expression changed dramatically when he asked whether I thought they really might care. I suggested he come and find out. He ended up sharing a lot of very real concerns that contributed to the effort being designed in a way that allowed it to work.

3. STRUCTURE

If structure creates behavior in organizations, what are the strengths in the way the organization is structured in terms of creating a diverse, inclusive, culturally competent culture? What are the drawbacks in the present structure? What structural changes need to be made? Do people have a clear sense of their roles and responsibilities? Do people have a clear sense of the business flow of the organization and how it is affected by diversity? Is the business flow consistent with producing the results the organization wants? Do the policies and procedures of the organization support its success?

We recently worked with a large university that was beginning a global graduate program and had almost one hundred students from almost twenty countries. We were helping the students understand their different cultural orientations to things such as classroom participation when one of the white Americans said, "I can hear what you're saying and it makes sense that our culture is more extroverted than some others, but 20 percent of our grade is based on classroom participation." The structure of the grading system was encouraging students to do the exact opposite from the more culturally competent behavior we were encouraging.

4. FINANCIAL HEALTH

What is the overall financial health of the organization, and how is it impacted by diversity, inclusion, and cultural competency? How does the organization make money, and what potential is there for diversity to contribute to the organization's financial health? What are the major expenditures of the organization? Are there ways that diversity, inclusion, and cultural competency can increase revenue or decrease expenditures?

What does where we put our money tell us about our commitment? The leaders in one organization I worked with talked all the time about their commitment to training and development, but when you looked at their budgets there were no resources allocated for it and no metrics to measure it. No big surprise to see the results of that financial structure.

5. INTERNAL AND EXTERNAL FORCES

Are there external concerns that are now affecting, or will soon affect, the organization's ability to be successful? How do diversity-related issues affect those concerns? Are there internal concerns that are now affecting, or will soon affect, the organization's ability to be successful? How do diversity-related issues impact those concerns? How is the marketplace changing? Will the organization have to do things differently in order to be successful in the future? What and when?

After September 11, 2001, many of the health-care organizations we were working with expressed concerns about the number of patients who said they didn't want to be treated by Arab or Muslim nurses or house physicians. It was not a localized issue, but a generalized, societal one. We helped the hospitals learn how to surface the concern and address it.

6. ORGANIZATIONAL MOOD

What is the general mood of the organization? What is it like to work there on a day-to-day basis? What emotions come to mind? What is the mood of employees like? Is it the same for all of the employees, or are some more satisfied than others? Are people in the organization optimistic? Pessimistic? Cynical? Happy? Angry? Sad?

There are times when you encounter an organizational culture in which anything seems possible. One of my clients in the food market industry has such a culture. Other clients have cultures that make it seem like anything will be a struggle. I've found that it is important for the mood to be looked at honestly and addressed. The simple act of turning complaints into requests can begin to transform an organizational culture.

7. RELATIONSHIPS (INTERNAL AND EXTERNAL)

What is the quality of communication and interactions between people within the organization? Do people relate well across lines of diverse identity? How well do diverse people collaborate? Do people seem to recognize their interdependence and work to one another's support and benefit? How do people get along within departments? Between departments? How do different parts of the organization interact? Is the organization aware of its social responsibility and its relationship to outside communities? How do employees relate to customers? What would customers say about the organization? Vendors? Neighbors? Is there any difference between relationships to diverse customer groups? Do people understand how to treat customers with cultural competence, understanding their distinctive cultural needs? Do public relations and marketing reflect an understanding of the diverse communities with which the organization interacts?

This is an especially important area in which to look for subtleties. I remember one organization in which the sales team couldn't work effectively with either the marketing team or the acquisition team because the head of the sales team didn't get along with the other two leaders. Anybody in his team who was seen as cooperating too much was seen as virtually "fraternizing with the enemy."

8. FEEDBACK PROCESSES (INTERNAL/EXTERNAL)

What behavior is rewarded in the organization? Do those rewards go to people from diverse groups? How is behavior considered outside of the desired culture confronted? Are leaders willing to confront customers who show a lack of respect for all associates, regardless of their diversity? How is performance evaluated? Who are the people who are rewarded, and for what? What do people get praised for within the organization? For what do people get criticized? On balance, what is there more of, praise or criticism? Is performance reviewed and feedback given regularly? Do some people get more feedback than others?

One of the challenges that we have discovered where diversity, inclusion, and cultural competency are concerned is that most of the feedback we give people in organizations around their behavior is negative. We tell people far more often what not to do than we tell them what behaviors they can engage in to be considered successful. This often results in people expressing concern about "walking on eggshells." We have to give people clear instruction as to the kinds of things that can build an inclusive, culturally competent culture and then hold them accountable to those behaviors.

9. KNOWLEDGE SHARING

How do people find out about things in the organization? How is knowledge shared? Are people able to benefit from the knowledge of their colleagues? What is the formal and informal communication structure within the organization? Is technology used effectively to keep people inside and outside of the organization informed? How does the organization utilize the collective knowledge of its diverse employee base? What information gets shared, and with whom? What is the quality of communication within the organization? Is everything said that needs to be said? What isn't being said? Who gets heard? Who doesn't get heard? Are certain groups of people "in the loop" more than others?

Many years ago, we had a client for whom we conducted a cultural mapping process. We conducted interviews and focus groups and then designed an online "organizational meme indicator" to allow employees to weigh in with their view of how the organizational culture functioned. One of the questions we asked people to agree or disagree with was this: "In this organization, is it a norm for people to get the information they need to do their jobs effectively?" The overall positive response was around 60 percent, which was not a bad result. However, when we looked at the breakdown by gender, 68 percent of men had responded positively, but only 44 percent of women felt the same way. The findings pointed us to a cultural dynamic. Women, who were about a third of the population, were widely dispersed and had little access to a great deal of what was going on. Identifying these patterns and transforming them had a huge impact on the gender dynamics of the culture.

10. HISTORY/TRADITION

What are the historical origins and traditions of the organization? Of what is the organization most proud? What key significant events have influenced the development of the culture and the organizational focus? What impact does the history have on what the organization is and how it acts today? What are some of the organizational taboos and "sacred cows"? Which of these are spoken, and which are unspoken?

The history of an organization can cast a long shadow on the current issues the organization is facing. One of our client companies almost went bankrupt during the 1970s. We were asked to help them develop a more diverse and inclusive culture after they had run into some challenges more than twenty years later, in the mid-1990s, though they had one of the strongest financial operations in their industry. It was very clear what needed to be done, yet there was resistance to trying almost any new approaches to the way they were doing things. In talking with the key leaders we discovered that the hesitance came from a culture that evolved after the bankruptcy scare. They had developed a conservative culture that was designed to keep them safe *in the 1970s* but was now limiting their growth. When they began to realize how unconscious these organizational patterns were and began to look at them, they were able to change their culture in constructive ways.

11. ORGANIZATIONAL LEARNING

How are people developed in the organization? What kind of orientation is used to clearly communicate what is expected? Does the orientation process do an adequate job of preparing people to work effectively within the organization? What kind of formal or informal career development planning is in place? How does the organization use technology and knowledge sharing to create a learning organization? Is adequate training provided? Which training programs have been particularly effective and beneficial in the past? Which have failed? Why? What kind of training programs are currently being offered, and how effective are they? Is there a need for individual coaching of some key people? Is there a formal or informal mentoring process?

One of the real challenges that organizations have faced in the world of diversity and inclusion has been the proliferation of diversity training programs that seem interesting and valuable on the surface (sometimes!), but are not always tied to the needs of the particular organization. This is especially true with "one-size-fits-all" models. We have found that it is critically important to consider content, process, and delivery in training programs. We find that the content has to be relevant to the work of the organization, and the process has to be a good fit for the culture. The delivery may best be done by outside consultants, or by internal trainers, or by a combination. Sometimes e-learning also can be applied, but any of these must be a good match for the culture

12. PERSONAL SKILLS

How would you assess the overall talent of the organization? What are the strengths people possess? What talents or skills are missing that the organization needs in order to be successful in today's marketplace? To what degree do people in the organization feel a sense of ownership? Do people take responsibility for themselves in the organization? Do people have enough experience to do their jobs well? Are people in the organization willing to look at their own areas for development, or do they place blame on others? Do people do a good job of balancing their work and family concerns? What do people need more or less of to be successful in their job?

The culture of the organization is at the heart of the organizational unconscious. It will ultimately determine the success or failure of our efforts to create more diversity, inclusion, and cultural competency.

How do we change a culture?

Start with your commitment and then, step by step, move into action.

CHAPTER 12

Creating Cultures That Work

> Great things are not done by impulse, but by a series of
> things brought together.
>
> Vincent van Gogh

> As a rule of thumb, involve everyone in everything.
>
> Tom Peters[1]

The good news is that cultures can be transformed. They can be made more vibrant, more inclusive, more alive, and more successful. At a time when it seems like we have a collectively short attention span, it is important to realize that changing an organizational culture is not a project or an activity, but a sustained process of creating a new way of being.

Over the course of my career I have seen some very exciting examples of how organizations have transformed themselves, and I will share one of them later. But first I want to talk about the way we can approach change, and I specifically want to talk about a methodology you can use within your own organization to create a stronger sense of organizational community. It works whether your organization is a hospital, a corporation, a not-for-profit, or an entire community.

I want to emphasize that while this is a complete approach, many of you reading this book are probably already engaged in some kinds of diversity and inclusion efforts. I am not suggesting that you abandon them and start over. On the contrary, it is important to build on efforts rather than abandon them altogether. Yet the question I encourage you to ask is this: "Have our efforts really been producing the results we have sought?" A U.S. Government Accounting Office report issued in October 2010[2] indicated that during the past ten years, women's salaries have increased from 79 percent of what men earn to only 81 percent, and the number of women in management had increased from 40 percent to only 41 percent. Shouldn't we be seeing more dramatic results than that at this point in time?

The simple truth is that most diversity processes do not succeed in changing the culture of the organizations they are trying to change. Parts of them might be successful; they might increase recruiting; people might conduct good training programs that participants gain value from; and marketing may increase to select groups. But rarely do organizations succeed in fundamentally changing the culture into one that is inclusive. The reason for this frustrating phenomenon is not that people do not care. They care very deeply. It's not that they don't spend money, because heaven knows millions of dollars are spent every year. And it's not because people are not smart. At the most basic level, the reason so many diversity efforts fail is because people do not understand change, and that lack of understanding creates a series of roadblocks that stop even the most committed organizations from achieving the success they want.

It may be time to try some new approaches.

Cultures develop patterns of memes that are invented, discovered, or adopted by the people in them to address what seems to be the best way for them to survive at a given time. At some point, though, the memes may take on a life of their own and, like human personalities, work to stay in place. As a background, culture defines the way its members behave and usually is seen as being successful enough that new members are taught to adopt it when they enter society. Thus it sustains itself.

Cultures are always creating themselves. It is the nature of the way they function. The question is, will you consciously create the culture in your organization, or will it unconsciously create itself while you try to survive it?

To bring consciousness to the process, it is important to put a structure in place that organizes the people and resources of the organization to build the kind of culture that you want. It is very much like the metaphor I used earlier regarding losing weight. Very few people sustainably create their personal health by "wanting to" or by trying this or that technique. Sustainable change invariably requires people to put themselves into a new mindset and then onto a new regimen of behaviors that, over time, becomes habitual.

Organizations are the same way. Special programs rarely work because they are predicated on the notion that "once we complete this special program, everything will be okay." As with our health, our ability to truly develop twenty-first-century inclusive and culturally competent organizations depends on our ability to develop a new "lifestyle" for our organization.

Our ability to create change begins with a new mindset. It begins when we realize we have to look at diversity, inclusion, and cultural competency not as something to fix, but as a set of distinctions that our organization can master to increase our productivity and success. And it also begins when we realize that if we want to develop an organization that is inclusive, we have to be inclusive ourselves. That may be what we talk about in a lot of cases, but only rarely do we really act in such a way. When we are willing to do our own work, we will then be prepared to lead. As the old saying goes, you can take people only as far as you are prepared to go yourself. Then we can really understand that most of the behaviors in our organization that stand in the way of what we are trying to create are unconscious and find ways to surface those unconscious drives so that we consciously can develop new ones. And we have to learn to appreciate the nature of the system we inhabit. That's where we can truly create organizational community.

Doing this may not be easy, but if we go about it strategically, it can work. I have created an eight-phase approach that can become an organization's way of being.

The Organizational Community Change Model

The organizational community change model, depicted in figure 12.1, is a process that can help bring the organizational unconscious out of "hiding" and create a course of action to transform an organization's culture.

Figure 12.1

PHASE 1: CREATING A SHIFT IN CONSCIOUSNESS

The foundation for creating a new background of thinking for the organization lies in a shift in consciousness as to how we approach the work of diversity and inclusion. The challenge with too many diversity and inclusion efforts is that they are built on "fixing" the existing culture rather than creating and empowering a vision for the future. I'm not saying that sometimes things don't need to be fixed, because things sometimes do require some fixing. But when that repair process becomes our primary raison d'être, it is not inspiring. At some point, people burn out and move away from the process. The vision should be one that completely integrates diversity, inclusion, and cultural competency into the fabric of the organization, which means it must be aligned with the business of the business.

How do we create a vision? First, leaders and other stakeholders engage in a series of conversations that introduce a contextual framework for the organization's transformation. How do we begin to break through old ways of thinking to create a culturally competent approach that serves all of the stakeholders of the organization?

Actually, there are many ways to do so, but the most successful usually involves gathering a strong, diverse group of people from the organization into an ongoing team that can guide the process. We might call this an organizational community development team (OCDT), or diversity guide team, or organizational culture team, but what you call it is less important than how it functions.

To function effectively, the OCDT should be a microcosm of the organization. That doesn't mean it has to be mathematically configured that way, but it is amazing how often I see diversity leadership groups of one kind or another that are missing key functions of the organization, lacking leadership representation, or have almost no white men in them (within organizations that are predominantly composed of white males). How can that possibly lead to anything other than the team, and therefore the culture change effort, being seen as an outside influence? The team should include a generous grouping of all levels of associates within the organization, including senior leadership to the degree that it is possible.

One of the most important aspects of the development of the OCDT is that the people in the group have an opportunity to create a sense of community among themselves before they start doing their work for the organization. All too often teams come together with the best of intentions but with many different agendas and levels of understanding. The group's efforts are frustrated by the lack of full engagement and alignment. Taking the time to create alignment is critical to the team's success.

There are times when bringing together a larger group can give the effort a real boost. We have often conducted future search conferences as a way to get representatives from the entire organization to align in a new direction. Future search is a model originally created by Marvin Weisbord[3] that allows us to bring large numbers of people together in the room at the same time and create a dramatic shift in the nature of the way people relate to one another and the challenge at hand.

For example, in 2007, we worked with the American Dental Association (ADA) to create a plan to address the dramatic dental disparities among Native American Indians and Alaskan Natives. We gathered at the Tamaya Pueblo Reservation in New Mexico with more than 150 representatives of more than sixty native tribes, the ADA, the Indian Health Service, tribal health practitioners, dental educators, dentists, academics, and an assortment of other stakeholders. In three days, we were collectively able to create a plan that has been in action for the past three years.

> "I came into the Future Search Conference knowing that there was a long history of antipathy between many of the stakeholders in the meeting. Over the course of three days, I watched with increasing admiration as the facilitator repetitively created consensus on point after point from a large group of health-related professionals with diverse titles, backgrounds, goals, experiences and agendas. The room was suffused with high energy, positive thinking and mutual collegial respect. The result was a strategy that is still in action now more than two years later."
>
> Ronald Chez, MD
> Participant in American Dental Association
> Access to Dental Care Summit

There are more ways to create this vision than I have space to describe here, but the key is to create a positive, affirmative vision that people can see and *feel.* That sets the tone for the rest of the process.

PHASE 2: ORGANIZATIONAL DISCOVERY

Once we have a vision as to where we want to go, we have to figure out where we are right now. It's somewhat like going to the mall and looking for the shoe store. If we have never been to the mall before, most of us will start by going to the information map. And the first thing we look for is the arrow that says, "You are here," because without knowing where we are, the map is pretty much worthless to us.

The process of uncovering the organization's unconscious usually involves three major parts: an organizational survey, focus groups, and individual interviews with key players and representatives of various stakeholder groups. The three parts of the process serve as three legs of a stool, supporting one another in getting a good sense as to how the organization functions. The survey, which I like to call an organizational community indicator, is designed to learn about more than people's individual experience. Instead, we ask people how they view the culture. A question might read, "In this organization, people are clear about what they have to do to be successful." Participant's agreement or disagreement levels with the statement help us determine the way the culture functions. In addition, by looking at relative responses by group identity we also can see patterns as to how different groups experience the culture in different ways. We also have conducted similar surveys for customer and community groups in order to get the outside perspective.

As a way of identifying the memes and behavioral patterns of the culture, we have created the Diversity Systems Map™.

The Diversity Systems Map creates an effective template for both viewing the organizational culture and understanding the interaction between various aspects of the culture. It may seem obvious, but I stumbled upon the notion of it some years ago. I had conducted a couple of diversity trainings, which were received very well, for a client company. A few months later I ran into one of the participants. He saw me and immediately began telling me how valuable he thought the training. "How has it been going since then?" I asked him. "You've got to get my boss to do that training!" he replied.

I had heard similar things so many times. The best trainings, recruiting programs, mentoring programs, employee resources groups, and so on that we had helped clients to set up seemed to be enthusiastically received in and of themselves but often didn't have the lasting impact we sought. I began to think about what I had learned about organizational culture development and systems theory and tried to figure out a design for looking at the whole system. Thus, the Diversity Systems Map was born, as shown in figure 12.2.

The Diversity Systems Map provides a way of looking at the various leverage points that can impact organizational diversity and inclusion. It is not meant to be exclusive, as I'm sure there are other ways it could be structured or other elements that might be highlighted. Our experience has been that it provides a very effective structure for looking at an organization holistically and for planning and monitoring diversity and inclusion within the organization. Each of the identified areas has a series of inquiry questions that are designed to help an organization explore it.

The way the map is structured includes four background elements. The first is the *mission, vision, and values* of the company. What does the company really

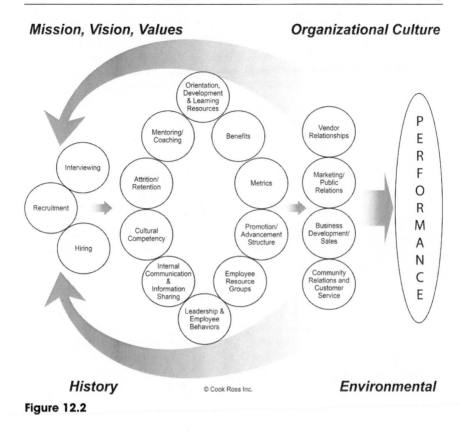

Mission, Vision, Values   **Organizational Culture**

History   © Cook Ross Inc.   **Environmental**

Figure 12.2

stand for, and how does diversity and inclusion fit into that mindset? If diversity and inclusion are not among the stated values of the organization and it is not clear how they fit into the "business of the business," you can be almost assured that it will be viewed as a secondary focus. I'll share some of the questions that we encourage organizations to ask about the company's *mission/vision/values*. You may want to think about them in relation to your own organization.

• Is diversity a stated value in your organization?
• Is there a clear understanding of the business reasons and strategic importance of diversity?
• Does diversity appear in your organization's mission/vision/value statements?
• Is your organization aware of its current state of diversity?
• Is your organization aware of its current vulnerability regarding diversity issues?
• Has your organization issued a definition of diversity?

The second background area focuses on the *organizational culture*. The nature of the culture has a lot to do with the effectiveness of the diversity effort. If the culture is a very left-brain, fact-based culture, diversity must be addressed from that framework. A lot of data must be provided to ensure that people understand the business case. If it is a more affective-oriented culture that has already focused on people's needs within the organization, the diversity efforts can fit well into that mindset. The key is to understand and match your efforts to the cultural pattern. Some of the kinds of questions you might ask include:

- Is your organization's history fully articulated and understood with respect to diversity and its impact on the current culture?
- Does your organization regularly promote cultural understanding and appreciation of differences as a part of its culture?
- To what degree does the culture of your organization focus on human interaction and relationship?
- How open is your culture to new ideas and approaches?
- What are the best ways to transform patterns within your culture?

The third background area of focus is the organization's *history*. As I discussed earlier, events from the history of the organization can teach us a lot about why the organization does things the way it does. One of our client organizations had a major lawsuit filed against it some years ago that resulted in a lot of public scrutiny and embarrassment. Any discussion of diversity had pain associated with it among many of the leaders that had to be addressed before we could move forward. This is especially true since many organizations have pictures of their former leaders lining the walls—and all of them are white men.

To understand the *history*, questions might include:

- Are there historical events that may reflect on the way your organization addresses diversity and inclusion?
- Are there symbols or artifacts within your organization that communicate something about its history with diversity?
- Who are the people who are remembered and celebrated, and what was their history regarding diversity?
- Are there things that have happened in the past that might affect your organization's relationship with change or with trying new approaches to things?

The final background area focuses on the *environment* that the organization and its diversity efforts are occurring within. Environmental issues can have both a dramatic and subtle impact on diversity and inclusion. In October 2008, the collapse of the economy led to a tightening of resources in many organizations and a requisite contraction of some diversity and inclusion efforts. External events such as the O. J. Simpson trial, Hurricane Katrina, or September 11 also created reactions that stimulated discussion or tension among employees. Environmental factors within the company or specific to the company also may affect the outlook. One merger I worked on brought together two companies. One was "all-American," with very few employees who were born outside of the country, and the other was a company that had a vast array of people from all over the world. The two companies had completely different levels of understanding of diversity and culture that had to be addressed in order for the merger to succeed. Company layoffs also can create a sense of tension that might impact diversity and inclusion efforts, even if in an irrational fashion. A factory worker who sees one of his friends laid off might turn a hostile eye to another co-worker who has a "foreign" accent, even if that co-worker is a naturalized citizen who has lived in the United States for thirty years.

Some questions you might ask about the *environment* include:

- Are there things happening in the community or in the world that might impact the culture of your organization?
- Are there things that are happening within your organization that might affect the way people view diversity and inclusion?
- Are there events occurring outside of your organization that your willingness to engage in might impact the way people see diversity within your organization?
- Is there a general mood in the world, the country, the community, or within the organization that might affect the way people experience diversity efforts?

The next group of leverage points, *recruitment, interviewing, and hiring*, focuses on the ways we bring people into our organizations. I often find it fascinating that organizations are so fearful of created diversity hiring goals. They are afraid that the "Q" word (quotas) will be used. Yet what organizational goal doesn't have numbers associated with it? How else are we to know when we are successful and to plan our activities accordingly? These three areas focus on what we are doing to manage patterns of representation throughout the organization.

Recruitment

- Does your organization have clear recruitment goals relating to key diversity areas?
- Are search firms identified who have experience recruiting from target groups?
- Are recruitment areas selected (geographical areas, schools, etc.) that are likely to offer the diversity your organization wants?

- Are media sources used for recruiting that are likely to reach the diverse audiences your organization seeks?
- What is your organization's reputation among members of the nondominant communities it serves?
- Do employees involved in recruiting fully understand all legal issues related to discrimination?
- Are you effectively recruiting in diverse markets?
- Are "pipeline measurements" (the demographics of people applying for jobs) tracked?
- What diversity-associated activities or organizations is your organization affiliated with (e.g., Urban League, Inroads, HBCUs [Historically Black Colleges and Universities], and professional associations for people of color)?
- Are members within diversity groups utilized in recruiting efforts?
- Do your organization's employee resource groups (ERGs) partner in recruitment?

Interviewing

- Are there clear criteria and skills established for the position before the interview process begins?
- What is the skill level required to do the job?
- Are interviewers educated to understand their own biases so that they are less likely to impact the interviewees' opportunities? Can they discuss them with each other?
- Is the interview process structured and monitored in a way that ensures equity?
- Does the interview process include a diverse panel of interviewers?
- Do interviewers understand all legal issues related to discrimination in the interviewing process?

Hiring

- Is the element of bias (especially unconscious) considered and discussed in making final hiring decisions?
- Are hiring patterns observed and tracked?
- Do interviewers understand all legal issues related to discrimination in the hiring process?
- Is there a formal process for communicating the hire/no hire decision?

All of these questions help in determining the goals and process through which people are brought into the organization. Through the years, we have consistently found that structured processes tend to create more equity in organizational processes, while unstructured processes tend to support the organizational status quo and lead to more unconscious behavior.

The large group of ten circles in the middle of the Diversity Systems Map points to some of the things that the organization can focus on within the culture itself. There are many more specifics that I could delineate here, but our experience is that these ten areas are a good place to start.

Orientation, Development, and Learning Resources

How do people learn within the organization? Beginning with the orientation that employees are exposed to, the process of organizational learning is crucial to understanding how employees get the message about what is important in the organization and get the skills to perform consistently with what is deemed important. One of my clients was determined to make this very clear to new employees, even before they were hired. In the office where people came to apply for jobs was a sign that read, "We believe in diversity and inclusion and count on every employee to support us. If you share that commitment, we welcome your application!"

The following questions focus on functions that are ongoing within any organization and that often determine where employees put their focus:

- Is diversity an element in each stage of orientation?
- Are new hires prepared to understand the history of the environment they are entering?
- Are new hires scheduled for organization-wide, departmental, and job-specific orientation?
- Are employees exposed to educational experiences that create clear behavioral objectives, skills development, and a higher level of consciousness about diversity issues and other important organizational concerns?
- Are there any special training needs (e.g., sexual harassment, gay, lesbian, bisexual, and transgender issues, specific cultural groups, and so forth)?
- Is there a career development structure in place that monitors how all employees are developing and creates an opportunity to move employees to the next level?

Benefits

Organizational benefits and the way they are managed can be very important to diversity and inclusion areas. They also can be a key to understanding some of the unconscious patterns of the culture. I have had several professional services clients over the years, and many of them have struggled with adapting to changing demographics. Law firms, for example, are dealing with a dramatic change in their new hires. As more and more women have graduated from law school, firms have been dealing with a new employee population that is much more focused on work-life balance issues than ever before. As a result, many have instituted "flextime" policies, which allow people (mostly women, although more and more men are asking for this benefit as well) to work less demanding schedules while they have young children at home. The policies make good business sense because they can help the firms hold onto talented attorneys, but they often don't work as well as they should work.

One reason for this seems to be that many women are concerned that, even though they are "allowed" to take flextime, they will still be viewed as less committed to the organization and to their career. In some cases these beliefs become deeply internalized. In addition, studies tracking unconscious patterns show that both men *and* women have unconscious biases about women (and especially mothers) being at work. Understanding these dynamics and being able to bring them to the surface and reflect on them can help in bringing a higher level of consciousness to the issue of gender within the culture of the organization.[4]

The mindset behind many of our organizational leaders contributes to this challenge. I spoke with the managing partner of one of the law firms I was working with, and he was resistant to the idea of flextime. I asked him why, and he said, "Our expectation is that partners will bill 2,400 hours per year." I asked whether three people, billing 1,600 hours, couldn't do the same job as two people billing 2,400, assuming they were willing to work for about two-thirds the salary? "No," he answered, "we still have overhead." So then I asked whether they could share support services and even "hotel" their office space? "No," he replied again. "Even if they did that it would be hard for them to serve their clients." "Even if they handled fewer clients?" I asked. "Well," he replied, "our clients expect us to be available. I can't see somebody leaving at four o'clock every day to pick up the children." Given that these attorneys would still be making high six-figure salaries, I asked, "What if they had support at home and could work when they needed to, but over the year they still billed 1,600 hours?" Still more resistance. Why? Because *that's the way we do it around here.* Old patterns are hard to break.

Here are some of the questions that we ask about benefits:

- Is there flexible time off in the organization for religious observation?
- Are domestic partner benefits offered for lesbian, gay, bisexual, transgender (LGBT) couples?
- What work-life programs are offered that would allow your organization to tap into talent pools unable to commit to a fixed schedule, such as parental leave, elder care, and flextime?

- Are educational/development benefits widely offered, or only to a select group?
- If a benefit is offered to everyone, is there a trend in use between one group and another?
- Are periodic audits conducted to ensure equitable compensation between groups at the same level?
- To what extent have employees contributed their ideas to the work-life program?
- What are the usage rates? Is usage dependent on level?
- How regularly is feedback sought from users and nonusers to determine how to improve the program?

Metrics

There is an old saying that we should "expect what we inspect," and with regard to diversity, it could not be truer. We notice what we measure, which is why it is so important to build strong metrics around diversity and inclusion and why we have metrics built into every aspect of the Diversity Systems Map. It also is important to understand the relationship among metrics. Too often organizations use random metrics without realizing that the way they are used may be counterproductive. One of our clients was a large corporation with five distinct business units, each headed by presidents, all of whom were white men. The chief executive officer of the corporation wanted to increase diversity hiring and told the five presidents that 15 percent of their annual bonus would be based on their hiring results. Two of the men took this quite seriously, but the other three privately complained about it being "affirmative action BS." They did very little until they got to the later part of the year and remembered what 15 percent of their bonus meant to their pockets. Then they encouraged the hiring of anybody who fit the identity specifications. The problem, of course, was that the way they did the hiring almost assured that it was poorly done, giving them more justification for their point of view.

We recommend that metrics be viewed in "batches." For example, imagine your goal is that 30 percent of your new hires will be people of color. You can create four metrics that work together to create a result: pipeline measurements (number of people who apply for jobs), jobs offered, jobs accepted, and employees deemed successful after six months on the job. Let's assume that only 12 percent of job applicants are people of color. Obviously, we have to do a better job of reaching out and finding the places to draw talent. Let's say that 30 percent of the applicants are people of color, but only 12 percent are offered jobs. Then we may either have a problem in terms of the people we are drawing, or there may be some issues in our hiring process. Let's say that 30 percent of job offers are made to people of color, but only 12 percent accept. This points to an interviewing process that may be turning off some of the applicants. Finally, let's say that 30 percent of those who accept job offers are people of color, but only 12 percent are deemed successful at six months, based on job review. This may mean that something is happening on the job, or in orientation, where people turn out to be less successful, or that our hiring process is focused on the wrong skills.

In any case, this kind of approach makes it far easier to focus where the concern is rather than take an arbitrary approach. Batches of metrics can be created in almost any part of the organization. We also work with our clients to encourage them to develop a "report card" or "dashboard" that gives them regular feedback as to how they are doing in their quest to become more inclusive and culturally competent.

Here are some of the questions you might ask:

- Are clear metrics established for monitoring organizational performance regarding diversity objectives? Is the relationship among metrics understood?
- Are metrics reviewed along with other business information on a regular basis?
- Are legal issues and vulnerabilities monitored?
- Are metrics studied to ensure that they are reinforcing the appropriate behaviors?
- Are diversity metrics easily available and usable by senior leadership in monitoring the evolution of your organization?
- Does the organization have a diversity "scorecard" or "dashboard" that allows it to easily see the current status of diversity efforts?
- Are all leaders held accountable for their diversity metrics, along with their other business metrics?

Promotion/Advancement Structure

How are people promoted within the organization? Many organizations have good diverse representation, but the numbers fall off dramatically when we look at leadership. Understanding the promotional process is critical to addressing this factor.

- Are practices consistent with the mission/vision/values and objectives of your organization?
- Are managers aware of inherent biases that may impact the promotion process?
- Are records maintained that allow for comparing promotion rates between population groups?
- Have leaders developed succession plans that draw from a diverse pool?
- How much flexibility is built into the promotion process? Is there only one way to be promoted?

- How inclusive is the process?
- Are there areas within your organization in which certain people seem to have special difficulty getting promoted?

Employee Resource Groups

Employee resource groups (ERGs), sometimes called business resource groups, have become increasingly important to organizations that have demonstrated a high level of success in their diversity and inclusion efforts. ERGs can provide support for their members but also can provide a valuable resource to the organization. They can help the organization understand their respective communities, provide input into the development of products and services, assist in the hiring process, and recommend systems and structures to help the organization develop a healthier, more inclusive culture. Some of the things to look for in evaluating ERGs include:

- Are there formally or informally recognized internal resource groups that are shared with new hires?
- Are your ERGs (assuming you have them) seen as a business asset to the organization or simply as something for the people in the ERG?
- Are there broad ranges of ERGs?
- Do they get the support they need in terms of resource and time allocation?
- Are employees encouraged to participate?
- Do leaders participate with and use the ERGs as a resource?
- Is information about the ERGs widely communicated throughout the organization?
- Do ERGs work together to create an understanding of the relationships among the issues they face?

Leadership and Employee Behaviors

One of the challenges with diversity and inclusion work has been that much of the behavioral feedback that leaders and employees get is about what *not to do* rather than about *what to do*. Clear behavioral standards contribute to the success of any organizational objective, and diversity and inclusion is no exception. Some questions for employees to ask include:

- Do clear standards of behavior exist for diversity? What are they?
- Are expectations communicated to employees at all levels regarding expected behaviors?
- Are standards incorporated into performance evaluation processes?

- Do employees receive direct feedback regarding their diversity-related behavior?
- Is there a clear policy regarding discrimination or harassment behavior?
- Are employees helped to understand what specific behaviors on their part can contribute to an inclusive environment?
- How much positive role modeling is available to employees on inclusive behavior? Does this role modeling come from people of influence?

Some questions for leaders to ask include:

- Are leaders engaged as to how they can develop a greater sense of inclusion and diversity awareness?
- Are leaders engaged with the organizational community development team?
- Do leaders participate in diversity training?
- Are leaders aware of legal issues regarding diversity?
- Do leaders recognize and communicate the business rationale associated with issues of diversity?
- Is the leadership team representative of the diversity of the organization?
- Are different points of view considered when making business decisions on a daily basis?
- Do leaders model the espoused diversity behaviors?
- Are standards incorporated into leadership assessment processes?
- Do leaders have regular opportunities to get feedback from employees as to their diversity-related performance (e.g., 360-degree feedback)?
- Are diversity standards for retention included in reward and bonus systems?
- Are managers/leaders prepared to communicate about and discuss these standards with all employees?
- Do organizational policies and practices promote an inclusive environment and support the principles of diversity?
- Are there nontraditional leaders in the organization—those who work reduced hours, job sharers, and so on?

Internal Communication and Information Sharing

An organization is run by the conversations that occur within it. Who is a part of those conversations and who gets certain information is one of the ways that cultural norms are proliferated. As Francis Bacon said, "Knowledge is power." Communication strategy is a critical part of the diversity and inclusion transformation because the messaging around the effort lets people know what it is about, what it is trying to accomplish, and whether or not it is successful. In addition, watching for who is involved in critical conversations is one of the real measures of inclusion.

- What internal communication plan exists? Does it include a strong statement of the business case for diversity, inclusion, and cultural competency?
- Does it have different paths, depending on the message?
- Does the plan compensate for different communication styles of employees?
- Does it compensate for different levels of English comprehension as well as comprehension of other languages?
- Do leaders engage in dialogue with diverse employee groups about diversity issues?
- Do leaders engage in dialogue with diverse community members about diversity issues?
- Do all in your organization have the same access to information that they need to do their jobs effectively, regardless of race, gender, age, sexual orientation, and other differences?

Cultural Competency

In chapter 6, I discussed the importance of cultural competency in the increasingly global environment we now inhabit. Culture impacts every organization, but it does so for each organization in different ways, depending on the nature of the business, its location, and the nature of the cultures and communities with which the organization deals. Culture impacts everything from how we interact with fellow employees to how people manage. It affects product development, sales, marketing, and customer service. Some of the questions we explore regarding this area include:

- How does culture play a part in the internal relationships within your organization?
- How do people from different cultures interact with your business?
- Are there specific needs from your organization for customers from various cultures?
- Are there products or services that are specifically needed or not needed by particular cultural or diverse groups?
- Do employees understand differences in communication styles among people of different demographic groups?
- Do customers from different cultures have different expectations regarding interaction with your company's employees?
- Are there normal business activities that might be considered offensive by particular cultures?
- Does your organization have a tool or reference to help prepare for successful interactions with people from different cultures?
- What kind of language accommodation is offered in your organization?

Attrition and Retention

The attrition and retention patterns of an organization can yield a lot of information about how the culture functions. The ultimate gauge of any organizational culture is whether people want to be there or not. In fact, while most people believe that money is the prime motivator for determining whether or not we keep our jobs, study after study shows that it is far more likely to be how much people believe that the culture they are a part of meets their needs, and particularly their direct boss. We often are unaware of these patterns and what we can learn from them because we look at each situation in a unique way.

I remember one organization we worked with a number of years ago that had a high level of turnover among female leaders that it didn't recognize at first because each had a good excuse for leaving. Only after research and interviews did we discover that under the stated reasons were some that were less obvious but far more indicative of the culture and its impact. One woman we interviewed had left six months before to have a baby but she was now working with a different company. "Why didn't you come back?" I asked. "I guess I just never thought I'd be successful there," she answered.

Some of the questions we ask in this area include:

- Is a regular attrition and retention analysis of employees by ethnicity, gender, and level done in order to monitor trends?
- Are exit interviews conducted by a diverse group of interviewers? Does a third party conduct these interviews six months after the individuals leave the organization?
- Are exiting employees tracked demographically to observe trends?
- Is information from exit interviews regularly communicated to leaders along with other key employee data?
- Are there retention policies and incentives in place?
- Are there patterns of some groups of employees leaving or staying at different rates than others? Does this pattern extend to certain departments, divisions, or leaders?

Mentoring and Coaching

The final area of inquiry in this "inner circle" is the area of mentoring and coaching. These are critical areas, particularly for people who might be in groups seen as outside of the organization's mainstream. Mentors and coaches can help employees learn how to be successful within the culture and can maximize the potential of the talent base of the organization. Questions to consider include:

- Are formal and/or informal mentors available to assist new hires in their transition?
- Are formal and/or informal mentors available to assist employees in their development?
- Are mentors and protégés trained to know how to make their relationships as successful as possible?
- If mentoring does exist, are special efforts created where appropriate (e.g., for women in nontraditional jobs), and are those efforts communicated in a way that encourages participation?
- What considerations have been made for mentoring employees from non-dominant groups?
- Are mentoring relationships monitored to track effectiveness and performance?
- Are coaches provided, where appropriate, to assist leaders in developing their inclusive and culturally competent leadership behaviors?

The final groups of leverage points, on the far right side of the Diversity Systems Map, address the external focus of the organization. These areas ultimately measure our diversity and inclusion efforts because organizations live or die by how they are seen by the outside world. We focus on four major areas: *vendor relationships; marketing and public relations; business development and sales; and community relations and customer service.*

Vendor Relationships

Vendor relationships are important because they send a message to the marketplace as to how interested an organization is in creating relationships with different community groups. In some cases there are mandated standards for percentages of vendors from different groups, but even when that's not the case, an organization can make an important statement to certain groups by reaching out to their representative vendor groups. Questions include the following:

- Does a supplier diversity process exist?
- Is your organization in compliance with the policy?
- Are employees instructed how to develop relationships with new vendors representing diverse organizations?
- Does your organization seek out vendors whose products and services expand their abilities to meet the needs of a wide range of customer groups?

Marketing and Public Relations

What could be more important than how an organization is seen in its marketplace? And where diversity and inclusion are concerned, this can be critical to the success of the business and also can send a message that makes the organization a magnet: one that either attracts the best talent or repels it. In the increasingly diverse marketplace, in which the spending power of people of color is increasing far more rapidly than that of the white population, the ability to communicate to these diverse markets may mean success or failure to the organization. Some of the questions we might address include:

- Are key market opportunities in ethnic communities or communities of color explored?
- What specific goals have been set regarding increased market share in diverse communities?
- Are marketing materials consistent with the strategic marketing plan in terms of populations?
- Are those materials printed in languages other than English?
- Does your employee base reflect the demographics of the constituents you serve?
- Is the marketing approach designed to address the concerns of particular communities?
- Is organizational signage reflective of the language and demographics of community members?
- Is the product or service provided by your organization reflective of the needs and desires of community members?
- Does advertising reach out appropriately to members of nontraditional communities?
- Are concerns of the local community considered when adding new services?
- Are marketing experts employed who know and understand diverse population, trends, purchasing practices, and so on?
- Do public relations efforts consider media and communication outlets that various communities look to for their information?
- Do marketing and public relations efforts appreciate the different values and behaviors of the various diverse groups with whom your organization is attempting to communicate?

Business Development and Sales

The ultimate measure of business success is in the business that gets developed. Whether that is measured simply in dollars or in the number of people the organization provides service for, every organization ultimately provides service to somebody. Diversity, inclusion, and cultural competency can affect the business development and sales process in numerous ways. Some of the factors we look for include:

- How culturally intelligent is your organization when sending sales teams to meet prospective clients? Do they understand the ethnic/cultural makeup of the prospective clients?
- Are these teams aware of the cultural patterns of potential sales groups?
- Has your organization ever lost potential business because of the composition of the sales team?
- Are salespeople aware of different cultural norms regarding selling?
- Does the diversity mix of the sales force approximately match that of the potential client population?
- Does the sales team approach people throughout the community or just those in particular areas?
- Do salespeople have the cultural competence to relate to people from different racial, cultural, and ethnic groups?

Community Relations and Customer Service

The final leverage point addresses the provision of service, whether to the customers the organization serves[5] or to the various communities the organization engages. Communities and customers can be deeply affected by cultural competency, or the lack of it, or sometimes by a simple lack of awareness. Many years ago we were asked to work with a clothing company located in Toronto, Ontario, Canada. While we were asked to help develop a customer service initiative, it became evident that there might be some diversity issues involved. Toronto had (and has) a substantial Asian population, but very few of the women from this community shopped in the company's stores. When we asked the leadership why, their response was always the same: "They're just not our customer base." We finally convinced them to allow us to conduct a few focus groups of community members from this group, and what we found was blindingly simple. The reason the women did not come to the store, they told us, was because the clothing sizes were too big. The Asian women were, on average, smaller than the other shoppers. All the company needed to do to increase sales was stock more clothes of smaller sizes, which they did, along with an appropriate advertising campaign, thus resulting in a dramatic increase in sales.

Some of the areas we explore in this domain include:

- What cultural competencies would you need to have to provide even better service to your customers?
- Are customers asked regularly for feedback regarding their service? How they are being served?
- Are there products or services that your organization can provide that might meet the special needs of certain racial, ethnic, or cultural groups?

- Are customer feedback responses evaluated demographically in order to identify patterns in responses by different groups?
- Are patterns in individual sites or regions monitored?
- Do diverse interviewers occasionally interview customers to identify any concerns that might exist regarding diversity-related issues?
- Are noncustomers asked for feedback that might help your organization understand why they are not customers?

After the survey, focus groups and interviews are conducted, and then we use the information gathered to create an organizational culture map. The mapping process creates a way to look at the organization, people's attitudes toward it, and the way the current memes of the culture are creating the results that members see.

PHASE 3: DEVELOPING TRUST

Trust can be a major issue when interacting with people in cultures that have been previously marginalized or ignored or with other people who have been demonized as perpetrators. Some of the mistrust may come from historic social injustices and some from personal experience, but in either case it must be addressed directly in order to create new opportunities to establish trust and allow it to move forward. The question of "who delivers the message" is a key element of any successful culture change effort. This is an important role for the OCDT and one of the reasons the team should have representation from all parts of the organization. This will encourage broad buy-in and avoid having the transformation effort seem like a "top-down" or human resources or diversity department–driven process.

PHASE 4: STRATEGIC PLANNING

Once the organizational culture map has been created and the memes of the existing culture understood, the organizational community development team works in alignment with the organization's leaders to create a new, clearly articulated set of memes and a strategic plan for the organization. This plan becomes an aspirational behavioral template for the organization to follow. It is important that it be viewed from a systems standpoint. The Diversity Systems Map can provide an excellent template for accomplishing that goal. The impact of each behavior on others must be explored, as well as the anticipated impact on the business.

It's not necessary to implement all of the new memes at the same time, nor is it helpful to throw out the baby with the bathwater. Existing organizational memes that are working should be maintained, enhanced, or modified as needed. Ultimately, this cultural design becomes the blueprint for the new culture.

PHASE 5: STAKEHOLDER EDUCATION AND DEVELOPMENT

Once the cultural blueprint is established, the population of the organization has to be exposed to and enrolled in the new cultural model. This may include some new sense of consciousness raising about how diversity and inclusion issues play out in the organization and about how the current organizational culture supports those behaviors. Quality education includes three major parts:

- *Informational* content, which helps participants understand why diversity, inclusion, and cultural competency are important to the business of the organization, how it is objectively impacting the organization today, and what the goals are for the future.
- *Transformational* experiences, which help participants obtain a better understanding of their own unconscious beliefs and behaviors and those of others, and the various ways different people view the organization, its culture, and its practices.
- *Operational* guidelines, which help participants develop skills that will help them become more inclusive and culturally competent.

Often, many questions arise in the development of education efforts. My belief is that it is critical that each effort be designed for the organization it will serve. There are no "cookie-cutter" solutions that work for everybody because each organization has had different experiences, a different culture, a different language, different employees, and different customers. Some of the things to consider might include:

- Is the education a separate, stand-alone program or part of a broader educational effort?
- Is management educated separately, or along with other employees, or both?
- What kind of education is provided? Does it have a compliance focus? A behavioral focus? A culture-change focus?
- How much time is or should be committed to education?
- Should education initiatives be designed and conducted by internal facilitators, external facilitators, or a combination of both?
- Should education occur as a one-time program, a series of programs, or a program with follow-up?

- What modalities will be most effective (e.g., live instructors, train-the-trainer programs, web seminars or e-learning programs, and so on)?
- Are resources available to do interventions in departments where special concerns have been identified?

PHASE 6: BUILDING SYSTEMS AND STRUCTURES

As I stated earlier, structure creates behaviors, and so in conjunction with the development of the education effort, a plan should be developed to create systems and structures that are consistent with the new vision of the organization and the aspirational memes that have been created. Once again, the Diversity Systems Map can provide a template. These structures and systems may include a new recruiting process, interviewing process, or hiring process. They may include new mentoring programs, career development programs, or new benefits. A new promotional structure or employee performance review process may be put in place. Or they may include new ways to deal with the organization's customers or communities.

Whatever systems and structures are developed, it is important that they be thoughtfully constructed with a mind to how they affect one another.

PHASE 7: CREATING A STRUCTURE FOR ACCOUNTABILITY

For the organization to fulfill the promise of the culture change, there must an ongoing structure to measure how accountable people are to the aspirational goals. The metrics I described earlier in this chapter must be designed in ways that allow the organization to get regular feedback as to how the culture change is progressing. These metrics also should provide a window into what the next generation of culture development should look like. Remember, strong organizational cultures do not get "fixed." They are always evolving. Years ago, Kurt Lewin, one of the giants of organizational development, created a maxim that became a mantra in organizational change: "unfreeze, change, refreeze." This approach may have made sense at one point, but with the rapidity of change and the need for adaptation that we face in today's world, a more appropriate mantra for today might be "unfreeze, change, change, change, change . . ."

PHASE 8: REGENERATION

The culture either will design itself or will be consciously designed. The purpose of the regeneration phase is to stop with regularity, acknowledge your accomplishments, and build on them so that the organization continues to develop a consciously culturally competent organization. The regular renewal of the organizational culture keeps it fresh, vibrant, and ready to respond to the needs of the workforce, the workplace, and the marketplace.

I know to some people this may seem overwhelming. Some may say, "Are you kidding? It's everything I can do to simply get my company to pay for a diversity training, so how will I be able to get all of this?"

I completely understand that reaction. The reality is that changing a culture and transforming an organization is a substantial undertaking. The good news is that it doesn't all have to be done at once. Each step moves you closer. The important thing is that your organization is taking the right steps and, even more critically, that the steps are in the right direction. Each movement forward creates more engagement and makes the next step more doable. But timing is everything. Forcing an organization to move faster than it is ready to move can shut down the process as quickly as not moving at all. As I have said to my clients many times, even if somebody is starving to death, shoving food down his throat is not the answer.

And, as you'll see in the next chapter, it is possible to fundamentally transform an organization. It is well worth the effort!

Perhaps the answer lies in a well-known quote from the Scottish mountaineer William Hutchison Murray in his study, *The Scottish Himalayan Expedition*:

> Until one is committed, there is hesitancy, the chance to draw back, always ineffectiveness. Concerning all acts of initiative (and creation), there is one elementary truth the ignorance of which kills countless ideas and splendid plans: that the moment one definitely commits oneself, then Providence moves too. A whole stream of events issues from the decision, raising in one's favor all manner of unforeseen incidents, meetings and material assistance, which no man could have dreamt would have come his way. I learned a deep respect for one of Goethe's couplets: "Whatever you can do or dream you can, begin it. Boldness has genius, power and magic in it!"

CHAPTER 13

Walls Come Tumbling Down

> Change means movement. Movement means friction.
> Only in the frictionless vacuum of a nonexistent abstract
> world can movement or change occur without that abrasive
> friction of conflict.
>
> Saul Alinsky[1]

I know that diversity and inclusion efforts often must confront resistance within organizations. Sometimes that is because of a lack of understanding, sometimes because of inherent bias, and sometimes because the organization has not been adequately and systematically prepared for the change. I have found that it is helpful to attempt to diagnose the source of the frustration in the organization by using a particular set of distinctions that can help an organization understand the components of a change process. It can then diagnose where the breakdowns are occurring when change is frustrated so that the appropriate corrections can be put in place that will allow the organization to be successful.

I've found that the change process has core components, the absence of which almost always results in frustration and ultimately failure. The challenge is that depending on what part of the process is left incomplete, different dynamics can occur. The diagram in figure 13.1 outlines these core components.

The change process comprises eight key components, and while they tend to build upon one another, they are not as much sequential as they are links in a chain:

- *Dissatisfaction*—Any time a change process is started, there must be some sense that the current state that is existing "today" is either problematic in some way (the proverbial "burning platform") or is insufficient to the per- ceived future needs of an organization. This might mean a reaction to some

237

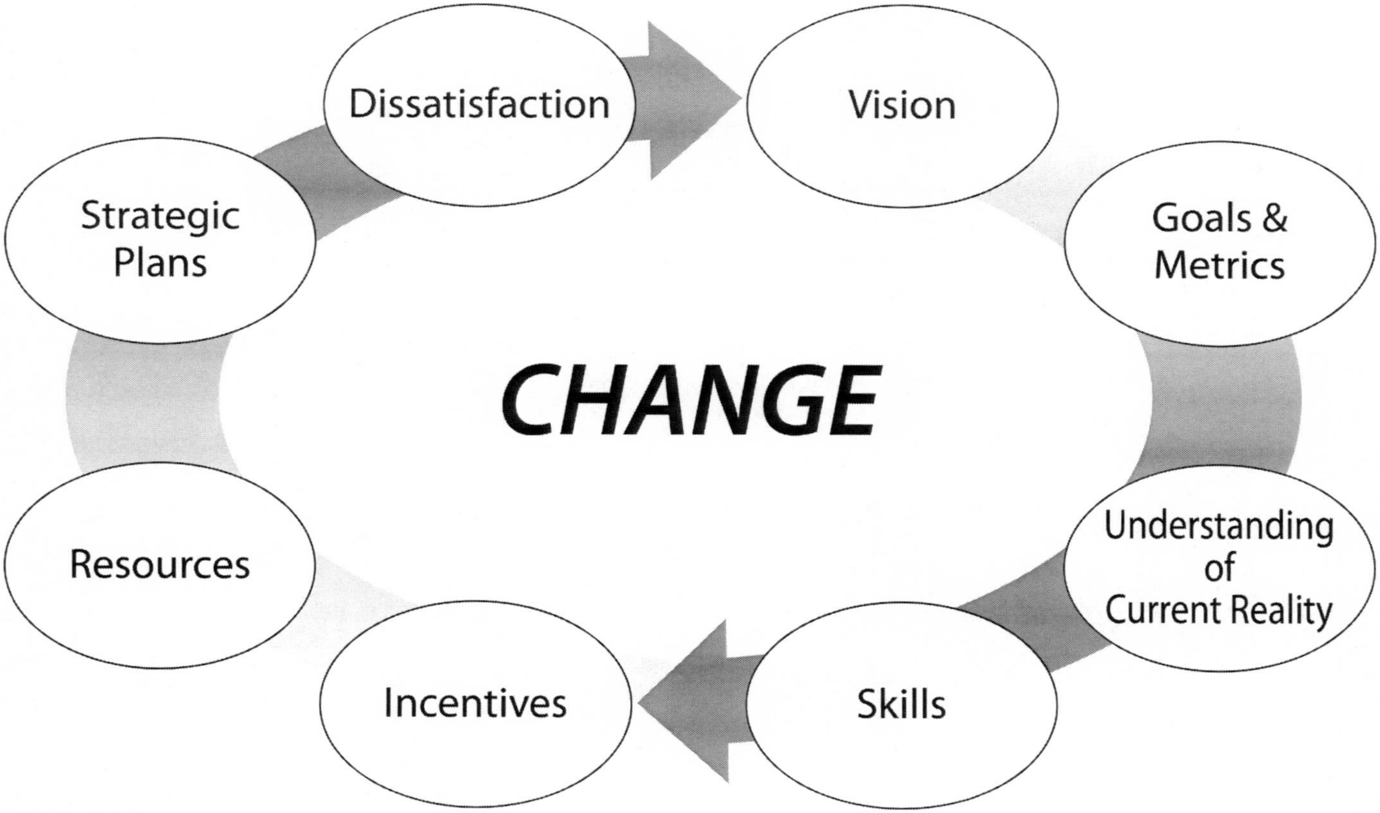

Figure 13.1

"diversity emergency," a lawsuit, a shortage of market share, or insufficient staff. Or it might mean a perceived sense that there could be a lost opportunity in the future, or future embarrassment, or detrimental public relations if an organization is perceived to be not inclusive.

- *Vision*—As I've said before, this is a particularly critical area for diversity processes because so often they are driven by a desire to correct past challenges rather than by a vision of a desired future. Creating an inspiring vision of the future is motivational for people. It gives them a sense of what they are working toward and helps provide grounding for "righting the ship" when the natural ebbs and flows of a process occur. Very few processes are linear, but with a clear vision of a desired future state, the times when the process gets pulled off course can be corrected and brought back into alignment.
- *Goals and Metrics*—Historically, we have been unsophisticated regarding the goals we have set and the way we have measured diversity. As I've stated earlier, many aspects of diversity efforts can and must be measured. We can set goals for, and measure, how many people apply for jobs, how many are offered jobs, how many accept them, and, yes, how many we hire. We can set goals for and measure promotion and advancement rates, track attrition and retention along with percentage of market share, and so on. We can identify literally dozens of goals and measurements once we recognize how critical they are to our success.
- *Understanding Current Reality*—My experience has been that it is critical to clearly identify the current reality the organization is facing in order to move forward productively with a diversity effort. What are people really feeling? How are the dynamics affecting them? What is the impact on the business? Questions like this give clarity to where you are beginning.
- *Skills*—Once people know where they are and where they want to go, they must have the skills that enable them to get there. These skills include both individual tools that allow people to deal with both day-to-day and longer-term strategic issues that emerge, as well as organizational tools that allow people to make the kind of process choices that are necessary to move the organization as a whole in the direction that they would like it to go.
- *Incentives*—I remember, not that long ago, that the buzz was all about the leisure time we were going to enjoy. People were writing books with titles like "The End of Work" that suggested that technology was going to create large amounts of free time. My experience has been the opposite. In most organizations that I have been in during the past several years, people are working harder than ever and, as a result, are forced to make choices about where they can devote their time. In most cases, they devote their time to things for which they are held accountable. Things for which they are rewarded when they happen or for which they are rebuked in some way when they don't are the things that consistently get people's attention. Diversity and inclusion

programs are no different. People have to be given incentives to produce the right results and held accountable when they don't in order for them to stay focused and in action.

- *Resources*—The best business plan in the world will not be successful if it is undercapitalized. The best diversity and inclusion plan in the world will not be successful if it doesn't have the resources to support it. Resources come in many ways: adequate staffing, staff time commitment to participate in trainings and activities, access to leaders' time when necessary, communication resources, budget, and so on. All of these and more, as in the case of any business venture, are necessary for support.
- *Strategic Plans*—Fundamental organizational culture change does not occur in the context of a constant flow of ad hoc decisions. Planning is critical to success. A successful change effort often will be thought out years in advance, anticipating what will be needed, and will include specific action plans drawn in order to ensure success.

I realize that many of you in reading this may be saying, "So what else is new? I already know this." Yet time after time, in organization after organization, diversity and inclusion efforts do not reach their potential. It is not because we don't do any of these things, but because not doing even one can have a detrimental effect on the potential success of the effort. That being the case, let's revisit each of the links in this "chain of change" and take a look at what happens when one is weakened or left out.

When *dissatisfaction* with the current state is not clear, complacency can be the result. This is often characterized by the familiar refrain, "If it ain't broke, don't fix it." It is not enough to create a general case for diversity. It also is important to be able to clearly show the impact that poor diversity practices are having on the fundamental business of the organization. That awareness of the "business case" has the capacity to propel an organization into action.

When a *clear vision* is missing, the result is an enormous amount of confusion around the diversity process. What is it that we're trying to create? For people to be inspired by the process, the vision should create a clear sense of a future for the organization. This eases the confusion and has the potential to create alignment.

Without *clear goals and metrics* for the diversity process, it will be challenging to keep people focused. How can people know when they're successful if there are no measurements of that success? Without these measurements, people are left to determine for themselves which activities they like or don't, and which are having an impact. This almost always results in an unfocused, scattered effort.

The lack of *understanding of the current reality* of the organization creates a dynamic in which people are blindly trying to move forward with a program. Imagine going into that shopping mall and trying to find a shoe store on the information map without being able to use the "you are here" arrow. You may as well not have the map at all. Understanding the reality of what's going on in the organization creates a starting point that allows you to map the way to get from here to there.

When people in the organization know what needs to be done but don't have the *skills* to do it, it can be a cause of great anxiety. Diversity issues are challenging. Often people are fearful about how to approach issues that have a history of being contentious and of attempting to engage in activities that could worsen rather than help the situation. When people within the organization develop the appropriate skills, the level of anxiety decreases and real change can occur.

Said very simply, what is not given *incentive* in organizations usually doesn't get done—or, in some cases, gets done only once in a while. Diversity efforts without any incentives may result in occasional victories because many people care enough about diversity to make occasional things happen. However, in the long run the changes will be sporadic because people's attention and their actions will constantly be pulled back to the things for which they are ultimately held accountable.

When people know what needs to be done but aren't given the *resources* to do it, frustration is a natural reaction. This can be among the most insidious of the challenges because it tends to also breed a sense of cynicism about what kind of commitment the organization has to the diversity effort. Committing resources is a foundational action that says, "We are committed to change."

When the diversity process is left to a random selection of actions rather than a clearly developed *strategic plan*, the result is often a series of false starts. Things get under way hopefully and then disappear or are replaced by the next "program du jour." Every challenge runs the risk of derailing the effort. Sustainability suffers.

If you're like me, you are probably skeptical, but creating a successful, sustainable diversity and inclusion effort is possible. It takes a real understanding of change, a comprehensive sense of all parts of the process, and a commitment to making them happen. Diversity and inclusion cannot be accomplished by a bits-and-pieces approach. All of the links have to be present for the chain to be strong. Let me give you an example of how it works when it works well.

Case Study: The Walls to Diversity Come Tumbling Down in an Inner-City Hospital

One of the most inspiring examples of how organizational community can work occurred in a project that our company, Cook Ross, engaged in with a large Midwestern inner-city hospital. When we first began consulting with the hospital, the once venerable, city-owned hospital was a shadow of its former self. The story is not an unfamiliar one. Decades old, the hospital had been a leader in the city and the state's medical community when the city was financially strong. But things began to change in the 1960s and 1970s, when local businesses began to move jobs elsewhere. The wealthy fled the urban center, businesses followed, and the city showed increasing signs of racial strife, urban poverty, and crime.

Located in one of the "tougher" sections of the city, this background contributed to a gradual decline in performance at the hospital. By the 1980s, the hospital's contentious relationship with its unions had resulted in major work stoppages. Racial tension was rampant in an institution that reflected a racial makeup similar to that of the surrounding community, the population of which was more than half people of color. Physicians had begun sending their patients to other hospitals and felt deeply resigned and hopeless about the future. Employee morale was at an all-time low, and the 1992 financial results indicated that the hospital had suffered record losses.

The chief executive officer knew that unless they could break down the "us/them" attitude that existed between the unions and management, between the physicians and the hospital, and between the hospital and the community, they had no hope of moving the hospital forward. One of their greatest diversity challenges was in the relationship between unions and management. While not seen in the classic sense of race, gender, and so on, union/management relationships are a great example of a more expanded view of diversity. Each group has a distinct view of the world. They see what is important and what they are willing to do to make the organization successful. In this organization, there also was a racial component to this tension because the unions were much more racially diverse than the management team.

The first step was in bringing the union leadership and management together to create a new vision for the process. Both groups knew that the current situation was untenable, but they had no idea how to get past the deep resentments that existed between each group. Leaders from the two groups spent several days working to heal the rift. They voiced their concerns and feelings about past confrontations before they could reestablish trust and agree on a future for the hospital that was dramatically different. Their détente was tentative, but their mutual concern for the future gave them cause to at least try to work together. They also chose representatives to form an organizational community development team to lead the process, a team that included the chief executive officer himself.

The next step was to identify the core issues. It was clear that people understood the major challenges in the organization. The first were diversity concerns (particularly around race and social class) that made it difficult for employees to work together and affected their relationship with patients, guests, and customers. Within the community, the hospital was seen more and more as the "black hospital," and patients from other racial groups, especially Whites, were shying away from it. Second, the internal strife at the hospital was affecting the level of service that employees were providing to the patients and guests of the hospital. The service levels in the hospital were considered poor, and that belief was reflected in the community's view of the institution.

The OCDT knew that they had challenges in customer relations, internal staff relations, physician relations, community image and perception. They met with the leadership team for a planning process. They told each other the truth of how they were feeling and what they were seeing. They hashed out the critical issues, engaged in simulations, and put their individual and group perspectives "on the table." Finally, a shared understanding began to emerge, and people from all groups began to see that their desires for the future were not as far apart as they had originally thought. In fact, they were able to agree on a new vision. They wanted to create an organization that

- valued and celebrated individual differences;
- recognized everyone as important and worthy of compassion and courtesy;
- encouraged all employees to participate fully;
- allowed members of all cultural and economic groups to be recognized, appreciated, and valued, and to contribute and reach their full potential;
- recognized and addressed patient and customer cultural differences and needs; and
- would be recognized as a diversity champion throughout the community.

The leadership agreed to conduct a future search conference in order to get a broad range of input as to how to make the vision a reality for the hospital. More than 150 stakeholders were invited to spend three days together, including senior management leaders, union leaders, physicians, nurses, a wide array of employees representing different functions, community leaders and neighborhood residents, patients and guests who had been in the hospital within the past year, and health department and regulatory officials.

The participants engaged in an honest inquiry, openly talking about how the hospital had gotten into the condition it was in. They looked at the role that each had played in that history and took responsibility for the things they had done to contribute and the things that they had done to get in the way. They identified areas they could all agree were essential to address in order to move forward, and they created strategies for moving forward that they could all share. Everyone was eager to move the organization forward, but they first had to create a clear sense of what "forward" looked like. We suggested that they come up with a clear plan that everybody in the institution could work together to create. They knew their diversity issues were about more than race and class and included ethnicity, gender, culture, sexual orientation, employee hierarchy, and political constituencies. But they also knew that unless they could share a common vision for the future, they were not going anywhere.

Rather than simply develop a flowery vision statement on the wall that had little real impact on the way the hospital ran on a day-to-day basis, the hospital chose to develop a bold strategic approach. As opposed to dealing with simply correcting past problems, the hospital wanted to establish a sense of a positive movement for the future. With our assistance, it adopted a strategic approach that allowed it to create an exciting future.

It became clear that it was not enough to simply identify the problems that the organization was facing but that a deeper understanding was needed of why these problems were taking place. It also was clear that once there was an understanding of the issues, a "game plan" for addressing them had to be created. In order to accomplish this, the group members identified five strategic objectives that they felt would move them in the right direction:

1. Conducting an organizational culture audit, which was a study of the organization as it related to diversity issues for all constituencies, would allow the OCDT and the leadership team to really get a picture of how the people within the organization were seeing it, reacting to it, and living it.
2. In order to create a context for the effort, it was clear that the organization had to develop an understanding of how diversity issues related to the organization's vision and mission. People had to really understand diversity as a core competency for success, and not just the success of the hospital. Their personal success was involved as well.
3. They had to clarify the motivation for a managing diversity initiative by identifying it as a key business strategy for managers, physicians, and staff.
4. They had to educate the staff and managers (senior, middle, and entry level) about the nature of managing diversity and valuing differences. We had to help them understand the information they needed to appreciate the impact diversity was having on them and would continue to have in the future. We also had to help them experience a transformation in the way they were seeing the issue, and particularly confront how "stuck" they were in their particular point of view about it. And we had to motivate them to develop new behaviors.
5. Finally, they had to develop a strategy to communicate to the public, patients, physicians, and staff that something was happening at the hospital and that it valued and celebrated diversity. It was critical that while the organization was changing on the inside, the outside world would begin to respond to it in a new way, with new expectations.

Then we set about making it happen. First, we talked to people within the organization. Lots of people. We interviewed key leaders, those with titles, and those who didn't have particular titles but were the proverbial "straws that stir the drink." We spoke with some of them individually, and we spoke with many in small groups. We spoke with mixed groups of employees, but we also spoke to specific, homogeneous groups of Whites, Blacks, doctors, nurses, managers, and so on. We wanted to find out how employees really saw their organization and how that view was different for different people. We also conducted a survey to give all employees an opportunity to have input.

The results were starker than we expected. People seemed to be living in almost parallel universes within the organization. The view of the world was completely different, depending on what identity one possessed. Blacks saw it very differently from Whites, union members differently from management, and doctors from nurses. However, the one thing everybody agreed on was that the situation was unpleasant. Only 9 percent of all of those who responded to the survey said that they enjoyed working at the hospital! It was time to go to work.

How did it work? In this case, we worked on several parallel tracks. We developed a comprehensive curriculum that addressed diversity issues as they emerged, one that gave employees an opportunity to talk about their concerns and also to engage in self-reflection about the role that they were playing in the dynamic as it existed. This then gave them specific behaviors that they could follow to make the changes happen.

We then trained more than fifty employees of the hospital to begin to deliver training to the approximately three thousand employees. All kinds of people were trained as facilitators: executives, physicians, nurses, food service workers, and custodians. We didn't necessarily choose people with training experience. We chose people with passion for the process, people who the other employees would be able to relate to in an easy manner. They weren't being trained to be "experts" in front of the room, they were being trained to guide the conversation in a way that allowed participants to tap into their own wisdom about what was needed and work together to find solutions and new ways of being.

One of the greatest examples of this was a man named Alan, an African American man in his fifties who worked in custodial services. Alan told a remarkable story about how he came to apply for the facilitator position:

> When the flyer inviting people to apply came out, people in my department didn't buy it. Most of them said it was a waste of time and wouldn't make a bit of difference anyway. I took it home with me one night and got to talking to my mother about it. She is a retired schoolteacher. She said something that really stuck with me. She said, "You know, if nobody tries then they'll be right . . . it won't make any difference." So I figured I'd give it a shot.

Alan epitomizes what people are capable of when given an opportunity to step up into leadership. He had very little experience with any sort of training, yet he jumped into the material. With coaching from our team he became comfortable with the concepts and when it came time for him to actually lead the sessions, his down-to-earth style and passion for what the hospital and its employees needed to do far outweighed the need for sophisticated training skills. He could really reach people.

> "The separation and distrust between management and unions as well as race, gender and culture was so distinct and disruptive that everyone agreed that something must be done. While the engagement of the CEO and union leaders was critical, the participation of employees as trainers was as an important factor in its success. The significance of the program was not limited to the workplace alone. A number of people stated that this 'influenced their behavior as parents and members of the community.' This may be the best measure of its value."
>
> Glenn Fosdick
> President and CEO, Nebraska Health System
> Former CEO, Hurley Medical Center, Flint, Michigan

The training began to be rolled out. All employees participated. We even conducted training for the board of directors. At the same time, policies, procedures, and practices within the organization were reviewed and changed. The medical center joined forces with various groups in the community to form coalitions that demonstrated community leadership in diversity. Other organizations came on board and started programs of their own. We worked with a local bank, a college in the community, and the local community coalition. Local political leaders got involved. And the hospital was at the core of it all, demonstrating leadership.

Over time things began to change, and much faster and more dramatically than we could imagine. And the results were nothing short of miraculous. People who had given up on the hospital came to life again. People who had become adversaries began to work together. Patient satisfaction statistics began to rise, and the local newspaper, which had written a scathing editorial about the hospital three years earlier (which had been one of the low points in the hospital's journey), wrote a new editorial citing them as leaders in the region in healthcare *and* diversity.

Oh, and the bottom line? Within two years, the hospital went from an operating loss of almost $10 million to an operating gain of more than $10 million.

Not every organization is in the difficult position that this hospital was, and many have already started their diversity and inclusion journey. Yet this is just one example of what is possible when people organize themselves and create a real sense of organizational community. It is hard work, but it does work.

Can you feel the plaster from the tumbling walls?

CHAPTER 14

A New Way Home

Courage is the most important of all the virtues, because without courage you can't practice any other virtue consistently. You can practice any virtue erratically, but nothing consistently without courage.

Maya Angelou[1]

When we speak we are afraid our words will not be heard nor welcomed. But when we are silent we are still afraid. So it is better to speak, remembering we were never meant to survive.

Audre Lorde[2]

So where do we go from here? The past few chapters have been very specific about how to create a diverse, inclusive, and culturally competent organization. I know that every organization is in a different place in terms of the challenges you face, the things you've tried, the specifics of your marketplace, your employee group, and your organizational culture. As I stated in the introductory chapters, I don't intend for anything in this book to be read as "the truth," as I fully recognize that every personal and organizational strategy is built upon unique qualities and experiences.

I also recognize that this book is mostly directed toward a U.S.-based audience, which doesn't mean that the same principles do not apply to organizations outside of the United States, but I have chosen to address the dynamics that are particularly dominant in U.S.-based organizations in this particular text.

The three general paradigm shifts that I've described require us to approach this subject in a different way than most organizations have approached it before. Creating a culturally competent, culturally flexible, and culturally intelligent organization will require a new way of operating for each of us, but also a new way of being. Becoming culturally competent will require us to learn more about our native cultures than we've ever known before, and even more importantly, to actually embrace our cultural memes as "our" rather than "the" cultural memes. On paper this may seem easy, but doing so will require us to develop a deeper sense of cultural humility than we may have ever considered before. That doesn't mean we have no right to an opinion about which cultural patterns we feel more comfortable with and want to adhere to, but it does call us to question our judgmental assumptions and seek to understand the cultural models of our employees, customers, and marketplace.

Perhaps the most challenging of the paradigm shifts will be to escape from the righteousness of our position and truly understand why the world looks so different in the minds of others. Breaking out of the "us/them," "good person/ bad person" mentality about diversity and inclusion may even seem like an affront to some of us. How can we even question that certain behaviors are just wrong?

But I am not suggesting that I don't have strong opinions about the things people believe and the way they behave. Of course I do. And so do the people who disagree with me. That is the challenge, and the opportunity. We do not need to let go of our beliefs, our values, or our sense of right and wrong, but we do need to rigorously attempt to understand the way others have come to believe what they believe. And, most importantly, we can learn to honor their humanity at the same time as we disagree with their beliefs and values. There may not be a greater challenge to us, especially when we believe so deeply in something as important, and I believe even *noble*, as diversity and inclusion. Yet only when we can "get some altitude" on the conversation (almost like a helicopter lifting off the ground) and see our predicament in a clearer way will we be able to create ways of being and interacting with one another that will truly create a breakthrough.

How do we do so? First, we need to ask more questions and resist the urge to provide all of the answers as we seek to really understand how the world looks the way it does to the people we are trying to understand. What are their fears (even if they seem irrational to us)? What are their challenges? What are their hopes for the future? Next, we must reflect back to them what we have heard them say, so that we are sure they feel heard. And third, we should seek to first identify the common beliefs we have before we start to tackle the differences. This is counterintuitive to most of us because our orientation is to believe "what's the point if we can't agree on the big things?" Yet mediation theory teaches us that beginning with establishing common ground on little things can make it easier for us to work toward understanding one another on the big ones.[3]

That process doesn't begin with them, it begins with us. It requires us to transform our way of being from righteous avengers to deep listeners, from "fixers" to facilitators, and from advocates to collaborators. That is why understanding the way the mind works is so important. Only when we really understand that we are *all* products of our programming and *all* responding to our unconscious triggering mechanisms can we see the humanity in the other point of view. Then we can truly engage in dialogue with each other rather than attempt to pound each other into submission.

The third paradigm shift will be very challenging because to create real organizational transformation, rather than simply conduct a series of exciting diversity activities, may require many of us to have patience, perseverance, and a deeper understanding of the way organizations run than we have ever had before. We will have to learn more, listen more, and study more than ever. And we will have to rely on our abilities to connect with people and enroll them in what we are doing, rather than simply be advocates for our agendas. In fact, we may have to be willing to surrender our certainty about the way to make things happen in exchange for the wisdom of the group.

All of these paths call on us to transform ourselves before we can expect to transform the environments we are living and working in. What greater challenge can we find? And what greater opportunity?

And let there be no doubt, it will be a challenge. Cultures, as I said earlier, want to sustain themselves every bit as much as individual human personalities want to be "right" about the way we see the world. If you are really moving your organization toward true diversity, inclusion, and cultural competency, you will inherently appear at times like an antibody to the system. And the system itself will do everything it can, in overt and covert ways, to stop you. As Machiavelli famously said, "There is nothing more difficult to take in hand, more perilous to conduct, or more uncertain in its success, than to take the lead in the introduction of a new order of things. Because the innovator has for enemies all those who have done well under the old conditions, and lukewarm defenders in those who may do well under the new."[4]

Doing the work of true organizational transformation is not work for the faint of heart.

Even as I write this book, the conversational network of contention exists even within my own field. The current duality is whether diversity and inclusion work is the work of business or the work of social justice. Some say, "Enough of the social justice stuff . . . let's just focus on business!" Others say the opposite. But this trap of dualism misses the point: the two sides are inexorably tied to each other. The driver of doing diversity work in businesses or organizational environments must be tied to the work of the organization. As the old saying goes, "The business of business is business." As practitioners, we have to learn the business, understand the business, speak in the language of the business, and focus our activities and efforts in ways that drive the business. But we must, at the same time, not forget that what occurs in the society that our co-workers and we confront every day *comes to work with everyone, too.*

At this time American society confronts a crisis point relative to issues of sexual orientation. Young gay men and women are taking their own lives in alarming numbers, four times as often as straight young people.[5] For the past seventeen years, the U.S. military has imposed a "don't ask, don't tell" policy that allows lesbian, gay, and bisexual men and women to serve, and perhaps die, in the military as long as they don't reveal their real identity. And the debate over marriage equality for gays and lesbians proliferates in our society.

Do we really think when gay men and women come to work every day in virtually every moderate-to-large organization in the country that these matters don't affect the way they relate to their straight co-workers? Or to how safe they feel? Can we really afford to have 5 to 6 percent[6] of our adult population feel that way at work and think we are getting their best talent?

Also at this time, American society confronts a crisis relative to issues regarding the full societal inclusion of Muslim Americans. The building of mosques and Islamic centers has triggered massive protest and resistance across the United States. None has been more virulent than the plans to build Park51, an Islamic center in New York City, a couple of blocks from the location of the destroyed World Trade Center buildings. At the same time, the Campbell Soup Company launched a new product line of halal products in Canada. This is a business decision designed to reach a large market share of Canadian Muslim shoppers and is akin to selling kosher products to observant Jews. This would seem to be a smart business decision, given the millions of peaceful, law-abiding Muslims who want to follow their dietary laws, right? But in response to this action, the company is being hit by a massive Internet-driven boycott of its products. This is happening because, according to some, providing halal products is "doing the 'bidding' of terrorist groups." Is this a social concern or a business concern? Can we really separate the two?

And we also continue to have massive examples of health disparities among people of color and lower-income people within our society.[7] Given these disparities, do we really think that the people of color who work in our organizations are not going to be impacted by these health issues?

There is no wall that separates the society we live in from the businesses and organizations we work in. If we expect to achieve all of the benefits of diversity and inclusion in our workplaces (greater creativity, productivity, and profit), then we will need to create a society to live in that values that diversity and inclusion as well. The business case and the social justice case are not competing interests. They are inexorably interwoven.

If you truly take on the mantle of change, you will encounter resistance. The important thing to recognize is that if you are not encountering resistance, you are not challenging the system to function in any other way. *Resistance is the acknowledgment that you are asking people to be and act a different way. It is an unavoidable part of the process.* To a certain extent, when resistance isn't present, we might ask ourselves, "Are we pushing hard enough?"

Within the hundreds of organizational transformation processes I have worked on, there has been a discernible pattern,[8] depicted in figure 14.1. There are usually about 5 to 10 percent of the people in the organization who buy into the change right from the start. They are "true believers" in the cause and are early adapters. Then there are 10 to 20 percent of the people I describe as "standing on the diving board trying to decide whether the water is warm enough." They generally believe in the direction but haven't quite made the commitment yet. The largest group, usually 40 to 70 percent of the people, is the group I refer to as the "dynamically apathetic."

Figure 14.1

They come to work every day and do their job, but they are not all that interested in the way the culture functions. We may see that as a problem, but it really is not. They will move with the culture whichever way it goes. They just want to do their job.

And then, on the outer fringes, we have the skeptics, usually 10 to 20 percent of the people. They are not enrolled in the change because they are just not sure that it's a good idea or that it can work. Skeptics engage in healthy questioning of the process. We sometimes see them as oppositional, but they often are asking important questions that need to be answered if the process is to move forward. Finally, about 5 to 10 percent of the organization is composed of cynics. Cynicism is significantly different from skepticism because cynics are often invested in the process not working. Sometimes it is because they are invested in the old order and don't want it to change. And sometimes cynicism is the last refuge of the idealist. It may be that they have believed in the past and been burned and they don't want to be disappointed again.

The key is not to be "captured" by the skeptics and cynics. All too often we put too much of our energy into defending what we are doing to the members of these groups. We exhaust ourselves trying to bring them over to "our side." Of course, when they are people in positions of power and influence they have to be dealt with, but the key lies in starting with the people who already believe. I have seen this proven true time and again. Build your coalition. Encourage those who are "waiting and seeing" to jump into the water. This is not usually a difficult task. It can start by looking for the "low-hanging fruit" and is a quick example of things you can do to start moving the process forward.

If we are lucky, some of these activities, and some of us, will become trim tabs. R. Buckminster Fuller described trim tabs as small things that can make a big difference by influencing larger things to move into action:

> Something hit me very hard once, thinking about what one little man could do. Think of the Queen Mary—the whole ship goes by and then comes the rudder. And there's a tiny thing at the edge of the rudder called a trim tab. It's a miniature rudder. Just moving the little trim tab builds a low pressure that pulls the rudder around. Takes almost no effort at all. So I said that the little individual can be a trim tab. Society thinks it's going right by you, that it's left you altogether. But if you're doing dynamic things mentally, the fact is that you can just put your foot out like that and the whole big ship of state is going to go. So I said, call me Trim Tab.[9]

As the center groups begin to move into action, the natural flow of the dynamically apathetic, the largest part of the organization, will move toward the center. A "new normal" will begin to develop whereby diversity, inclusion, and cultural competency simply become things we concern ourselves with because they have become part of our cultural conversation. New memes will begin to emerge.

And what of the outer circles? My experience has been that they will flail against the windmills of change. They will need to be addressed, but if we stay focused on building the new culture around the principles of diversity, inclusion, and cultural competency, eventually they will either jump into the center or fall to the wayside. The incontrovertible evidence is clear: our workforce, workplaces, and marketplaces have to move toward a better understanding and management of diversity if we are to survive. The inevitable flow of history is clear. Since the signing of the Magna Carta in 1215, history has moved steadily toward more freedom, more inclusion, and more diversity. This has been true throughout the world as well as in the United States. So, yes, we have to deal with resistance, but first and foremost, we stay the course.

Creating diverse, inclusive, and culturally competent organizations is hard work. There are times when we will feel frustrated. There are times when we will stumble and fall. There are times when we will wonder why we are spending our time investing in something so mentally challenging and emotionally confronting. There are times when we will feel alone and as if every victory is followed by a seeming defeat. The nature of the universe is that expansion is usually followed by contraction and regrouping.

But we are not alone in this effort. We are part of a flow of history that has brought our society to this very moment.[10]

We might begin looking in the early nineteenth century, when the notable transcendentalist Ralph Waldo Emerson went to Europe after the death of his wife and came back talking about two new major themes: how we treat nature and how we treat one another. He studied the Bhagavad Gita and the Upanishads, the sacred Hindu scriptures.[11] He began an association with Margaret Fuller, the journalist and early women's rights advocate whose ideas influenced Emerson and who took Emerson's ideas into her conversations with Susan B. Anthony and Elizabeth Cady Stanton, and then brought their ideas to Emerson. He also was connected to the orator and former slave, Frederick Douglass, who exposed him to the horrors of slavery and eventually extended his interest to abolitionism. Douglass had traveled to England, where he had met Thomas Clarkson,[12] who, along with Josiah Wedgwood, Granville Sharpe, and others, had been instrumental in launching the British abolitionist movement. This was perhaps the first time in human history that a group of people had launched a movement for the liberation of a group of people to which they did not belong.

Emerson's most noted student and friend was, of course, Henry David Thoreau, who became a lifelong abolitionist. Thoreau had done his own study of Eastern philosophy, having also read the Bhagavad Gita. He was a student of

Buddhism, which, he wrote, made "our modern world and its literature seem puny and trivial."[13] In July 1846, Thoreau was jailed for having refused to pay poll taxes for more than six years as a protest against slavery, the disenfranchisement of freed blacks, and the Mexican-American War. While he actually only spent one night in jail, his jail experience propelled Thoreau to write one of his most well-known essays, "Resistance to Civil Government" (later to be renamed "Civil Disobedience," though the term is never actually used in the essay). In it he wrote, "If the machine of government is of such a nature that it requires you to be the agent of injustice to another, then, I say, break the law!"[14]

Thoreau is thought to have influenced other members of the abolitionist movement and was known to speak on the same platform as William Lloyd Garrison, publisher of the *Liberator*, among others. It is without question that he had an impact on a young Indian attorney, Mohandas K. Gandhi, who read the essay while in South Africa in either 1906 or 1907 and proceeded to frequently refer to it for the rest of his life.[15] Gandhi used the ideals of civil disobedience to lead a nation of hundreds of millions of people to liberate themselves from the grip of what was then the world's greatest superpower, the British Empire.

Years later, the same stream of thought would result in Rosa Parks refusing to give up her bus seat in Montgomery, Alabama, beginning what most consider the modern civil rights movement. Contrary to some popular belief, Parks's action was not unique or impetuous. In 1946, Irene Morgan had used the same tactic in Virginia, resulting in a U.S. Supreme Court decision that declared segregation illegal in interstate buses, *Irene Morgan v. Commonwealth of Virginia*, 328 U.S. 373 (1946).[16] The case was argued by Thurgood Marshall, who later would argue the famous *Brown v. Board of Education of Topeka, Kansas* case and in 1967 would become the first African American to be named to the Supreme Court of the United States.

In 1955, Sarah Louise Keys similarly refused to give up her seat in a bus in North Carolina, resulting in yet another ruling banning discrimination, *Sarah Keys v. Carolina Coach Company*, 64 MCC 769 (1955).[17] And just nine months before Parks refused to give up her seat, Claudette Colvin, an Alabama high-school student, had refused to give up her own seat.[18]

Of course, the action by Parks became historic because it sparked the boycott of the Montgomery bus system. Clifford and Virginia Durr, white Southern aristocrats, had previously employed her in their home.[19] Clifford Durr, who had served in the Roosevelt and Truman administrations, became her lawyer, and Virginia Durr was a friend of Eleanor Roosevelt and of Dr. Mary McLeod Bethune, who had been in President Roosevelt's "black cabinet" and had started the National Council of Negro Women (NCNW) in 1935. Bethune was to become the mentor of Dr. Dorothy Height, who would follow her as president of the NCNW, create the Black Family Reunion, and win the Presidential Medal of Freedom before her death in 2010.

Virginia Durr paid for Parks to attend training in nonviolent resistance that was run by Myles Horton, a white Gandhian integrationist.[20] Other attendees in Horton's Highlander School included Stokely Carmichael, who would become a founder of the Student Non-Violent Coordinating Committee (SNCC); the Reverend Ralph David Abernathy, who organized the first mass meeting of the Montgomery bus boycott; SNCC organizer and later congressman John Lewis; Bernard Lafayette, who was to lead the Selma Voting Rights Campaign; and Fannie Lou Hamer, who led the Mississippi Freedom delegation at the 1964 Democratic National Convention and famously said, "We didn't come all the way up here to compromise for no more than we'd gotten here. We didn't come all this way for no two seats, 'cause all of us is tired. And I am sick of being tired of being sick and tired."[21] Of course, Highlander School's most famous attendee was a young minister named Dr. Martin Luther King Jr., who had been hired as a junior minister at the Dexter Avenue Baptist Church by Vernon Johns, and whom many consider the father of the modern civil rights movement.[22]

Jo Ann Robinson, a member of the Montgomery Women's Political Council, called for the bus boycott after Parks was arrested and stayed up all night mimeographing thirty-five thousand handbills to distribute. Juliette Morgan, a white librarian, journalist, and social activist who was the descendant of a Confederate general and upper-class traditional Southerners, supported the boycott. Morgan became the victim of such ferocious criticism from the white community of Montgomery that she eventually took her own life.[23]

The proposed one-day boycott was so successful that the Montgomery Improvement Association was formed and Dr. King was chosen as its president. Dr. King, fearing for his family's safety and his own life, obtained guns and bodyguards. His own turn to nonviolence was influenced powerfully when he met Bayard Rustin.[24] An African American who also was gay and a Socialist, Rustin was raised by his grandmother, Julia Rustin, who was a member of the NAACP. Frequent visitors in his home included W. E. B. DuBois and James Weldon Johnson. He also was an accomplished singer who knew and performed with Paul Robeson and Josh White.[25]

Rustin became an advisor to King and convinced him to develop nonviolent civil disobedience as a protest tool. He introduced him to Glenn Smiley, a Methodist minister and member of the Fellowship of Reconciliation (FOR), who was to introduce King to the works of Gandhi, Thoreau, and Richard Gregg, who had gone to India to study with Gandhi and had written *The Power of Non-Violence*.[26] The executive director of the FOR was the noted pacifist and antiwar advocate A. J. Muste, who also became an advisor to King.[27]

King and the civil rights movement were, of course, to go on and inspire others, notably a group of gay men whose civil action at the Stonewall Inn in New York on June 28, 1969, is widely considered the first time in American history that gay citizens fought back against government-sanctioned discrimination and persecution. Yet, as with Parks, this view of Stonewall obscures the fact that other actions preceded it. For example, in August 1966, a similar action among gays had occurred at Compton's Cafeteria in San Francisco when police tried to enforce a statute against cross-dressing. Nonetheless, it is reasonable to say that few would disagree that Stonewall was the birthplace of the modern gay rights movement. These expressions of protest against homophobia and heterosexism led to the formation of PFLAG (Parents and Friends of Lesbians and Gays), when Jeanne Manford was watching a news report covering a protest in 1972 and saw her son Morty being thrown down an escalator while police stood by and watched. PFLAG now has five hundred chapters around the United States and 250,000 members.[28] Stonewall also inspired Harvey Milk, who was to become the first openly gay man to be elected to public office in California. He inspired countless others, including Cleve Jones, who later started the Names Project AIDS Memorial Quilt[29] and several of the earliest organizations to fight the spread of AIDS.

Also inspired by King and the civil rights movement were Cesar Chavez and Dolores Huerta, who used the same tactics of nonviolence to build the United Farm Workers (UFW) movement, which led to the growth of La Raza,[30] the nation's largest Latino civil rights and advocacy organization.[31] Chavez had been trained by Fred Ross, a community organizer who was associated with Saul Alinsky, the famed community organizer who developed the organizing strategies that contributed to the election of President Barack Obama.[32] Alinsky was inspired by hearing stories of the Chicago stockyards and of the 1911 Triangle Shirtwaist factory fire. The fire killed 146 garment workers, mostly women, when their supervisors locked them in a building that then caught on fire. The Triangle fire led to the growth of the International Ladies Garment Workers Union.

Dr. King, Dr. Height, and Dr. Bethune also inspired Shirley Chisholm, who became the first African American woman elected to Congress in 1968, and in 1972 became the first African American woman to run for president. Feminist activists Betty Friedan and Gloria Steinem, who had been inspired by the women's suffrage movement, supported Congresswoman Chisholm in her presidential quest.

So we've just traveled quite a crowded road of history: Ralph Waldo Emerson, Henry David Thoreau, Margaret Fuller, Susan B. Anthony, Elizabeth Cady Stanton, Frederick Douglass, Thomas Clarkson, Josiah Wedgwood, Granville Sharpe, William Lloyd Garrison, Mohandas K. Gandhi, Rosa Parks, Irene Morgan, Thurgood Marshall, Sarah Louise Keys, Claudette Colvin, Clifford and Virginia Durr, Eleanor Roosevelt, Dr. Mary McLeod Bethune, Dr. Dorothy Height, Myles Horton, Stokely Carmichael, Reverend Ralph David Abernathy, Congressman John Lewis, Bernard Lafayette, Fannie Lou Hamer, Dr. Martin Luther King, Vernon Johns, Jo Ann Robinson, Juliette Morgan, Bayard Rustin, Julia Rustin, W. E. B. DuBois, James Weldon Johnson, Paul Robeson, Josh White, Glenn Smiley, A. J. Muste, Richard Gregg, Jeanne and Morty Manford, Harvey Milk, Cleve Jones, Cesar Chavez, Dolores Huerta, Fred Ross, Saul Alinsky, President Barack Obama, Congresswoman Shirley Chisholm, Betty Friedan, and Gloria Steinem. And, of course, we could include hundreds more names of people who have been inspired by this historic stream of liberation: Mordecai Anielewicz, who led the Warsaw ghetto uprising against the Nazis; Nelson Mandela and Desmond Tutu, who fought apartheid in South Africa; Daw Aung San Suu Kyi, the recently released Myanmar liberation leader; Bhimrao Ramji Ambedkar, the leader of the liberation movement for the Dalit in India; Dennis Banks, George Mitchell, Herb Powless, Clyde Bellecourt, Harold Goodsky, and Eddie Benton-Banai, who founded the American Indian Movement; and Liu Xiaobo of China, who was awarded the Nobel Peace Prize in 2010. The list can, and does, go on and on.

And when we do this work, we are part of this stream. We stand on the shoulders of all of those who have come before us, and we help build the platform for all of those who will come after us. The question is, what will our legacy be once the future arrives?

I once heard it said that "if you expect to see the fruits of your labor in your own lifetime, you're not asking a big enough question."[33] Human history has now evolved to the point where human liberation contributes to good business. We are at a time in that history when we are blessed with the reality that we can "do well by doing good."[34]

So even though it can be frustrating to tackle these difficult issues, and even though it sometimes seems as if we take two steps forward and one step back or that we are running in place, still we have to keep moving forward. The real work starts within us. We must continue to develop our own humility, to look at our own inherent blind spots. We must create real partnerships with those who are different from ourselves if we are to be champions for diversity, inclusion, and cultural competency in our organizations, our communities, and the world.

A. J. Muste said, "There is no way to peace. Peace is the way." Perhaps there is wisdom for us in a slight modification of that statement. We will not fundamentally transform our organizations until we transform ourselves. We will not be able to lead organizations or communities into inclusion until we can see the bias in ourselves. Only when we are living inclusion and cultural competency in our interaction with others will our message and the benefits of it have an opportunity to grow. It starts when we, as advocates for diversity, inclusion, and cultural competency, accept our own humanity and set the bar of inclusion at its highest for ourselves.

To accomplish that on a grand scale will require a revolution in human consciousness. The good news is that it is not a revolution without a road map. It is a way of being that travels a path that dates back thousands of years, through traditions throughout time in which people have tried to understand the human condition. It runs through modern psychology and now through the cognitive sciences. It is a path that relies on our learning to observe ourselves, both as individuals and organizations, and an understanding that unless we stop to watch ourselves, even we will be run by our preconceptions and biases. It requires us to practice what we preach in ways that we haven't generally understood. And, finally, it necessitates the realization that there is no way to inclusion. Inclusion *is* the way.

Notes

Opening Poem

1. Coleman Barks, Barry Phillips, and Shelley Phillips. Recitation of poems by Jalaluddin Rumi, *What Was Said to the Rose* (Athens, GA: Maypop Books, 2003), compact disc. Reprinted with permission.

Introduction

1. Margaret Mead, *Sex and Temperament in Three Primitive Societies* (New York: William Morrow, 1935).
2. Robert F. Allen, *Beat the System! A Way to Create More Human Environments* (New York: McGraw-Hill, 1980).

Chapter 1

1. Paulo Freire, *Pedagogy of the Oppressed* (New York: Herder & Herder, 1970).
2. Rita Mae Brown, *Sudden Death* (New York: Bantam, 1983), 68.
3. Kurt Lewin, *Field Theory in Social Science: Selected Theoretical Papers by Kurt Lewin* (London: Tavistock, 1952).
4. I have used the term *diversity* in the title of this book, as well as generally throughout the text, to describe the entire topic of diversity, inclusion, and cultural competency or cultural flexibility. I want to be clear that all of these distinctions are powerful and important, but I have used this shortcut mostly for the ease of language.
5. U.S. Census Bureau.
6. Salt Lake City Chamber of Commerce.

7. This collection of information was inspired by Karl Fisch, a high-school administrator in Littleton, Colorado, whose "Did You Know" slide show has been viewed by millions over the Internet.

8. One Laptop per Child, http://laptop.org/en/.

9. Robert D. Putnam, *Bowling Alone: The Collapse and Revival of American Community* (New York: Simon & Schuster, 2000).

10. Ibid, 18–24, for a broader explanation of the term.

11. Robert D. Putnam, "E Pluribus Unum: Diversity and Community in the Twenty-first Century, The 2006 Johan Skytte Prize Lecture," *Journal of the Nordic Political Science Association* (2007): 137.

12. Gordon Allport, *The Nature of Prejudice* (New York: Perseus, 1954), 261–82.

13. Putnam, "E Pluribus Unum," 147.

14. Ibid., 149.

15. Ibid., 151.

16. Daniel Henninger, "The Death of Diversity," *Wall Street Journal*, August 16, 2007.

17. Putnam, "E Pluribus Unum," 137–39.

18. Scott E. Page, *The Difference: How the Power of Diversity Creates Better Groups, Firms, Schools, and Societies* (Princeton, N.J.: Princeton University Press, 2007).

19. James Surowiecki, *The Wisdom of Crowds* (New York: Anchor Books/Random House, 2004).

20. Ibid., xvii–xviii.

21. U.S. Department of Labor, Bureau of Labor Statistics.

22. I use the term *people of color* throughout this book to refer to people who are often referred to as "minorities" (Black, Hispanic/Latino, Asian, Native-American Indian or Alaskan Native, etc.). While I know that most people understand this change in terminology, I think it bears explanation because the story of diversity in our country is a story of language. First, the term *minority* has a power differential in it that is framed by our democratic system. "Minorities" are those with less power; "majorities" get to rule. In the context of race, this not only minimizes people in those groups, but the term *minority* is simply an inaccurate description when in so many places in the country, people of color outnumber Whites. This was demonstrated not long ago when I had a conversation with the director of human resources of a client company of mine in the Washington, D.C., area. I asked her what the demographics of her company were, and she responded by saying, "We are about 63 percent minority." Point made.

23. Jeffrey M. Humphreys, "The Multicultural Economy: 1990–2013," Selig Center for Economic Growth, Terry College of Business, University of Georgia, 2008, 2.

24. Helen Keller, *The Open Door* (New York: Doubleday, 1957).

Chapter 2

1. Chris Argyris, *Teaching Smart People How to Learn* (Cambridge, Mass.: Harvard Business School Press, 2008).

2. A. A. Milne, *Winnie-the-Pooh* (London: Methuen, 1926).

3. Alexander Kalev, Frank Dobbin, and Erin Kelly, *Best Practices or Best Guesses? Diversity Management and the Remediation of Inequality* (Berkeley: University of California Press, 2007).

4. The term was first cited in 1992 by Massachusetts Institute of Technology researchers Arien Mack and Irvin Rock.

Chapter 3

1. Gregory Bateson, *Mind and Nature: A Necessary Unity* (New York: Macmillan, 1991).

2. Rwandan proverb.

3. In fact, as an example of how small the world is today, I was recently speaking at a conference in Singapore and went down to the ATM to get some cash. When I looked at the screen, a quotation from Helen Keller appeared!

4. Helen Keller, *My Religion* (New York: Doubleday, 1927), 200–202.

5. Ibid., 203.

6. The moment in the play when Keller says the word "water" is actually a fictionalization added for dramatic purposes so that the normally hearing and sighted could relate. It was years later that she learned to speak through a painstaking process of touching her teacher's lips and throat as Sullivan spoke and then repeating the physical manifestations in her own lips and throat.

7. John R. Searle, *The Construction of Social Reality* (New York: Free Press, 1995), 129.

8. Ibid., 132–33.

9. Carlos Castaneda, *A Separate Reality: Further Conversations with Don Juan* (New York: Pocket Books, 1971).

10. Dictionary.com, s.v. "ideology."

11. Ibid., s.v. "schema."

12. John Medina, *Brain Rules: 12 Principles for Surviving and Thriving at Work, Home, and School* (Seattle: Pear Press, 2008).

13. Terry Winograd and Fernando Flores, *Understanding Computers and Cognition* (Norwood, N.J.: Abelex, 1986), 57–58 (emphasis added).

14. I have seen this quoted so many times by so many people that it is difficult, if not impossible, to attribute authorship. I believe its original source is the Talmud, the record of interpretations of Jewish law that dates to as early as 200 CE.

15. *The Gods Must Be Crazy*, 109 min. (Ster Kinekor, Jensen Farley Pictures, 20th Century Fox, 1981).

16. Humberto R. Maturana and Francisco J. Varela, *The Tree of Knowledge: The Biological Roots of Human Understanding* (Boston: New Science Library, 1988), 16.

17. Philip Slater, *The Pursuit of Loneliness: American Culture at the Breaking Point* (Boston: Beacon Press, 1970).

18. Ibid., 19.

19. Erich Fromm, *Escape from Freedom* (New York: Rinehart, 1941), 51.

20. Ibid., 279.

21. S. E. Asch, "Effects of Group Pressure upon the Modification and Distortion of Judgment," in *Groups, Leadership and Men*, ed. H. Guetzkow (Pittsburgh: Carnegie Press, 1951).

22. Stanley Milgram, "Behavioral Study of Obedience," *Journal of Abnormal and Social Psychology* 24 (1963): 371–78.

23. Stanley Milgram, *Obedience to Authority: An Experimental View* (New York: Perennial Classics, 1974).

24. Albert Einstein and Leopold Infeld, *The Evolution of Physics: From Early Concept to Relativity and Quanta* (Cambridge: Cambridge University Press, 1938).

25. *The Truman Show*, 102 min. (Paramount Pictures, 1998).

Chapter 4

1. Wendell Berry, *The Long-Legged House* (Washington, DC: Shoemaker & Hoard, 1969).

2. *American Heritage Dictionary of the English Language*, 4th ed. (Boston: Houghton Mifflin Harcourt, 2000), s.v. "organization."

3. Ibid., s.v. "community."

4. Daniel Henninger, "The Death of Diversity," August 16, 2007. Retrieved from Real Clear Politics, www.realclearpolitics.com/articles/2007/08/the_death_of_diversity.html.

5. Richard Dawkins, *The Selfish Gene* (Oxford: Oxford University Press, 1976).

6. Susan Blackmore, *The Meme Machine* (Oxford: Oxford University Press, 1999).

7. Daniel Dennett, *Consciousness Explained* (Boston: Little, Brown, 1991) and *Darwin's Dangerous Idea: Evolution and the Meanings of Life* (New York: Simon & Schuster, 1995).

8. Dana Milbank and Claudia Dean, "Hussein Link to 9-11 Lingers in Many Minds," *Washington Post*, September 6, 2003.

9. Pew Research Center and the Pew Forum on Religion and Public Life (poll), August 18, 2010.

10. For an excellent study of this dysfunctional phenomenon see Colin Trumbull, *The Mountain People* (New York: Simon & Schuster, 1972). Trumbull studied the decline of the Ik, an Ugandan mountain-based tribe, in the face of severe environmental hardship.

11. Robert Greenleaf, *Servant Leadership: A Journey into the Nature of Legitimate Power and Greatness* (New York: Paulist Press, 1977), 83.

12. Albert Einstein, *The World As I See It* (Amsterdam: Querido, 1933).

13. George Orwell, *The Principles of Newspeak: An Appendix to Nineteen Eighty-Four* (London: Secker and Warburg, 1949).

14. Erich Fromm, *Beyond Chains of Illusion: My Encounter with Marx and Freud* (New York: Simon & Schuster, 1962).

15. Humberto R. Maturana and Francisco J. Varela, *The Tree of Knowledge: The Biological Roots of Human Understanding* (Boston: Shambhala, 1992), 9.

16. Jane Wagner and Lily Tomlin, *The Search for Signs of Intelligent Life in the Universe*, directed by Jane Wagner (1991).

17. Thomas Jefferson, "Letter to the Danbury Baptist Association" (1802). Retrieved on February 17, 2011, from www.loc.gov/loc/lcib/9806/danbury.html.

18. American Psychological Association, "Lesbian & Gay Parenting" (2005). Retrieved on February 17, 2011, from www.apaorg/pi/lgbt/resources/parenting-full.pdf.

19. Terry Winograd and Fernando Flores, *Understanding Computers and Cognition* (Reading, Mass.: Addison-Wesley Professional, 1987), 31.

20. Frederick Jackson Turner, "The Significance of the Frontier in American History," *Proceedings of the State Historical Society of Wisconsin*, 1893.

21. Robert Reich, "Government in Your Business," *Harvard Business Review* (July/August 2009), 78.

22. Unfortunately, I do not recall the name of this extraordinary woman, but her recollection of her experience is not unlike many others that I heard among the rescuers I met.

23. Robert N. Bellah, Richard Madsen, William M. Sullivan, Ann Swidler, and Steven Tipton, *Habits of the Heart: Individualism and Commitment in American Life* (Berkeley: University of California Press, 2007), 150–51.

Chapter 5

1. Saul Alinsky, *Rules for Radicals: A Pragmatic Primer for Realistic Radicals* (New York: Random House, 1971).

2. Thomas S. Kuhn, *The Structure of Scientific Revolutions* (Chicago: University of Chicago Press, 1962).

3. Ibid., 10.

4. Thomas S. Kuhn, *The Essential Tension: Selected Studies in Scientific Tradition and Change* (Chicago and London: University of Chicago Press, 1977), 460.

5. D. J. Simons, G. Nevarez, and W. R. Boot, "Visual Sensing Is Seeing: Why 'Mindsight,' in Hindsight, Is Blind," *Psychological Science* 16 (2005): 520–24.

6. T. Nørretranders, *The User Illusion*, trans. J. Sydenham (New York: Viking, 1998), cited in Timothy Wilson, *Strangers to Ourselves: Discovering the Adaptive Unconscious* (Cambridge, Mass.: Belknap Press of Harvard University Press, 2002), 24.

7. If you weren't able to get it, the sentences read, "Can you read this? You are not reading this. What are you reading?" The experiment was created by the brilliant experimental neuroscientist Beau Lotto.

8. Richard Rorty, *Philosophy and the Mirror of Nature* (Princeton, N.J.: Princeton University Press, 1980).

9. Shirley Sherrod, "Address at the Georgia NAACP Twentieth Annual Freedom Fund Banquet," March 27, 2010. Retrieved from www.americanrhetoric.com/speeches/shirleysherrodnaacpfreedom.htm.

10. Sherrod, "Address."

11. Ernst von Glasersfeld, *Distinguishing the Observer: An Attempt at Interpreting Maturana* (Frankfurt, Germany: Zuhrkamp, 1990).

12. Humberto R. Maturana and Francisco J. Varela, *The Tree of Knowledge: The Biological Roots of Human Understanding* (Boston: New Science Library, 1988).

13. "The Story of Dick Fosbury at the XIX Olympiad," Oregon State University Alumni Association, 1968. Retrieved on February 2, 2011, from www.osualum.com/s/359/index.aspx?sid=359&gid=1&verbiagebuilder=1&pgid=387.

14. William B. Johnston and Arnold H. Packer, *Workforce 2000* (Washington, D.C.: Hudson Institute Press, 1987). Retrieved on February 17, 2011, from www.hudson.org/booksore/itemdetail.cfm?item=1035.

15. Krissah Thompson, "Harvard Professor Arrested at Home," *Washington Post*, July 21, 2009.

16. Idries Shah, *Tales of the Dervishes* (London: Penguin, 1967), 29.

17. This metaphor was created by my dear friend and colleague, Michael Schiesser.

Chapter 6

1. Geert Hofstede, *Culture and Organizations: Software of the Mind* (New York: McGraw-Hill, 1991).

2. The term originated in anthropology as a means of explaining the "observer effect." Scientists have long understood that the act of observing is a phenomenon that impacts the behavior and culture of those being observed.

3. Thomas Friedman, *The World Is Flat: A Brief History of the Twenty-first Century* (New York: Farrar, Straus & Giroux, 2005).

4. Adapted from T. Cross, B. Bazron, K. Dennis, and M. Isaacs, "Towards a Culturally Competent System of Care" (Washington, D.C.: CASSP Technical Assistance Center, Center for Child Health and Mental Health Policy, Georgetown University Child Development Center, 1989. Retrieved June 16, 2010, from www.nccccurricula.info/documents/TheContinuumRevised.doc.

5. Scott E. Page, *The Difference: How the Power of Diversity Creates Better Groups, Firms, Schools, and Societies* (Princeton, N.J.: Princeton University Press, 2007).

6. Surowiecki, James, *The Wisdom of Crowds* (New York: Anchor Books/Random House, 2004).

7. C. M. Pearson, L. Andersson, and C. L. Porath, "Assessing and Attacking Workplace Incivility," *Organizational Dynamics* 29 (2000): 123–37.

8. U.S. Department of Labor, Bureau of Labor Statistics, "The Employment Projections for 2008–18," retrieved December 14, 2009, from www.bls.gov/opub/mlr/2009/11/art1full.pdf; U.S. Department of Labor, Bureau of Labor Statistics, "Job Openings and Labor Turnover Survey," retrieved February 11, 2010, from www.bls.gov/jlt/.

9. National Association of Social Workers, "Diversity and Cultural Competence Fact Sheet." Retrieved September 11, 2009, from www.socialworkers.org/pressroom/features/issue/diversity.asp.

10. Stephen R. Covey, *The Seven Habits of Highly Effective People* (Glencoe, Ill.: Free Press, 1989).

11. With thanks to Robert F. Allen and Edgar Schein.

12. John H. Bodley, *Cultural Anthropology: Tribes, States, and the Global System* (Mountain View, Calif.: Mayfield, 1994), 12.

13. Wendy's television commercial, 1984. Retrieved February 23, 2011, from http://en.wikipedia.org/wiki/Where%27s_the_beef%3F.

14. Erving Goffman, *Stigma: Notes on the Management of Spoiled Identity* (Upper Saddle River, N.J.: Prentice Hall, 1963).

15. Shiri Lev-Ari and Boaz Keysar, "Why Don't We Believe Non-Native Speakers? The Influence of Accent on Credibility," *Journal of Experimental Social Psychology* 46, no. 3 (2010).

16. Milton J. Bennett, "Towards a Developmental Model of Intercultural Sensitivity," www.library.wisc.edu/EDVRC/docs/public/pdfs/SEEDReadings/intCulSens.pdf.

17. "What Is Cultural Competency?" U.S. Department of Health and Human Services, Office of Minority Health. Retrieved September 11, 2009, from: www.omhrc.gov/templates/browse.aspx?lvl=2&lvlID=11.

18. Patricia St. Onge, "Introduction: Conversation as a Tool for Transformation," in *Embracing Cultural Competency: A Roadmap for Nonprofit Capacity Builders*, ed. Patricia St. Onge (St. Paul, Minn.: Fieldstone Alliance, 2009).

Chapter 7

1. Maha Sthavira Sangharakshita, *The Essense of Zen* (Cambridge: Windhorse Publications, 1997). Retrieved on February 17, 2011, from www.sangharakshita.org/_books/essence-of-zen.pdf.

2. These ideas are adapted from the work of Alan Page Fiske, associate professor of anthropology at the University of California, Los Angeles.

3. Joseph LeDoux, *The Emotional Brain: The Mysterious Underpinnings of Emotional Life* (New York: Simon & Schuster, 1996).

4. Gordon Allport, *The Nature of Prejudice* (New York: Basic Books, 1979), 23.

5. Encarta World English Dictionary, CD-ROM (Microsoft Corporation, 1999).

6. Timothy D. Wilson, *Strangers to Ourselves* (Cambridge, Mass.: Harvard University Press, 2004).

7. N. E. Miller and J. Dollard, *Social Learning and Imitation* (New Haven, Conn.: Yale University Press, 1941).

8. J. B. Rotter, *Social Learning and Clinical Psychology* (Upper Saddle River, N.J.: Prentice-Hall, 1954).

9. A. Bandura, *Social Learning through Imitation* (Lincoln: University of Nebraska Press, 1962).

10. Malcom Gladwell discusses this phenomenon in his book *Blink*, based on research conducted by Timothy Judge and Daniel Cable.

11. Timothy A. Judge and Daniel M. Cable, "The Effect of Physical Height on Workplace Success and Income," *Journal of Applied Psychology* (June 2004): 435.

12. Ibid., 428.

13. These dynamics are less consistent for women because shorter men, and sometimes even women, may be intimidated by, or feel uncomfortable with, taller women.

14. D. J. Simons and C. F. Chabris, "Gorillas in Our Midst: Sustained Inattentional Blindness for Dynamic Events," *Perception* 28 (1999): 1059–74.

15. Ian Ayres, *Pervasive Prejudice: Unconventional Evidence of Race and Gender Discrimination* (Chicago: University of Chicago Press, 2001), 19–44. This work is also discussed in Malcolm Gladwell's *Blink*. For the original study, refer to the work Ayres published as "Fair Driving: Gender and Race Discrimination in Retail Car Negotiations," *Harvard Law Review* 817 (1991).

16. ABC News, *20/20*, "True Colors," September 26, 1991 (viewable at www.youtube.com/watch?v=YyL5EcAwB9c).

17. Ian Ayres, Fred Vars, and Nasser Zakariya, "To Insure Prejudice: Racial Disparities in Taxicab Tipping," *Yale Law Journal* 1613 (2005):114.

18. Roger Shepard, *Mind Sights: Original Visual Illusions, Ambiguities, and Other Anomalies* (New York: Freeman, 1990), 48.

19. Ibid., 46.

20. Ibid., 128.

21. Samuel R. Sommers and Michael I. Norton, "Race-Based Judgments, Race-Neutral Justifications: Experimental Examination of Peremptory Use and the Batson Challenge Procedure," *Law and Human Behavior* 31, no. 3 (June 2007):261–73.

22. For a more complete look at this study, see J. L. Eberhardt, P. A. Goff, V. J. Purdie, and P. G. Davies, "Seeing Black: Race, Crime, and Visual Processing," *Journal of Personality and Social Psychology* (2004) and J. L. Eberhardt and P. A. Goff, "Seeing Race," in *Social Psychology of Prejudice: Historical and Contemporary Issues*, ed. C. S. Crandall and M. Schaller (Seattle: Lewinian Press, 2005), 215–32.

23. Katherine Beckett and Theodore Sasson, *The Politics of Injustice: Crime and Punishment in America* (Thousand Oaks, Calif.: Sage, 2004), 173.

24. J. L. Eberhardt, P. G. Davies, V. J. Purdie-Vaughns, and S. L. Johnson, "Looking Deathworthy: Perceived Stereotypicality of Black Defendants Predicts Capital Sentencing Outcomes," *Psychological Science* 17 (2006):383–86.

25. To take the Implicit Association Test or to learn more about this research, view https://implicit.harvard.edu/implicit.

26. Shankar Vedantam, "See No Bias," *Washington Post*, January 23, 2005.

27. Davis showed her study being conducted in a wonderful seven-minute film titled *A Girl Like Me*, which can be seen online on a number of websites. It is particularly poignant because the film actually shows several of the children taking the test.

28. Mahzarin Banaji, quoted by Shankar Vedantam, "See No Bias," *Washington Post*, January 23, 2005.

29. Alexander R. Green, M.D., MPh, Dana R. Carney, PhD, Daniel J. Pallin, M.D., MPh, Long H. Ngo, PhD, Kristal L. Raymond, MPh, Lisa I. Iezzoni, M.D., MSc; Mahzarin R. Banaji, PhD, "Implicit Bias among Physicians and Its Prediction of Throm-

bolysis Decisions for Black and White Patients," *Journal of General Internal Medicine*, September 2007.

30. This study was referenced in Shankar Vedantam, "See No Bias," *Washington Post*, January 23, 2005.

31. Marianne Bertrand and Sendhil Mullainathan, "Are Emily and Greg More Employable Than Lakisha and Jamal? A Field Experiment on Labor Market Discrimination" (Working Paper No. 03-22, MIT Department of Economics, May 27, 2003).

32. Nicholas D. Kristof, "What? Me Biased?" *New York Times*, October 29, 2008.

33. Charles C. Ballew II, and Alexander Todorov, "Predicting Political Elections from Rapid and Unreflective Face Judgments," *National Academy of Sciences*, June 2007.

34. R. Rosenthal and L. Jacobson, "Pygmalion in the Classroom," *Urban Review*, 1968.

35. Lawrence E. Williams and John Bargh, "Experiencing Physical Warmth Promotes Interpersonal Warmth," *Science* 322, no.5901 (October 24, 2008):606–7.

36. Michelle R. Hebl and Laura M. Mannix, "The Weight of Obesity in Evaluating Others: A Mere Proximity Effect," *Personality and Social Psychology Bulletin* 29 (2003): 28.

37. Melissa Bateson, Daniel Nettles, and Gilbert Roberts, "Cues of Being Watched Enhance Cooperation in a Real-World Setting," *Biology Letters*, The Royal Society, June 2006.

38. Daniel Arielly, *Predictably Irrational: The Hidden Forces That Shape Our Decisions* (New York: Harper Collins, 2008).

39. Margaret Shih, Todd L. Pittinsky, and Nalini Ambady, "Stereotype Susceptibility: Shifts in Quantitative Performance from Socio-Cultural Identification," *Psychological Science* 10, no. 1 (January 1999): 80–83.

40. Claude M. Steele, "A Threat in the Air: How Stereotypes Shape Intellectual Identity and Performance," *American Psychologist* (June 1997): 613–29.

41. A. J. C. Cuddy, "Just Because I'm Nice, Don't Assume I'm Dumb," *Harvard Business Review* 87 (2009): 24.

42. CNN, January 31, 2007.

43. Shanto Iyengar and Richard Morin, "Natural Disasters in Black and White," *Washington Post*, June 8, 2006.

44. Timothy D. Wilson, *Strangers to Ourselves: Discovering the Adaptive Unconscious* (Cambridge, Mass.: Belknap Press of Harvard University Press), 2002, 16.

45. Mahzarin Banaji, quoted by Shankar Vedantam, "See No Bias," *Washington Post*, January 23, 2005.

Chapter 8

1. Malcolm X (with Alex Haley), *The Autobiography of Malcolm X* (New York: Grove, 1965).

2. Oscar Wilde, *De Profundis* (London: Methuen, 1905).

3. G. H. Mead, *Mind, Self and Society* (Chicago: University of Chicago Press, 1934).

4. Jeff Pearlman, "At Full Blast," *Sports Illustrated*, December 23, 1999.

5. I am referring to groups that represent the predominant influence in societal norms, values, power, and privilege. In the United States, that generally refers to Whites, men, Christians, heterosexuals, and so on.

6. Yolanda Woodlee, "Williams Aide Resigns in Language Dispute," *Washington Post*, January 27, 1999.

Chapter 9

1. Ken Wilber, *The Collected Works of Ken Wilber*, vol. 8, *The Marriage of Sense and Soul—Integrating Science and Religion/One Taste* (Boston: Shambhala, 2000).

2. A special thanks to my colleague Howie Schaffer for his assistance with this chapter.

3. Viktor Frankl, *Man's Search for Meaning: An Introduction to Logotherapy* (Boston: Beacon, 1959).

Chapter 10

1. Chief Seattle is believed to have used this language in 1851, when the Suquamish and other Puget Sound tribes were presented with a treaty that in part persuaded them to sell some two million acres of land for approximately $150,000.

2. Eric Watson, in conversation with Howard Ross.

3. Ken Keyes Jr., *The Hundredth Monkey* (Los Angeles: DeVorss, 1984), 11–16.

4. Brigid Schulte, "Breast Cancer Awareness Goes Viral on Facebook . . . with Bra Color Updates," *Washington Post*, January 9, 2010, retrieved March 2, 2011 from www.washingtonpost.com/wp-dyn/content/article/2010/01/08/AR2010010803693 .html.

5. Hannah Arendt, *Eichmann in Jerusalem: A Report on the Banality of Evil* (New York: Penguin, 1977), 287–88.

Chapter 11

1. Lewis Carroll, *Alice's Adventures in Wonderland* (London: Macmillan).

2. John Gardner, "The Life and Death of Institutions," retrieved March 2, 2011, from http://findarticles.com/p/articles/mi_7566/is_200803/ai_n32280016/pg_2/.

3. Robert Fritz, *The Path of Least Resistance: Learning to Become the Creative Force in Your Own Life* (New York: Random House, 1989).

4. Martin Luther King Jr., "Letter from Birmingham Jail," in *Why We Can't Wait* (New York: Harper & Row, 1964).

5. Professor Emeritus Chris Argyris of Harvard University Business School described these as "undiscussible undiscussibles."

6. Scott Peck, *The Different Drum: Community Making and Peace* (New York: Simon & Schuster, 1987).

Chapter 12

1. Tom Peters and Robert H. Waterman Jr., *In Search of Excellence* (New York: HarperCollins, 1982).

2. Government Accounting Office, *Women in Management: Female Managers' Representation, Characteristics, and Pay* (Washington, D.C.: GAO-10-1064T, September 28, 2010).

3. Marvin Ross Weisbord, *Discovering Common Ground: How Future Search Conferences Bring People Together to Achieve Breakthrough Innovation, Empowerment, Shared Vision, and Collaborative Action* (San Francisco: Barrett-Koehler, 1992).

4. My wife and business partner, Leslie Traub, has created a program called "Dynamic Choices for Women," which specifically focuses on helping women better understand the internal impact of this and make choices that encourage them to stay with their organization. Some six hundred female employees of one client attended this program, and 19 percent said that they had been thinking of leaving but now would stay.

5. I use the term *customers* to generally address any people served by an organization. You may use *clients*, *patients*, *guests*, and so on, depending upon your organization.

Chapter 13

1. Saul Alinsky, *Rules for Radicals: A Pragmatic Primer for Realistic Radicals* (New York: Vintage, 1989).

Chapter 14

1. Stedman Graham, *Diversity: Leaders, Not Labels—A New Plan for the Twenty-first Century* (New York: Free Press, 2006), 224.

2. Audre Lorde, *The Black Unicorn* (New York: Norton, 1978).

3. I strongly recommend Roger Fisher and William L. Ury's simple and powerful book, *Getting to Yes: Negotiating Agreement without Giving In* (New York: Penguin Books, 1983), as a good way to learn about this approach. The training I did with their colleagues at the Harvard Negotiation Project twenty years ago fundamentally changed my view of ways to develop understanding between people on even the most difficult of issues.

4. Nicolo Machiavelli, *The Prince* (1532), 6.

5. Caitlin Ryan, David Huebner, Rafael M. Diaz, and Jorge Sanchez, "Family Rejection as a Predictor of Negative Health Outcomes in White and Latino Lesbian, Gay, and Bisexual Young Adults," *Journal of the American Academy of Pediatrics* 16, no. 1 (January 2009), 346–52.

6. The exact percentage of lesbian, gay, bisexual, and transgender (LGBT) people in our society is hard to calculate and greatly disputed. I choose to use the percentage cited by the Human Rights Campaign, the nation's largest advocacy group for LGBT rights, because I believe they have taken a studied approach to determining the number.

7. Brian D. Smedley, Adrienne Y. Stith, and Alan R. Nelson, eds., *Unequal Treatment: Confronting Racial and Ethnic Disparities in Health Care* (Washington, D.C.: National Academies Press, Institute of Medicine of the National Academies, Committee on Understanding and Eliminating Racial and Ethnic Disparities in Health Care, 2003).

8. Another lesson from my mentor, Robert F. Allen.

9. Interview with R. Buckminster Fuller, *Playboy*, February 1972.

10. I am deeply indebted to my friend and colleague Paul Hawken, who began my thinking on this piece in his brilliant book *Blessed Unrest* and who has granted me permission to build on it here. Paul Hawken, *Blessed Unrest: How the Largest Movement In the World Came into Being and Why No One Saw It Coming* (New York: Viking, 2007), 71–85.

11. Robert D. Richardson, *Emerson: The Mind on Fire* (Alexandria, Va.: Centennial, 1996).

12. Simon Schama, *Rough Crossings: Britain, the Slaves, and the American Revolution* (New York: HarperCollins, 2006).

13. Henry David Thoreau, *Walden: On Life in the Woods* (Boston: Ticknor and Fields, 1854), 393–94.

14. Henry David Thoreau, "On the Duty of Civil Disobedience" (1849).

15. Mohandas K. Gandhi, *Speeches and Writings of Mahatma Gandhi* (Madras, India: G. A. Natesan, 1933), 227, as cited in Paul Hawken, *Blessed Unrest: How the Largest Movement in the World Came Into Being and Why No One Saw It Coming* (New York: Viking, 2007).

16. Carol Morello, "The Freedom Rider a Nation Nearly Forgot: Woman Who Defied Segregation Finally Gets Her Due," *Washington Post*, July 30, 2000, A1.

17. Catherine A. Barnes, *Journey from Jim Crow: The Desegregation of Southern Transit* (New York: Columbia University Press, 1983), 86–107.

18. Brooks Barnes, "From Footnote to Fame in Civil Rights History," *New York Times*, November 5, 2009.

19. Taylor Branch, *Parting the Waters: America in the King Years 1954–63* (New York: Simon & Schuster, 1989), 121–35.

20. Rosa Parks, *Rosa Parks: My Story* (New York: Dial, 1992), 101, as cited in Hawken, *Blessed Unrest*, 80.

21. The latter part of this quote is on Ms. Hamer's tombstone in her hometown of Ruleville, Mississippi.

22. Myles Horton (with Judith and Herbert Kohl), *The Long Haul: An Autobiography* (New York: Teachers College Press, 1998).

23. Stewart Burns, *To the Mountaintop: Martin Luther King Jr.'s Sacred Mission to Save America: 1955–1968* (San Francisco: HarperCollins, 2004), 14–18, as cited in Paul Hawken, *Blessed Unrest: How the Largest Movement in the World Came Into Being and Why No One Saw It Coming*, p. 83.

24. Hawken, *Blessed Unrest*, 83.

25. Branch, *Parting the Waters*, 174.

26. Richard B. Gregg, *The Power of Non-Violence* (Philadelphia: Lippincott, 1934).

27. Nat Hentoff, *Peace Agitator: The Story of A. J. Muste* (New York: A. J. Muste Memorial Institute, 1982).

28. Richard Rankin, "Talking Tolerance," *Wo!* (November/December 2006).

29. See www.aidsquilt.org.

30. See www.nclr.org.

31. Here the story intertwines with my own because as a teenager, I volunteered for the UFW in the early grape boycott and had a brief chance to meet Chavez. This still ranks as one of the most significant moments of my life.

32. Sanford D. Horwitt, *Let Them Call Me Rebel: Saul Alinsky: His Life and Legacy* (New York: Vintage, 1989).

33. I. F. Stone, retreived March 2, 2011, from www.babson.us/quotes/other_quotes.html.

34. Though I have never been able to confirm it, this quote has been attributed to Benjamin Franklin, Ralph Waldo Emerson, and the writer and journalist I. F. Stone.

Bibliography

Author's Note: I have tried very hard to include the writers and researchers who have influenced the ideas and perspectives presented in this book. I apologize for any who may have been omitted.

Adelson, E. H. "Lightness Perception and Lightness Illusions." In *The New Cognitive Neurosciences*. 2nd ed., edited by Michael S. Gazzaniga, 339–51. Cambridge, Mass.: MIT Press, 2000.

Alinsky, Saul. *Rules for Radicals: A Pragmatic Primer for Realistic Radicals*. New York: Random House, 1971.

Allen, Robert F. *Beat the System! A Way to Create More Human Environments*. New York: McGraw-Hill, 1980.

Allen, Robert F., and Stanley Silverzweig. "Changing Community and Organizational Cultures." *Training and Development Journal* (July 1977).

Allport, Gordon. *The Nature of Prejudice*. New York: Perseus, 1954.

Arendt, Hannah. *Eichmann in Jerusalem: A Report on the Banality of Evil*. New York: Penguin Books, 1977.

Argyris, Chris. *Teaching Smart People How to Learn*. Cambridge, Mass.: Harvard Business School Press, 2008.

Arielly, Daniel. *Predictably Irrational: The Hidden Forces That Shape Our Decisions*. New York: Harper Collins, 2008.

Asch, Solomon E. "Effects of Group Pressure upon the Modification and Distortion of Judgments." In *Groups, Leadership and Men*, edited by H. Guetzkow, 177–90. Pittsburgh: Carnegie Press, 1951.

Ayres, Ian. *Pervasive Prejudice: Unconventional Evidence of Race and Gender Discrimination*. Chicago: University of Chicago Press, 2001.

Ayres, Ian, Fred Vars, and Nasser Zakariya. "To Insure Prejudice: Racial Disparities in Taxicab Tipping." *Yale Law Journal* 144 (2005): 1613.

Ballew, Charles C., and Alexander Todorov. "Predicting Political Elections from Rapid and Unreflective Face Judgments." *National Academy of Sciences* (June 2007).

Banaji, Mahzarin. "See No Bias." Interview by Shankar Vedantam. *Washington Post*, January 23, 2005.

Barnes, Brooks. "From Footnote to Fame in Civil Rights History." *New York Times*, November 5, 2009.

Barnes, Catherine A. *Journey from Jim Crow: The Desegregation of Southern Transit*, 86–107. New York: Columbia University Press, 1983.

Bateson, Gregory. *Mind and Nature: A Necessary Unity*. New York: Macmillan, 1991.

Bateson, Melissa, Daniel Nettles, and Gilbert Roberts. "Cues of Being Watched Enhance Cooperation in a Real-World Setting." *Biology Letters* (June 2006).

Bellah, Robert N., Richard Madsen, William M. Sullivan, Ann Swidler, and Steven Tipton. *Habits of the Heart: Individualism and Commitment in American Life*. Berkeley: University of California Press, 2007.

Bennett, Milton J. "Towards a Developmental Model of Intercultural Sensitivity." www.library.wisc.edu/EDVRC/docs/public/pdfs/SEEDReadings/intCulSens.pdf.

Berry, Wendell. *The Long-Legged House*. Washington, DC: Shoemaker and Hoard, 1969.

Bertrand, Marianne, and Sendhil Mullainathan. *Are Emily and Greg More Employable Than Lakisha and Jamal? A Field Experiment on Labor Market Discrimination*. MIT Department of Economics Working Paper, 2003.

Blackmore, Susan. *The Meme Machine*. Oxford: Oxford University Press, 1999.

Bodley, John H. *Cultural Anthropology: Tribes, States, and the Global System*. Mountain View, Calif.: Mayfield, 1994.

Branch, Taylor. *Parting the Waters: America in the King Years 1954–63*. New York: Simon & Schuster, 1989.

Brown, Rita Mae. *Sudden Death*. New York: Bantam, 1983.

Burns, Stewart. *To the Mountaintop: Martin Luther King Jr.'s Sacred Mission to Save America: 1955–1968*. San Francisco: HarperCollins, 2004.

Carroll, Lewis. *Alice's Adventures in Wonderland*. London: Macmillan, 1865.

Castaneda, Carlos. *A Separate Reality: Further Conversations with Don Juan*. New York: Pocket Books, 1971.

Covey, Stephen R. *The Seven Habits of Highly Effective People*. Glencoe, Ill.: Free Press, 1989.

Cross, T., B. Bazron, K. Dennis, and M. Isaacs. *Towards a Culturally Competent System of Care*. Vol. 1. Washington, DC: CASSP Technical Assistance Center, Center for Child Health and Mental Health Policy, Georgetown University Child Development Center, 1989. Accessed June 16, 2010. www.nccccurricula.info//.doc.

Cuddy, Amy J. C. "Just Because I'm Nice, Don't Assume I'm Dumb." *Harvard Business Review* no. 87 (2009): 24.

Cuddy, Amy J. C., Susan T. Fiske, and Peter Glick. "Warmth and Competence as Universal Dimensions of Social Perception: The Stereotype Content Model and the BIAS Map." *Advances in Experimental Social Psychology*, vol. 40 (2008).

Damasio, Antonio. *Self Comes to Mind: Constructing the Conscious Brain*. New York: Pantheon, 2010.

Dawkins, Richard. *The Selfish Gene*. Oxford: Oxford University Press, 1976.

Dennett, Daniel. *Consciousness Explained*. Boston: Little, Brown, 1991.

————. *Darwin's Dangerous Idea: Evolution and the Meanings of Life.* New York: Simon & Schuster, 1995.

"Diversity and Cultural Competence Fact Sheet." National Association of Social Workers. Accessed September 11, 2009. www.socialworkers.org/pressroom/features/issue/diversity.asp.

Dobbs, Richard, and Rajat Gupta. "An Indian Approach to Global M&A: An Interview with the CFO of Tata Steel." *McKinsey Quarterly* (October 2009).

Eberhardt, J. L., P. G. Davies, V. J. Purdie-Vaughns, and S. L. Johnson. "Looking Deathworthy: Perceived Stereotypicality of Black Defendants Predicts Capital Sentencing Outcomes." *Psychological Science* 17 (2006): 383–86.

Eberhardt, J. L., and P. A. Goff. "Seeing Race." In *Social Psychology of Prejudice: Historical and Contemporary Issues*, edited by C. S. Crandall and M. Schaller, 215–32. Seattle: Lewinian Press, 2005.

Eberhardt, J. L., P. A. Goff, V. J. Purdie, and P. G. Davies. "Seeing Black: Race, Crime, and Visual Processing." *Journal of Personality and Social Psychology* (2004).

Einstein, Albert. *The World As I See It.* Amsterdam: Querido, 1933.

Einstein, Albert, and Leopold Infeld. *The Evolution of Physics: From Early Concept to Relativity and Quanta.* Cambridge: Cambridge University Press, 1938.

Frankl, Viktor. *Man's Search for Meaning: An Introduction to Logotherapy.* Boston: Beacon Press, 1959.

Frantz, Cynthia M., Amy J. C. Cuddy, Molly Burnett, Heidi Ray, and Allen Hart. "A Threat in the Computer: The Race Implicit Association Test as a Stereotype Threat Experience." *Personality and Social Psychology Bulletin* 30: 1611–24.

Freire, Paulo. *Pedagogy of the Oppressed.* New York: Herder & Herder, 1970.

Friedman, Thomas. *The World Is Flat: A Brief History of the Twenty-first Century.* New York: Farrar, Straus & Giroux, 2005.

Fritz, Robert. *The Path of Least Resistance: Learning to Become the Creative Force in Your Own Life.* New York: Random House, 1989.

Fromm, Erich. *Beyond Chains of Illusion: My Encounter with Marx and Freud.* New York: Simon & Schuster, 1962.

————. *Escape From Freedom.* New York: Rinehart, 1941.

Fuller, R. Buckminster. Interview. *Playboy*, February 1972.

Gandhi, Mohandas K. *Speeches and Writings of Mahatma Ghandhi.* Madras, India: G. A. Natesan, 1933.

Gladwell, Malcolm. *Blink: The Power of Thinking without Thinking.* New York: Little, Brown, 2005.

Goffman, Erving. *Stigma: Notes on the Management of Spoiled Identity.* Upper Saddle River, N.J.: Prentice Hall, 1963.

Graham, Stedman. *Diversity: Leaders, Not Labels—A New Plan for the Twenty-first Century.* New York: Free Press, 2006.

Green, Alexander R., Dana R. Carney, Daniel J. Pallin, Long H. Ngo, Kristal L. Raymond, Lisa I. Iezzoni, and Mahzarin R. Banaji. "Implicit Bias among Physicians and Its Prediction of Thrombolysis Decisions for Black and White Patients." *Journal of General Internal Medicine* (September 2007).

Greenleaf, Robert. *Servant Leadership: A Journey into the Nature of Legitimate Power and Greatness.* New York: Paulist Press, 1977.

Greenwald, Anthony G., and Linda Hamilton Krieger. "Implicit Bias: Scientific Foundations." *California Law Review* 94, no. 4 (July 2006): 945–67.

Greenwald, Anthony G., Debbie E. McGhee, and Jordan L. K. Schwartz. "Measuring Individual Differences in Implicit Cognition: The Implicit Association Test." *Journal of Personality and Social Psychology* 74, no. 6 (1998): 1464–80.

Gregg, Richard B. *The Power of Non-Violence.* Philadelphia: Lippincott, 1934.

Grodsky, Eric, and Devah Pager. "The Structure of Disadvantage: Individual and Occupational Determinants of the Black-White Wage Gap." *American Sociological Review* 66 (August 2001): 542–67.

Hawken, Paul. *Blessed Unrest: How the Largest Movement in the World Came into Being and Why No One Saw It Coming.* New York: Viking, 2007.

Hebl, Michelle R., and Laura M. Mannix. "The Weight of Obesity in Evaluating Others: A Mere Proximity Effect." *Personality and Social Psychology Bulletin* 29 (2003): 28.

Heidegger, Martin. *On the Way to Language.* New York: HarperCollins, 1971.

Henninger, Daniel. "The Death of Diversity." *Wall Street Journal,* August 2007.

Hentoff, Nat. *Peace Agitator: The Story of A. J. Muste.* New York: A. J. Muste Memorial Institute, 1982.

Hofstede, Geert. *Culture and Organizations: Software of the Mind.* New York: McGraw-Hill, 1991.

Horton, Myles. *The Long Haul: An Autobiography.* New York: Teachers College Press, 1998.

Horwitt, Sanford D. *Let Them Call Me Rebel: Saul Alinsky: His Life and Legacy.* New York: Vintage, 1989.

Humphreys, Jeffrey M. *The Multicultural Economy: 1990–2013.* Selig Center for Economic Growth, Terry College of Business, University of Georgia, 2008.

Iyengar, Shanto, and Richard Morin. "Natural Disasters in Black and White." *Washington Post,* June 8, 2006.

Jost, John T., Mahzarin R. Banaji, and Brian A. Nosek. "A Decade of System Justification Theory: Accumulated Evidence of Conscious and Unconscious Bolstering of the Status Quo." *Political Psychology* 25, no. 6 (2004): 881–919.

Judge, Timothy A., and Daniel M. Cable. "The Effect of Physical Height on Workplace Success and Income." *Journal of Applied Psychology* (June 2004): 435.

Kalev, Alexander, Frank Dobbin, and Erin Kelly. *Best Practices or Best Guesses? Diversity Management and the Remediation of Inequality.* Berkeley: University of California Press, 2007.

Keller, Helen. *My Religion.* New York: Doubleday, 1927.

Keyes, Ken, Jr. *The Hundredth Monkey.* Los Angeles: DeVorss, 1984.

King, Martin Luther, Jr. "Letter from Birmingham Jail." In *Why We Can't Wait.* New York: Harper & Row, 1964.

Kluger, Jeffrey. "What Makes Us Moral." *Time,* December 3, 2007, 54–58, 60.

Kristof, Nicholas D. "What? Me Biased?" *New York Times,* October 29, 2008.

Kugler, M. B., J. Cooper, and B. A. Nosek. "Group-based Dominance and Support for Equality as Consequences of Different Psychological Motives." *Social Justice Research* 23 (2010): 117–55.

Kuhn, Thomas S. *The Essential Tension: Selected Studies in Scientific Tradition and Change*. Chicago: University of Chicago Press, 1977.

———. *The Structure of Scientific Revolutions*. Chicago: University of Chicago Press, 1962.

Lane, K. A., M. R. Banaji, B. A. Nosek, and A. G. Greenwald. "Understanding and Using the Implicit Association Test: IV: Procedures and Validity." In *Implicit Measures of Attitudes*, edited by Bernd Wittenbrink and Norbert Schwarz, 59–102. New York: Guilford, 2007.

LeDoux, Joseph. *The Emotional Brain: The Mysterious Underpinnings of Emotional Life*. New York: Simon & Schuster, 1996.

Lev-Ari, Shiri, and Boaz Keysar. "Why Don't We Believe Non-Native Speakers? The Influence of Accent on Credibility." *Journal of Experimental Social Psychology* (May 2009).

Lewin, Kurt. *Field Theory in Social Science: Selected Theoretical Papers*. London: Tavistock, 1952.

Living Compassion. www.livingcompassion.org.

Lorde, Audre. *The Black Unicorn*. New York: Norton, 1978.

Machiavelli, Nicolo. *The Prince*. 1532.

Marsh, A. A., and N. Ambady. "The Influence of the Fear Facial Expression on Prosocial Responding." *Cognition and Emotion*.

Maturana, Humberto R., and Francisco J. Varela. *The Tree of Knowledge: The Biological Roots of Human Understanding*. Boston: New Science Library, 1988.

Mead, G. H. *Mind, Self and Society*. Chicago: University of Chicago Press, 1934.

Mead, Margaret. *Sex and Temperament in Three Primitive Societies*. New York: William Morrow, 1935.

Medina, John. *Brain Rules: 12 Principles for Surviving and Thriving at Work, Home, and School*. Seattle: Pear Press, 2008.

Milbank, Dana, and Claudia Dean. "Hussein Link to 9-11 Lingers in Many Minds." *Washington Post*, September 6, 2003.

Milgram, Stanley. "Behavioral Study of Obedience." *Journal of Abnormal and Social Psychology* 24 (1963): 371–78.

———. *Obedience to Authority: An Experimental View*. New York: Perennial Classics, 1974.

Milne, A. A. *Winnie-the-Pooh*. London: Methuen, 1926.

Molinsky, A., M. Krabbenhoft, N. Ambady, and Y. S. Choi. "Cracking the Nonverbal Code: Intercultural Competence and the Diagnosis of Gestures across Cultures." *Journal of Cross Cultural Psychology* 36 (2005): 380–95.

Morello, Carol. "The Freedom Rider a Nation Nearly Forgot: Woman Who Defied Segregation Finally Gets Her Due." *Washington Post*, July 30, 2000.

Nørretranders, T. *The User Illusion*. Translated by J. Sydenham. New York: Viking, 1998.

The NAMES Project Foundation, AIDS Memorial Quilt. www.aidsquilt.org/.htm.

National Council of La Raza. www.nclr.org/.

Nosek, B. A., M. R. Banaji, and A. G. Greenwald. "Math = Male, Me = Female, Therefore Math ≠ Me." *Journal of Personality and Social Psychology* 83, no. 1 (2002): 44–59.

Nosek, B. A., M. R. Banaji, and J. T. Jost. "The Politics of Intergroup Attitudes." In *Social and Psychological Bases of Ideology and System Justification (Series in Political Psychology)*, edited by John T. Jost, Aaron C. Kay, and Hulda Thorisdottir, 480–506. Oxford: Oxford University Press, 2009.

One Laptop per Child. http://laptop.org/.

Oregon State University Alumni Magazine, 1968.

Orwell, George. "The Principles of Newspeak: An Appendix to Nineteen Eighty-Four." In *Nineteen Eighty-Four*. London: Secker & Warburg, 1949.

Page, Scott E. *The Difference: How the Power of Diversity Creates Better Groups, Firms, Schools, and Societies*. Princeton, N.J.: Princeton University Press, 2007.

Pager, Devah, and Lincoln Quillian. "Walking the Talk? What Employers Say versus What They Do." *American Sociological Review* 70 (June 2005): 355–80.

Parks, Rosa. *Rosa Parks: My Story*. New York: Dial Books, 1992.

Pearlman, Jeff. "At Full Blast." *Sports Illustrated*, December 23, 1999.

Pearson, C. M., L. Andersson, and C. L. Porath. "Assessing and Attacking Workplace Incivility." *Organizational Dynamics* no. 29 (200): 123–37.

Peck, Scott. *A Different Drum: Community Making and Peace*. New York: Simon & Schuster, 1987.

Peters, Tom, and Robert H. Waterman Jr. *In Search of Excellence*. New York: Harper-Collins, 1982.

"Pew Forum on Religion and Public Life." Pew Research Center. Last modified August 18, 2010.

Putnam, Robert D. *Bowling Alone: The Collapse and Revival of American Community*. New York: Simon & Schuster, 2000.

———. "E Pluribus Unum: Diversity and Community in the Twenty-first Century." *Journal of the Nordic Political Science Association* (2007): 137–39, 147.

Rankin, Richard. "Talking Tolerance." *Wo!* (November–December 2006).

Reich, Robert. "Government in Your Business." *Harvard Business Review* (July–August 2009): 78.

Richardson, Robert D. *Emerson: The Mind on Fire*. Alexandria, VA: Centennial, 1996.

Rosenthal, R., and L. Jacobson. "Pygmalion in the Classroom." *Urban Review* (1968).

Ross, Lee D., Teresa M. Amabile, and Julia L. Steinmetz. "Social Roles, Social Control, and Biases in Social-Perception Processes." *Journal of Personality and Social Psychology* 35, no. 7 (1977): 485–94.

Rowe, Mary. "Micro-affirmations & Micro-inequities." *Journal of the International Ombudsman Association* 1, no. 1 (March 2008).

Rowe, Mary P. "Barriers to Equality: The Power of Subtle Discrimination to Maintain Unequal Opportunity." *Employee Responsibilities and Rights Journal* 3, no. 2 (1990): 153–63.

Rudman, Laurie A., Richard D. Ashmore, and Melvin L. Gary. "'Unlearning' Automatic Biases: The Malleability of Implicit Prejudice and Stereotypes." *Journal of Personality and Social Psychology* 81, no. 5 (2001): 856–68. doi: 10.1037//0022-3514.81.5.856.

Rumi, Jalaluddin, Coleman Barks, Barry Phillips, and Shelley Phillips. *What Was Said to the Rose*. Athens, GA: Maypop Books. CD.

Ryan, Caitlin, David Huebner, Rafael M. Diaz, and Jorge Sanchez. "Family Rejection as a Predictor of Negative Health Outcomes in White and Latino Lesbian, Gay, and

Bisexual Young Adults." *Journal of the American Academy of Pediatrics* 16, no. 1 (January 2009): 346–52.

Sabin, J. A., B. A. Nosek, A. G. Greenwald, and F. P. Rivara. "Physician Implicit and Explicit Attitudes about Race by MD Gender, Race and Ethnicity." *Journal of Health Care for the Poor and Underserved* 20 (2009): 896–913.

Schama, Simon. *Rough Crossings: Britain, the Slaves, and the American Revolution.* New York: HarperCollins, 2006.

Searle, John R. *The Construction of Social Reality.* New York: Free Press, 1995.

Shah, Idries. *Tales of the Dervishes.* London: Penguin, n.d.

Shepard, Roger. *Sights: Original Visual Illusions, Ambiguities, and Other Anomalies.* New York: Freeman, 1990.

Simons, D. J., and C. F. Chabris. "Gorillas in Our Midst: Sustained Inattentional Blindness for Dynamic Events." *Perception* 28 (1999): 1059–74.

Simons, D. J., G. Nevarez, and W. R. Boot. "Visual Sensing Is Seeing: Why 'Mindsight,' in Hindsight, Is Blind." *Psychological Science* 16 (2005): 520–24.

Slater, Philip. *The Pursuit of Loneliness: American Culture at the Breaking Point.* Boston: Beacon Press, 1970.

Smedley, Brian D., Adrienne Y. Stith, and Alan R. Nelson. *Unequal Treatment: Confronting Racial and Ethnic Disparities in Health Care.* Edited by Committee on Understanding and Eliminating Racial and Ethnic Disparities in Health Care. Washington, DC: The National Academies Press, Institute of Medicine of the National Academies, 2003.

Sommers, Samuel R., and Michael I. Norton. "Race-Based Judgments, Race-Neutral Justifications: Experimental Examination of Peremptory Use and the Batson Challenge Procedure." *Law and Human Behavior* 31, no. 3 (June 2007): 261–73.

Steele, Claude M. "A Threat in the Air: How Stereotypes Shape Intellectual Identity and Performance." *American Psychologist* (June 1997): 613–29.

St. Onge, Patricia. "Conversation as a Tool for Transformation." Introduction to *Embracing Cultural Competency: A Tool for Nonprofit Capacity Builders.* St. Paul, Minn.: Fieldstone Alliance, 2009.

Surowiecki, James. *The Wisdom of Crowds.* New York: Anchor, 2004.

Teachman, Bethany A., Kathrine D. Gapinski, Melissa Rawlins, and Subathra Jeyaram. "Demonstrations of Implicit Anti-Fat Bias: The Impact of Providing Causal Information and Evoking Empathy." *Health Psychology* 22, no. 1 (2003): 68–78.

Thompson, Krissah. "Harvard Professor Arrested at Home." *Washington Post,* July 21, 2009.

Thoreau, Henry David. "On the Duty of Civil Disobedience." 1849.

———. *Walden: On Life in the Woods,* 393–94. Boston: Ticknor and Fields, 1854.

True Colors. 1991. ABC News, *20/20.* YouTube: www.youtube.com/?v=YyL5EcAwB9c.

The Truman Show. Paramount Pictures, 1998.

Turnbull, Colin. *The Mountain People.* New York: Simon & Schuster, 1972.

Turner, Frederick Jackson. "Significance of the Frontier in American History." In *Proceedings of the State Historical Society of Wisconsin.* 1893.

Ury, William L., and Roger Fisher. *Getting to Yes: Negotiating Agreement without Giving In.* New York: Penguin, 1983.

U.S. Department of Labor, Bureau of Labor Statistics. Accessed December 14, 2009. www.bls.gov/opub/mlr/2009/11/art1full.pdf.

U.S. Department of Labor, Bureau of Labor Statistics. Accessed February 11, 2010. www.bls.gov/jlt/.

Vedantam, Shankar. "See No Bias." *Washington Post*, January 23, 2005.

———. *The Hidden Brain: How Our Unconscious Minds Elect Presidents, Control Markets, Wage Wars, and Save Our Lives.* New York: Spiegel & Grau, 2010.

Voelkl, Kristin, Maria Testa, Jennifer Crocker, and Brenda Major. "Social Stigma: The Affective Consequences of Attributional Ambiguity." *Journal of Personality and Social Psychology* 60, no. 2 (1991): 218–28.

von Glasersfeld, Ernst. *Distinguishing the Observer: An Attempt at Interpreting Maturana.* Frankfurt, Germany: Zuhrkamp, 1990.

Wagner, Jane, and Lily Tomlin. *The Search for Signs of Intelligent Life in the Universe.* Directed by Jane Wagner. N.p., 1991.

Weisbord, Marvin Ross. *Discovering Common Ground: How Future Search Conferences Bring People Together to Achieve Breakthrough Innovation, Empowerment, Shared Vision, and Collaborative Action.* San Francisco: Barrett-Koehler, 1992.

"What Is Cultural Competency?" U.S. Department of Health & Human Services, Office of Minority Health. Accessed September 11, 2009. www.omhrc.gov//.aspx?lvl=2&lvlID=11.

Wilber, Ken. *The Marriage of Sense and Soul—Integrating Science and Religion and One Taste.* Vol. 8 of *The Collected Works of Ken Wilber.* Boston: Shambhala, 2000.

Wilde, Oscar. *De Profundis.* London: Methuen, 1905.

Williams, Lawrence E., and John Bargh. "Experiencing Physical Warmth Promotes Interpersonal Warmth." *Science* 322, no. 5901 (October 2008): 606–7.

Wilson, Timothy D. *Strangers to Ourselves: Discovering the Adaptive Unconscious.* Cambridge, Mass.: Belknap Press of Harvard University Press, 2002.

Winograd, Terry, and Fernando Flores. *Understanding Computers and Cognition.* Norword, N.J.: Abelex, 1986.

Woodlee, Yolanda. "Williams Aide Resigns in Language Dispute." *Washington Post*, January 27, 1999.

X, Malcolm, and Alex Haley. *The Autobiography of Malcolm X.* New York: Grove, 1965.

Index